Rollins

AFTER DARK

Rollins
AFTER DARK

The Hamilton Holt School's
Nontraditional Journeys

RANDY NOLES

ADDITIONAL CHAPTERS BY
Patricia A. Brown and Michael McLeod

STORY FARM

WINTER PARK • MIAMI • SANTA BARBARA

Rollins After Dark: The Hamilton Holt School's
Nontraditional Journeys

Published in the United States of America by Story Farm, Inc.
www.story-farm.com

Printed in Canada

Library of Congress Cataloging-in-Publication Data
available upon request
ISBN 978-1-7326456-4-6

EDITORIAL DIRECTOR Bob Morris
ART DIRECTOR Jason Farmand
COPY EDITOR Laura Paquette
INDEXING Harry Wessel
PRODUCTION MANAGEMENT Tina Dahl

10 9 8 7 6 5 4 3 2 1
First edition, January 2020

This work is respectfully dedicated to Jack C. Lane, the official historian of Rollins College, whose scholarship will continue to guide generations of researchers; to the late Thaddeus Seymour, president emeritus of Rollins College, whose vision shaped the modern Hamilton Holt School; and to Hamilton Holt School students of all ages, whose personal sacrifices to earn a degree are often heroic and just as often underappreciated.

CONTENTS

INTRODUCTION

CONTEXT IS EVERYTHING. When I was asked to write a 60th anniversary history of the Hamilton Holt School, I believed it would be necessary to cast a much wider net to tell the whole story — and to make it interesting. After all, the history of a program within an institution is rarely as interesting as the history of the institution itself. Anyone with enough time on his or her hands can trace the history of the Holt School, administratively at least, by reviewing course catalogs to determine when certain majors were introduced or eliminated, who was director or dean at any given point, and how many people were enrolled in classes.

But continuing education at Rollins College dates much further back than 60 years. In fact, what was initially called the Adult Education Program began in 1936, under President Hamilton Holt, who invited well-to-do winter visitors to campus to hear lectures and see cultural presentations such as plays and concerts. Holt, whose pioneering work was on behalf of undergraduates, never considered a degree-granting program for nontraditional students. The Adult Education Program under Holt was, as I call it later, "a kind of high-minded holiday for scholarly snowbirds."

Nonetheless, *Rollins After Dark* begins with Holt the

man. How could any work related to the college's history do otherwise? Many know, in a general way, that Holt was a very important person whose educational ideas made the college a hotbed of progressivism back in the 1920s and 1930s. Perhaps less well remembered, at least for those not steeped in college lore, is the fact that Holt was a world figure before he ever set foot on the campus — for reasons that had nothing to do with his educational philosophy.

What was the basis of his celebrity? And if he was such an international luminary, how did he come to helm a near-insolvent Deep South college with an enrollment of 264 students? The 60th anniversary of the school that now bears his name seemed an appropriate time to examine the converging circumstances and personalities that brought the Brooklyn-born editor and activist to lush but languid Winter Park.

Holt, at least, has not faded into obscurity even if some of the reasons for his renown have been long forgotten. The same cannot be said of early continuing education figures such as Edwin Osgood Grover, the quiet but consequential professor of books; John and Prestonia Mann Martin, the sophisticated socialists who became the toast of the town; and George Sauté, the mild-mannered mathematician who directed the Holt School's precursors while crusading to save the world from annihilation. Sauté, in fact, later claimed that the continuing education program was started primarily as a way to mend community fences following the unruly reign of President Paul Wagner, Holt's ill-fated successor. That contention provided an excuse to revisit the so-called Wagner Affair, a calamity that proves truth can indeed be stranger than fiction. Indeed, the helter-skelter history of what would become the Holt School is filled with colorful characters and more intrigue than a course catalog's unremarkable pages could ever reveal.

Which brings me to the notes found at the bottom of each page. Many people, places and things mentioned in the narrative were connected to the continuing education program only briefly or tangentially but were nonetheless fascinating upon closer examination. So, rather than clog the narrative with detours, I chose to tell some of these backstories through notes. If you are otherwise inclined to skip the small type, I encourage you not to do so in this case. As for traditional footnotes, there are none. The sources are almost entirely from archival files, old newspaper clippings and personal interviews. I attempted to reference sources within the text where possible, but footnotes would have been too tedious to bear — for either me or you.

Another caveat: I am neither a historian nor an academician. I have, however, written two nonfiction books and hundreds, if not thousands, of long-form newspaper and magazine articles, some of which have won local, regional and national awards. Therefore, as a writer, I am a generalist, not a specialist. Given that, my particular thanks to Wenxian Zhang and Darla Moore of the Olin Library Department of Archives and Special Collections for their patience and good-natured helpfulness, and to my research assistant, Barbara Hughes, for the hours she spent in the archives chasing down facts or making copies. And, of course, to Interim Dean Patricia A. Brown, who wanted this story told, warts and all, for her encouragement and guidance on big-picture issues related to continuing education.

Sometimes, I think you'll agree, the most interesting things that happen at Rollins happen after dark.

Randy Noles
July 2019

———— 66 ————

Seek truth wherever truth is found; follow truth wherever truth may lead; teach truth and nothing but the truth."

—Hamilton Holt

Rollins

AFTER DARK

Chapter 1

————

THE IDEAL
COLLEGE PRESIDENT

HAMILTON HOLT WAS never reticent about expressing opinions. As the owner/editor of an influential weekly opinion journal prior to his 24-year stint (1925-49) as president of Rollins College, Holt was a public intellectual whose high-profile crusades for social justice and world peace helped shape the national discourse preceding and following World War I. Although he had never run a college — he did not, in fact, hold an advanced degree[1] — he opined frequently about higher education's perceived shortcomings. Colleges were infected with three major ills, Holt wrote: "First, the insatiable impulse to expand materially; second, the glorification of research at the expense of teaching; and third, the lack of human contact between teacher and student."

---

1   Holt's numerous doctoral degrees were honorary: LL.D., Ursinus College, 1915; Litt.D., College of Wooster, 1916; LL.D., Wilberforce University, 1920; LL.D., Oberlin College, 1921; LL.D., Otterbein University, 1922; LL.D., Baylor University, 1927; L.H.D., Boston University, 1928; D.Sc., University of Tampa, 1948; L.H.D., Keuka College, 1948; and LL.D., Bethune-Cookman College, 1950.

Holt's educational reforms transformed the undergraduate experience at Rollins. But he was also interested in lifelong learning, and from the earliest days of his presidency he sought to entice year-round residents and winter visitors to campus with classes, lectures and cultural events. In 1936, he bundled such offerings into a catch-all adult education program that he described as "merely teaching an old dog new tricks." Today, Holt's concept would be correctly called cultural tourism. A 1948 *Chicago Tribune* story headlined "Sun Seekers Vacation in Classrooms" described the lively little college as "a place where most persons attending the four-month winter course are men and women who find recreation and relaxation in the lecture room more than on the beaches and the lakes. Many are retired professors, clergymen and professional men. The art classes attract many women."[2]

The Hamilton Holt School at Rollins College now offers a Bachelor of Arts degree with 12 majors and 17 minors, as well as seven graduate degrees, to a culturally and ethnically diverse student body made up primarily of working adults — few of whom likely consider themselves to be vacationing. Holt's Adult Education Program, the purposes of which were publicity, public service and personal enrichment, became Courses for the Community and Operation Bootstrap in 1951. The Rollins College Institute for General Studies, which encompassed the School of General Studies, the Graduate Programs and the School of Creative Arts, was formed in 1960. The name was changed to the Central Florida School for Continuing Studies in 1965, the School of Continuing Educa-

---

2 It was not the first nor would it be the last time that Holt's promotional efforts resulted in national media attention for Rollins, but often such attention focused on Holtian gimmicks and made the college appear frivolous. Despite its innovative academics, the combination of its subtropical location and Holt's headline hunting contributed to an image of the college as a country club run by eccentrics.

tion in 1972, the Division of Continuing Education in 1982 and back to the School of Continuing Education in 1986. Finally, under President Thaddeus Seymour (1978-90), the enigmatic night school was reorganized, revamped and renamed for the college's revered eighth president in 1987. "We needed a 'real college' name and the Hamilton Holt School has been a 'real college' ever since," said Seymour, now president emeritus, who added that he did not wish to "diminish the good education that a lot of people got from that program" prior to the administrative and curricular changes that were implemented following his arrival in Winter Park.

Continuing education had also generated significant nonrestricted income for the college — particularly through the 1970s — but had at times veered into such discordant disciplines as criminal justice and fire safety administration. "We would offer a degree in almost anything anybody wanted to get a degree in," said Seymour in a 2005 oral history interview with Wenxian Zhang, head of the Olin Library's Department of Archives and Special Collections.[3] "I had taken the position that the destiny of the institution would be determined by its quality ... the quality of the institution was our most important issue, period." Yet, despite strengthened standards and greater academic alignment between the day and night programs, the Holt School remained underappreciated — even on campus. When Leanza Cornett, later host of *Entertainment Tonight*, won the Miss America crown in 1992, she was criticized for representing herself as a Rollins

---

3   Zhang has conducted numerous oral history interviews with important figures in the college's history. Whenever an oral history is referenced, it is among those conducted by Zhang and members of his team as part of an oral history project completed in the summer of 2005 under the auspices of the college, the Winter Park Historical Society and the Winter Park Public Library.

student when, in fact, she "only attended a few night classes."[4] Because continuing education was supervised by a dizzying succession of deans — most of whom were transferred from other administrative positions — goals for the program were at times confusing or contradictory.

Criticism continued from some day-school faculty members who believed that the Holt School lacked sufficient rigor — reforms notwithstanding — and harmed the Rollins brand as an elite and selective liberal arts college. Although ingrained perceptions are difficult to overcome, in recent years many former naysayers have been won over by the program's public-relations prowess and the heart-tugging tenacity of its highly motivated students — whose feel-good stories always seem to leave commencement audiences cheering, wiping away tears, or both. Likewise, President Grant Cornwell's 2019 decision to conduct a national search for a permanent dean has confirmed his view of the Holt School not as an afterthought but as equal in importance to the College of Liberal Arts (the day school) and the Roy E. Crummer Graduate School of Business. "I believe the strength of Rollins College as a whole is that it has three educational programs of very high quality," said Cornwell. "While each is distinctive, a common set of values binds them together. That is the belief that deep learning takes place in the context of human relationships between students and faculty, and between and among students themselves — not mediated and made imper-

---

4   The controversy was first limited to the campus but became a national story when Cornett, an organizational communications major, appeared on the *Larry King Show* and was criticized by a caller for claiming to be a college student when she was, in fact, a professional entertainer enrolled in night school. At the time, Cornett played a live-action version of Ariel, the title character from *The Little Mermaid*, at the "Voyage of the Little Mermaid" show at Disney's Hollywood Studios at the Walt Disney World Resort.

sonal by technology or large lectures."

The Holt School has given opportunities to nontradition-al students — there are now 16,000 graduates and counting — who, for a variety of reasons, could not otherwise have pursued a prestigious degree from Rollins. "I came to appreciate the effort it took for most of these students to work full time and then attend and prepare for class in the evening," said Jack C. Lane, professor of history emeritus and college historian.[5] "As adults with more experience in the world, they tended to make interesting contributions to the classes. One woman was pregnant and barely made it through the finals before she gave birth. She never once asked for anything special. Those were memories that will stay with me." Added former President Rita Bornstein (1990-2004): "The Holt School commencement was very different from the others. There were many family members and friends who came to share the joy. Right at the beginning of the program, I said we understood that graduates often did homework to the sounds of a baby crying or a toddler wanting attention. I told the relatives that such noises were not a reason to take the children out of [Warden Arena]. I loved the payoff of seeing these students graduate."

---

5   Lane's book, *Rollins College Centennial History: A Story of Persever-ance, 1885-1985* (Story Farm, 2017) remains the definitive history of the college. It was written in 1985 for the communitywide centennial cele-bration but for budgetary reasons was not published at the time. When the manuscript's existence was made known to incoming President Grant Cornwell, he had it published with minor revisions and a new preface by Lane, who wrote that "one cannot read this story and not feel inspired by the efforts of so many to realize the original and evolving vision for Rollins and not feel obligated to do all one can to move Rollins forward into its next century. ... Liberal education will need to evolve to meet global challenges in the 21st century; however, any new direction for Rollins must be built upon the college's past. In this time of rapidly shifting changes, one that requires (re)envisioning of the role of liberal education in a global context, it is critical that present and future Rol-lins generations embrace the distinctive character of the college that previous Rollins communities strove to build."

So while the Hamilton Holt School may not have evolved exactly as Hamilton Holt would have expected, it is nonetheless instructive to explore the reasons why Seymour believed that attaching Holt's name would send a powerful message to the campus and the community about the direction of the college's once-unwieldy night program — and how a man of Holt's celebrity stature came to accept a position at a small (264 students), cash-strapped institution that had been on the brink of insolvency since its founding by civic boosters and the Florida Congregational Association in 1885.[6]

The improbable sequence of events that resulted in Holt relocating to Winter Park began decades earlier — in December 1894 and March 1895 — when back-to-back freezes wiped out citrus groves and devastated the local economy. As a result, the Winter Park Company — the city's primary developer and landholder — defaulted on payments to the estate of Francis Bangs Knowles,[7] who had been the company's largest

---

6   The story of the college's founding has been told several times in other books, most thoroughly by Lane. In 1884 the Florida Congregational Association announced plans to build a liberal arts college in Florida and sought inducements from various cities, with Jacksonville (then the state's largest city), Daytona, Mount Dora and Orange City competing with Winter Park, where the campaign was led by developer Frederick W. Lyman, president of the Winter Park Company, and Rev. Edward W. Hooker, pastor of the First Congregational Church of Winter Park. Both men were motivated; Lyman knew that the presence of a college would increase land value, and Hooker likely assumed that he would be named president if a college were built. Fortuitously, Lyman and Hooker also served on the selection committee and were thus able to gauge the strength of competing efforts. Winter Park's offer of $114,180 in cash and land — bolstered by a $50,000 donation from winter resident Alonzo Rollins, for whom the college was named — far outstripped those of other cities. Wrote Lane: "All the traditional elements — the frontier environment, denominationalism, booster spirit and real estate development — were present in the founding of Rollins."

7   Knowles, a New England industrialist and winter resident, was the largest shareholder in the Winter Park Land Company and an important donor during the formation of Rollins. He remained on the college's

shareholder, and surrendered 1,200 lots to satisfy the debt. Enter Chicago industrialist Charles Hosmer Morse, a seasonal resident who recognized an opportunity when he saw one.

LIKE MANY EARLY Winter Parkers, Morse originally hailed from New England. Born in St. Johnsbury, Vermont, he graduated from St. Johnsbury Academy in 1850 before joining his uncle, Zelotus Hosmer, as an apprentice in the Boston office of E. & T. Fairbanks Co., a manufacturer of weighing scales. Winter Park's Fairbanks Avenue is named for Franklin Fairbanks,[8] whose father, Erastus, and uncle, Thaddeus, founded E. & T. Fairbanks in 1824. Franklin also worked in the family business and, in 1888, became its president. He shared Morse's enthusiasm for Winter Park and joined his friend as both a seasonal resident and a property owner with a vested interest in seeing the city thrive. Morse worked his way up the ladder at E. & T. Fairbanks, and in 1855 was transferred to New York as a clerk and salesman. Two years later he was sent to help establish an affiliate company, Fairbanks & Greenleaf, in Chicago. In 1866, he founded Fairbanks, Morse & Co., which manufactured windmills, pumps, locomotives and other industrial equipment. (Fairbanks, Morse & Co. bought controlling interest in E. & T. Fairbanks in 1916.) Morse became a multimillionaire during the Second Industrial Revolution that followed the Civil War — a time when a cadre of magnates amassed great fortunes.

In 1904, with his business interests in the Midwest no

---

board of trustees until his death in 1890. His daughter, Frances "Fannie" Knowles Warren, donated funds for the building of the college's Knowles Memorial Chapel in 1932.

8   Franklin Fairbanks, a partner in the original Winter Park Company, was also an important donor during the formation of Rollins. A member of the Vermont House of Representatives, he remained on the college's board of trustees until his death in 1895.

longer requiring his undivided attention, Morse bought the Knowles estate's holdings in Winter Park for $10,000 (the equivalent of about $280,000 today). The tale of that transaction was told by Harold A. "Harley" Ward at a 1954 dinner commemorating his retirement from the Winter Park Land Company, where he was executive vice president.[9] A half-century earlier, Ward had worked at the Pioneer Store, located at the corner of Park Avenue and The Boulevard (later Morse Boulevard), a general-merchandise emporium that dabbled in real estate. Here is how Ward recalled perhaps the most consequential property purchase in Winter Park's history: "Well, as I had said, Mr. Morse came into the store and asked if I had the sale of the Knowles estate property. I said. 'That's correct. Would you like to buy a lot?' And we talked a little, and he said, 'What'll they take for the whole shebang?' That's the way he expressed it. It like to have knocked me down." Ward "blurted out the low price they'd given me" and Morse said he would take it — with one condition: "Provided you can get released from your present work here and take charge of the property for me." After all, Morse noted, his primary home was still in Chicago and he would need year-round local management.

When the deal was done, Morse and Ward — along with Morse's son, Charles H. Morse Jr. (who lived full-time in Chicago) — became the original directors of the newly formed Winter Park Land Company. Morse then bought a home built in 1888 by Francis Bangs Knowles and remodeled it for use as

---

9   Attorney Harold A. Ward III, grandson of Harold A. "Harley" Ward, provided a transcript of this fascinating dinner, which intersects with Rollins on multiple levels. The emcee was Hugh F. McKean, who had become president of Rollins in 1951. Also in attendance was McKean's wife, Jeannette Morse Genius McKean, granddaughter of Charles Hosmer Morse and president of the Winter Park Land Company. Jeannette had been a Rollins trustee since she was 26 years old.

his winter residence. Osceola Lodge — so named for the Seminole warrior thought to have camped along the creek connecting what are today lakes Virginia and Osceola — was filled with custom Mission-style oak furniture, walls of books and an array of Native American artifacts. From this comfortable setting, Morse supervised development of his properties and quietly, often anonymously, supported community causes.[10]

Morse moved to Winter Park permanently in 1915, and in 1920 pledged $100,000 to the college, provided an additional $400,000 could be raised in the community. When only $368,000 was committed, Morse waived his stipulation and gave the college $100,000 regardless. "Rollins is very dear to me and to every citizen interested in the best development of Florida," he said when announcing removal of the preconditions. "I am deeply moved by the splendid response ... from the people of Florida, and particularly those from Orlando and Winter Park, who know the institution best." The college's most generous benefactor to that time died just six months later, leaving an estate valued at $23 million (the equivalent of nearly $290 million today).

"While other boys were content to live upon the parental support which gladly would have been his had he so willed it, [Morse] went out to fight his own battle," eulogized George Morgan Ward, a clergyman who was then president of the college. "His was a phenomenal record even in these days of magic, which have seen so many Americans rise from humble

---

10   Morse, a college trustee and a generous donor over a period of years, funded Winter Park's first town hall but refused to be acknowledged for it. He donated Central Park on Park Avenue with the stipulation that it never be developed, and helped organize the Winter Park Country Club, leasing land for a golf course to the club for $1 per year. He also gave to the Women's Christian Temperance Union and the Winter Park Woman's Club. Morse was cited as Winter Park's "Citizen of the Century" in a 2015 issue of *Winter Park Magazine*.

origins to dignified positions of power." (Osceola Lodge, a surprisingly modest home for a man of Morse's wealth, still stands at the corner of Interlachen and Lincoln avenues and today is headquarters for the Bach Festival Society of Winter Park and the Winter Park Institute at Rollins College, which sponsors seminars, lectures, readings, classes and discussions with prominent thought leaders in an array of fields.)[11]

Although Morse died four years before Holt became president of the college, and it is not known if they ever met, the pair are inexorably linked through their mutual friend, popular novelist Irving Bacheller (*Eben Holden: A Tale of the North Country* and *D'ri and I* were among his bestsellers). Morse, who selected who could and who could not buy lots in Winter Park, was protective of the town and guided by his refined sensibilities in steering its development. He refused to sell to speculators, for example, explaining in no uncertain terms that *he* would do the speculating. Only people who planned to build homes could buy lots, and the homes had to be of acceptable quality. Morse even recruited relocators whom he deemed desirable, such as Bacheller, a winter denizen of the Seminole Hotel. "Now, Mr. Ward, we must keep Bacheller here," Morse told his manager in 1917. "He'll be a great asset to Winter Park. I want you to be sure to land him here, no matter what you have to do."

Bacheller, whose $75,000 home in Riverside, Connecticut, had just burned to the ground, was amenable to relocating. Still, he drove a hard bargain. Morse ended up taking

---

11 The Winter Park Institute, founded in 2008, was inspired by the college's Animated Magazine (see pages 38-49). Guests of the institute's Speaker Series have won Academy Awards, Tony Awards, Emmy Awards, Pulitzer Prizes, National Medals of the Arts, Presidential Medals of Freedom and even French Legions of Honor. Three have been Kennedy Center Honorees and one has earned a Nobel Peace Prize. Its distinguished senior fellow is former two-term U.S. Poet Laureate Billy Collins.

the author's property in trade and loaning him money to buy a large lakefront tract on the Isle of Sicily, where he built a handsome Asian-style home he dubbed Gate O' the Isles. "I think Bacheller missed his calling," Morse grumbled to Ward. "He should have been a horse trader." But the author did, indeed, prove to be a great asset — in ways that Morse could not have predicted. In the summer of 1925, when Bacheller chaired the search committee for a new Rollins president, he advocated for Holt, editor and publisher of *The Independent*, a progressive weekly journal based in Brooklyn, New York.

Ironically, *The Independent* had published Bacheller's first work of fiction, a heartbreaking poem called "Whisperin' Bill" (see page 293). The poem appeared in 1890, just as Holt was beginning his freshman year at Yale University, so the two were not then personally acquainted. They met later, probably in the late 1890s, when Holt was publishing the magazine and Bacheller was embarking on a literary career after founding and then selling arguably the first newspaper syndicate in the U.S.[12] Both lived in Brooklyn at the time and would have traveled in the same circles and shared mutual friends. "[Rollins] is a growing institution in the best section of a growing state," Bacheller wrote to Holt, either at the behest of the search committee or on his own volition. "You could make it a big thing ... it's a cinch for a man of your capacity." The compensation suggested by Bacheller: $5,000 per year (the equivalent of about $70,000 today) and a home.

Holt was no stranger to Rollins or to Winter Park. He first visited the campus in 1910 to deliver an address entitled "The

---

12   The Bacheller Syndicate, which at its peak serviced more than 50 daily and weekly newspapers, introduced American readers to the works of such authors as Joseph Conrad, Arthur Conan Doyle and Rudyard Kipling. Bacheller also serialized Stephen Crane's novel *The Red Badge of Courage*. He sold the syndicate in 1897 to concentrate full time on writing fiction.

Federation of the World." In 1914, he accepted an invitation from President William F. Blackman to join the college's board of trustees and served a single two-year term, resigning when it became apparent that he was too preoccupied trying to save mankind (not a hyperbolic statement in Holt's case) to meaningfully participate. In 1924, Holt returned to Rollins during another lecture tour and informally discussed the vacant presidency with several alumni. But the position was offered to William Clarence Weir, formerly president of Pacific University in Forest Grove, Oregon. Weir accepted but abruptly resigned after less than a year when, according to an announcement from the college, he was "suddenly and seriously stricken with apoplexy."[13]

The timing of Bacheller's letter was fortuitous for Holt; his recession-battered magazine — co-founded in 1848 as a pro-abolition religious journal by his maternal grandfather, Henry C. Bowen[14] — was absorbed in 1921 by *The Weekly Review*, a competitive publication, leaving Holt with $33,000 in personal debt. After disassociating himself from *The Independent's* successor publication, which ambiguously declared that its purpose was to "promote the principles of liberal conservatism," Holt continued to participate in internationalist organizations and was the 1924 Democratic nominee for U.S. Senate in Connecticut, enduring a bruising and ultimately unsuccessful campaign during which he was labeled

---

13 Whatever ailed Weir, he recovered quickly. The following year he and his wife, Nettie, opened The Weir System, a real estate office, in Orlando.

14 *The Independent* was founded by Bowen, Theodore McNamee, brothers Seth and Jonathan Hunt, and Simeon B. Chittenden, Congregationalists who opposed slavery. Eventually, Bowen became the sole owner and hired celebrity pastor Henry Ward Beecher as his editor, assisted by Theodore Tilton. A national scandal erupted when Tilton accused Beecher of seducing his wife, prompting Beecher to resign and Bowen to dismiss Tilton. The ailing Bowen, who died in 1896, was both editor and publisher when Holt joined the staff in 1894.

a subversive for his prewar peace activism.[15] With no steady source of income and nagged by concerns that he had for years neglected his health and his family, Holt was eager to settle in Florida — a place he believed offered boundless opportunity — and was intrigued by the challenge of testing his theories about higher education. Still, he responded to Bacheller with an audacious, even imperious, counteroffer:

> If Rollins College cares to give me a "preliminary" call to the presidency on the terms you mention I will accept the offer for the five free winter months. That will give me from December first to May first to study the problem, consider the present and future policies and work out a program. If after that the Board wants me to continue on a permanent basis, I will do so for not less than $10,000 a year and a home, although my income for the past decade has varied from $21,000 to $28,000 a year. I could not accept the terms you offer as I am unwilling to have any permanent connection with any educational institution that is compelled to underpay its President or Professors.
>
> As a result of my experience in money raising I have no doubt at all as to my ability to finance Rollins College adequately if the right policy is agreed upon. I have some doubts whether I have the requisite educational requirement for the task. Nor do I know

---

15 *The Hartford Courant*, in endorsing Holt's Republican opponent Hiram Bingham, contended that Holt's crusading had hindered preparedness and cost lives when the U.S. entered World War I. "We would not say that Mr. Holt knew that would be the result when he opposed preparedness," wrote the *Courant*. "But he is properly chargeable with bad judgement ... and we want no bad judgement in the handling of the votes of the state of Connecticut in the United States Senate." The editorial called Holt "a pronounced pacifist" in contrast to Bingham, who was described as "gallant and soldierly."

whether your Board is such as can be depended upon to get behind a sane, liberal expanding program. The "preliminary" arrangement suggested would seem to be the surest way to clarify these matters.

Holt's compensation demand, while roughly average for a college president in 1925, must be considered in context. Weir had earned $6,000 per year, while the average faculty salary was just over $1,000 per year. Still, perhaps out of regard for Bacheller's judgement — and after a less expensive but arguably more qualified candidate declined — the trustees appointed Holt in October 1925. Congratulatory messages from notables in politics and academia poured into the college, including one from former President and then U.S. Supreme Court Chief Justice William Howard Taft that read: "[Holt] is a man of the highest probity and character, a man of wide experience and great ability. I felicitate the college on securing him." On that mannerly note, the Holt Era began.

Born in Brooklyn in 1872, Hamilton Holt was the son of Judge George Chandler Holt[16] — a district court judge in the Southern District of New York — and Mary Louise Bowen Holt. Later his family, which included five younger siblings,[17] moved to Spuyten Duyvil in the Bronx, where he spent his childhood. Holt, an 1894 graduate of Yale University with a degree in economics, was an undistinguished student who despised the classical curriculum and mind-numbing

---

16 According to a 1903 edition of *The New York Times,* George Chandler Holt's name was floated as a possible Supreme Court justice, but it is unclear if the article references the U.S. or the State of New York courts. He was not formally nominated for either post.

17 Holt's siblings included Grace (1874-1937), Stuart (1876-1900), Constance (1879-1968), Henry (1881-1955) and Sylvia (1889-1945).

lecture-and-recitation pedagogy that he had been compelled to endure. He worked part time at the family-owned magazine while studying sociology at the Columbia University Graduate School of Arts and Sciences. But in 1897, when he was named managing editor, he abandoned his studies. In his expanded role at *The Independent*, Holt solicited manuscripts, edited copy and wrote editorials. He also composed a series of 75 "lifelets" — a memorable moniker for compact but compelling autobiographical sketches of "the humbler classes" representing various races and ethnicities. (He collected 16 lifelets for a 1906 book, *The Life Stories of Undistinguished Americans: As Told by Themselves,* which he described hopefully in the introduction as having "perhaps some sociological importance.") Edwin E. Slosson, *The Independent's* literary editor, provided the introduction to Holt's compilation, writing: "If Plutarch had given us the life stories of a slave and a hoplite, a peasant and a potter, we would willingly have dispensed with an equivalent number of kings and philosophers."

At *The Independent,* Holt came to believe that a lively, collaborative workplace was more intellectually stimulating, and more conducive to learning, than a stuffy classroom in which a professor pontificated while students struggled to remain awake. "The editors with whom I was associated ... were older, abler and more cultivated than myself," recalled Holt in a 1915 lecture at Yale, during which he described his early days as an editorial apprentice. "Now, these men did not consciously try to teach me anything. But I found that by working with them shoulder to shoulder and desk to desk eight solid hours a day, I soon began to absorb like blotting paper their spirit and acquire something of their attitudes towards the issues of life. All of which made me wonder why I had got so little from my professors at Yale, who were employed for the chief purpose of inspiring and imparting knowledge to a young man." The crux of the problem, Holt insisted, was that professors and students did not work collaboratively. Professors, he added, "sit on high and treat undergraduates as inferiors," offering little of themselves and expecting little of their charges. In his lecture, Holt eventually got around to the vicissitudes of the magazine business — the topic about which he had been invited to speak — but it was clear that his opinions on pedagogy were already strongly held.

In 1912, Holt formed the Independent Weekly Corporation and bought *The Independent* outright from his uncle, Clarence W. Bowen,[18] for $44,000, most of which was borrowed from friends. He then dropped the journal's historic affiliation with the Congregational church and steered the publication toward coverage of such issues as civil rights, organized labor, open government, universal suffrage and prison reform from a secular perspective, calling upon a who's who of prominent contributing writers. Holt believed that magazines offered an ideal format through which to convey opinion and information. Books quickly went out of date, he noted, while daily newspapers were hurriedly produced, leaving writers no time for reflection or analysis. "The weekly magazine is the ideal textbook of current events," Holt wrote in 1914. "Articles are not usually written under the heat and pressure of the event, but as a result of more mature thought. The writers are men who are specially fitted to discuss the problems upon which they write."

---

18 Bowen, son of founder Henry C. Bowen, was a reporter for the *New York Herald Tribune* in 1874 when he inherited *The Independent,* where he would spend his entire editorial career. He was also active in numerous historical and genealogical societies, including the American Antiquarian Society, the New York Genealogical and Biographical Society, the Connecticut Historical Society, the Grant Monument Association, Colonial Society of Massachusetts, the Rhode Island Historical Society and the American Scenic and Historic Preservation Society.

Between 1912 and 1917, *The Independent* absorbed three other magazines — *The Chautauquan, Harper's Weekly* and *Countryside* — pushing circulation to more than 125,000. But costs rose as well, causing Holt concern about the degree to which publishers (himself included) had come to depend upon paid advertising for survival. The solution, Holt believed, was that *The Independent* and others of its ilk should become endowed, much like universities. "If a journal is to have an eminent, enterprising and trustworthy staff capable of finding out the facts about current events with accuracy and dispatch, it cannot be expected to be self-supporting any more than a university can be self-supporting by fostering the arts and sciences and maintaining a faculty of nationwide repute," he maintained. "If a journal is to perform the two essential duties of careful newsgathering and competent comment, it must have an assured income sufficient to [withstand] the stress of sensational commercialized competitors, and to demonstrate its usefulness to large circles of readers all over the country."

An endowment of about $5 million, Holt figured, would fund *The Independent* in perpetuity. With basic expenses covered, additional income from subscribers and advertisers could be reinvested in expanding coverage, hiring eminent writers and improving the publication's graphic design. The idea — logical as it may have seemed to an idealistic publisher uncomfortable with commercialism — failed to attract interest. To the detriment of thoughtful mass-market journalism, most contemplative (if wordy) weeklies began to disappear in the early 1920s, when a sharp economic downturn pummeled the advertising market and the public clamored for lighter fare such as *The Saturday Evening Post* and *Ladies' Home Journal.*[19]

---

19 In a 1909 essay called *Commercialism and Journalism*, Holt wrote:

The peripatetic Holt — likely to the detriment of *The Independent,* which might have lasted longer with his undivided attention — expended more time and energy as an advocate for international peace, barnstorming the country from 1907 to 1914 and delivering his "Federation of the World" lecture under the auspices of the Peace Society of New York, the World Peace Foundation and the Carnegie Endowment for International Peace. "Now, my friends, the peace movement is no longer a little cult of cranks," said Holt in a typical stump speech, which was usually illustrated by stereopticon images of the second peace conference held at The Hague in 1907.

Holt, who covered the conference for *The Independent,* believed that the international Permanent Court of Arbitration — usually called the World Court — established there was a step in the right direction but ultimately inadequate because it lacked the authority to enforce its rulings. "Peace has at last become a practical political issue — soon *the* political issue before all the nations," he declared. "It seems destined that America should lead in this movement. The U.S. is the world in miniature. The U.S. is a demonstration that all the peoples of the world can live in peace. And when that golden period is at hand — and it cannot be very far distant — we shall have in very truth Tennyson's dream of 'The Parliament of Man, The Federation of the World,' and for the first time since the

---

"The danger from the advertising columns is not, as I have said, that the advertisements misrepresent the goods, but that the terms on which they are solicited tend to commercialize the whole tone of the paper and make the editor afraid to say what he believes. The advertiser is coming more and more to look on his patronage as a favor, and he seldom hesitates to withdraw his advertisement if anything appears that may injure his business or interfere with his personal fad or political ambition." Holt envisioned a department in *The Independent* that would offer frank evaluations of consumer goods, much as *Consumer Reports* offers now, but said that only an endowed journal could afford to offend advertisers by critiquing their products.

Prince of Peace died on Calvary, we shall have peace on earth and good will to men!"[20] This speech, with only slight modifications, would be delivered perhaps thousands of times over the next four decades.

In 1910, Holt chaired the World-Federation League and testified before the U.S. House of Representatives Committee on Foreign Affairs. He and other members spoke in favor of a league-authored resolution, introduced by Representative Richard Bartholdt[21] of Missouri, that called upon President Taft to appoint a commission that would draft "articles of federation" for the "maintenance of peace, through the establishment of a court that could decide any dispute between nations." The proposed court, unlike The Hague, could "enforce execution of its decrees by the arms of the federation, such arms to be provided to the federation and controlled by it." Wary of the policing provision, both houses of Congress instead unanimously passed a far less ambitious joint resolution that called for a commission to investigate both arms reduction and the creation of a multinational naval force to patrol the sea.[22]

---

20 The title of Holt's lecture was a line from Alfred Lord Tennyson's 1843 poem "Locksley Hall." The relevant portion reads: "Till the war-drum throbb'd no longer, and the battle-flags were furl'd / In the Parliament of man, the Federation of the world. There the common sense of most shall hold a fretful realm in awe / And the kindly earth shall slumber, lapt in universal law." The most famous line from the poem is: "In the spring a young man's fancy lightly turns to thoughts of love."

21 Holt and Bartholdt were kindred spirits indeed. In addition to being an advocate for world government, Bartholdt was a newspaper man interested in education. Prior to entering politics, he was connected with several newspapers as a reporter, legislative correspondent and editor, and at the time of his election to the U.S. Congress was editor in chief of the *St. Louis Tribune*. He served as member of the St. Louis Board of Education from 1888 to 1892 and was president from 1890 to 1892.

22 The resolution called for five members to be appointed by the president for the purpose of considering "the expediency of utilizing exist-

Holt, never one to take an all-or-nothing position, lobbied Taft to appoint the commission and asked former President Theodore Roosevelt — who had been awarded the Nobel Peace Prize in 1906 for negotiating an end the Russo-Japanese War — to serve as chairman. "It is said to be extremely likely that before many months have passed, a powerful peace commission will be in existence with the Colonel at its head," predicted one widely circulated editorial. Roosevelt declined, however, telling Holt that U.S. presidents should not pioneer international movements. "Let others sow the seed," said the Rough Rider, according to later accounts from Holt. "But let [the president] reap the harvest."

Holt may have been puzzled by the response, particularly considering Roosevelt's supportive public declarations. In his 1904 address to congress, Roosevelt had announced a "corollary" to the Monroe Doctrine vowing that the U.S. would act as an international police force to bar foreign intervention in Latin America. He had gone further recently, in a belated 1910 Nobel lecture in Oslo, Norway, during which he had called for treaties of arbitration between nations as well as "a league of peace, not only to keep the peace among [league members], but to prevent, by force if necessary, its being broken by others." In any case Taft, whose diplomats floated the idea and received discouraging feedback from their counterparts, let the matter of a commission drop for the time being.

At the outbreak of the Great War in 1914, Holt revisited the topic of an international federation in "The Way to Disarm: A Practical Proposal" (see page 282). The editorial,

---

ing international agencies for the purpose of limiting armaments of the nations of the world by international agreement, and of constituting the combined navies of the world [into] an international force for the preservation of universal peace, and to consider and report upon any other means to diminish the expenditures of government for military purposes and to lessen the possibilities of war."

which appeared in *The Independent* and other publications in September of that year, was widely praised. "That the world should go on after the appalling experiences it is now undergoing ... is a prospect to which no thinking mind can reconcile itself," wrote the *New York Post*. "When the bloodshed and devastation come to an end, the best thought in every nation must be centered upon the possibilities of remedy. And it is not improbable that it will be along such lines as those indicated by Mr. Holt that the remedy will be sought." Opined the *Kansas City Star*: "Doubtless Mr. Holt's suggestion will be dismissed as 'impractical' by many European statesmen. But is there anything less 'practical' than the work of the 'practical' statesmen which has resulted in the catastrophe of the present war?"

Encouraged, Holt marshalled his resources. The League to Enforce Peace, subsidized by industrialist Andrew Carnegie's World Peace Foundation, was formed in 1915 by Holt and Theodore Marburg, a long-time activist in international peace movements and a previous U.S. minister to Belgium. Now-former President Taft, at Holt's behest, agreed to chair the new organization.[23]

In June of that year, at Independence Hall in Philadelphia, league members after a spirited debate endorsed a federation of nations whose members would "jointly use their economic and military force against any one of their number that goes to war or commits acts of hostility against another."[24] Just weeks prior to the meeting, German subma-

---

23 In 1912, Taft finished third in a three-way race between Democrat Woodrow Wilson, governor of New Jersey, and former President Theodore Roosevelt, his friend and onetime supporter, who ran under the Progressive Party banner. Holt supported Taft, but later quipped that the Taft-Roosevelt feud was essentially "the survival of the fattest." The quote made its way into several newspapers.

24 Charter members of the League to Enforce Peace also included Elihu

R O L L I N S   A F T E R   D A R K

rines had sunk the British ocean liner *Lusitania*. The kaiser, league members agreed, must be held to account. The issue for Holt and others was how the world would be structured in the war's aftermath. "The momentous step of Holt's life was putting forward his proposal for a league of peace when the Great War was only a few weeks old," wrote Marburg in a 1928 edition of *World Unity Magazine*. "Holt's great service was in sifting the proposals of the past, selecting from among the sound and practical, and putting them forward at a moment when opinion was awakening for the vital need of their acceptance and application."

Holt, with a renewed sense of urgency, again crisscrossed the country with a somewhat more substantive lecture. Voluntary universal disarmament would not be possible in the short term, he admitted, because "there are too many medieval-minded nations still in existence." However, since ancient times, cities and states had resolved their differences with one another through legal means. Could nations not do the same? Said Holt: "The peace problem, then, is nothing but the problem of finding ways and means of doing *between* the nations what has already been done *within* the nations." Although federation members would have smaller individual armies, they would be under the protection of a combined military force larger than that of any nation or alliance of nations outside the federation. "The league therefore reconciles the demand of pacifists for the limitation of armaments

---

Root, former secretary of state under President Theodore Roosevelt; Alexander Graham Bell, scientist and inventor; Rabbi Stephen S. Wise, progressive social activist; James Gibbons, archbishop of Baltimore; and Edward A. Felene, a department store magnate representing the newly formed United States Chamber of Commerce. With Taft as president of the league, executive committee members included Holt as well as Abbott Lawrence Lowell, president of Harvard University; and Oscar S. Straus, secretary of commerce and labor under Roosevelt.

and eventual disarmament, and the demand of militarists for the protection that armament affords," Holt asserted. Because police power remained a delicate issue, Holt vowed that such a federation would exhaust every option before resorting to force against recalcitrant members.

In the meantime, German submarines continued to sink U.S. merchant ships. On April 2, 1917, President Woodrow Wilson appeared before Congress and called for a declaration of war. The league — which was not a pacifist organization — wholeheartedly supported the Allied effort to stamp out German militarism, distributing hundreds of thousands of pieces of pro-war literature and establishing a National Speakers Bureau through which some 3.8 million people were reached, according to league estimates. In the spring and early summer of 1918, Holt spent three months in Europe, sending surprisingly jingoistic dispatches from the front lines to *The Independent*. "The way our soldiers and sailors and marines have waded into the big fight and made good has electrified England and the continent," he told the *New York Sun* upon his return. "I don't think it is too much to say that the people in France, Italy and the other countries I visited look up to President Wilson as much or more than their own great leaders. They have come to revere him as their savior."

When the war ended with the signing of the Armistice in November 1918, "The Way to Disarm" and the League to Enforce Peace provided much of the philosophical underpinning for the League of Nations. In early 1919, Holt and Oscar S. Straus, a former secretary of commerce under President Theodore Roosevelt, traveled to Paris as observers for the League to Enforce Peace when Wilson negotiated and signed the Treaty of Versailles. Granted, the resulting League of Nations was no more than an organization of sovereign states, not a world government that could compel order and guarantee security.

Still, Holt and his allies championed the organization, reasoning that it was at least a start and could later be strengthened. "The dreams of the poets, prophets and philosophers have at last come true," Holt wrote in a dispatch from Paris published in *The Independent*. "There can be no doubt whatever about it. The peace conference itself is the germ from which a real united nations will eventually develop."

Holt, a lifelong Republican, had become an affirmed Wilsonite. In 1920, during Wilson's final year in office, the activist editor was named the first executive director of the endowment fund for the Woodrow Wilson Foundation, an educational nonprofit established to make cash awards to individuals and groups that advanced world peace.[25] Donors received a certificate imprinted with Wilson's words from his 1917 address to Congress seeking a declaration of war: "The world must be made safe for democracy. Peace must be planted upon the tested foundations of political liberty." Former Assistant Secretary of the Navy Franklin D. Roosevelt chaired the fundraising campaign, which sought an endowment of $1 million. Although only half that amount would be raised, the foundation would forge ahead regardless.

"At a critical time in the history of civilization, Mr. Wilson expressed the ideals of America, of humanity, and his words were as powerful as battalions upon Germany's autocratic leaders," wrote Holt in response to a critical editorial published in several newspapers. "Do not let me be misunderstood. I do not claim that Mr. Wilson won the war. But his contribution to that end was as great, or greater, than any other individual's. The foundation was not created to

---

25 The foundation existed until 1963, when the expense required to publish a 69-volume set of Wilson's papers, undertaken in partnership with Princeton University, exhausted its resources and it was forced to cease operations.

honor this act of public service. It was created to perpetuate the ideals that prompted him to act on behalf of humanity." Holt also became involved in various international friendship societies, including the Italy-America Society, the Netherlands American Foundation, the Friends of Poland, the American-Scandinavian Foundation and the Greek-American Club. In Holt's optimistic view, the world would inevitably become "federated in a brotherhood of universal peace" even if progress toward that noble goal was incremental.[26]

Then, despite Wilson's exhausting effort, the U.S. Senate failed to ratify the Treaty of Versailles. At issue was Article 10 of the League of Nations covenant, which regarded collective security. "I have loved but one flag and I cannot share that devotion and give affection to the mongrel banner invented for a league," thundered Massachusetts Republican Senator Henry Cabot Lodge, an opposition leader who contended that the article violated U.S. sovereignty and could lead to unwanted military entanglements. Holt, in a letter to Lodge, did not mince words: "I regard the actions of the Republican senators under your leadership ... in oppos-

---

26   Holt's outrage over war in general would be exemplified in mortar and steel on the Rollins campus in 1938, when his Peace Monument was unveiled in front of Lyman Hall. Dedicated on Armistice Day, the monument was emblazoned with a powerful message: "Pause, passer-by, and hang your head in shame" was written beneath a World War I–era German mortar shell presented to Holt by his friend Poultney Bigelow, co-owner of the *New York Evening Post*. Affixed to the monument's base was a plaque with text written by Holt that read: "This engine of destruction, torture and death symbolizes the prostitution of the inventor, the avarice of the manufacturer, the blood-guilt of the statesman, the savagery of the soldier, the perverted patriotism of the citizen, the debasement of the human race; that it can be employed as an instrument in defense of liberty, justice and right in nowise invalidates the truth of the words here graven." Ironically, the Peace Monument was destroyed in an act of vandalism in August 1943. The plaque was rediscovered in 1988 and is on display in the lobby of Mills Memorial Hall.

ing the League of Nations as the worst action of public men holding high public office in the history of the United States." Then in 1920, anti-league Republican Warren G. Harding was elected to succeed Wilson. Although Harding died in office three years later, the famously taciturn former Vice President Calvin Coolidge was no more receptive to league membership than his scandal-ridden predecessor had been. "The issue has been settled," said Coolidge.

Holt, though, was unwilling to capitulate; in 1922, he organized the League of Nations Non-Partisan Association and through it attempted to rally public opinion and exert political pressure. In the summer of 1923, he traveled to Paris to see the Third Assembly of the League of Nations, then returned the following summer to watch the league's World Court in action. "We cannot scrap the league," Holt told the *Hartford Courant*. "The United States should join if for no other reason than it is the best plan yet on the horizon looking toward a genuine solution to the armaments problem." He delivered the same message in lectures across the country, from Massachusetts to Montana and just about everywhere in between.

In 1924, after Coolidge won re-election, Holt bolted the party for good and ran as a Democrat for a vacant U.S. Senate seat in Connecticut, where he had registered to vote just months before in order to qualify for the race. (His summer residence was Roseland Cottage, the sprawling Bowen family homestead in Woodstock, a picturesque village in the northeastern corner of the state.) [27] Holt discovered, however, that

---

27 Built in 1846 by Holt's maternal grandfather, Henry Chandler Bowen, Roseland Cottage was a 6,000-square-foot Gothic Revival home with a distinctive pink exterior. Though primarily a retreat for Bowen's large family, Roseland Cottage also hosted many political luminaries, including three sitting U.S. presidents (Grant, Harrison and Hayes). Holt took ownership after the last of the Bowen siblings died in 1940. His unmarried sisters, Sylvia and Constance, occupied the home year-

League of Nations membership was not a compelling enough issue to overcome the statewide strategic advantage enjoyed by Republicans. Cast as subversive for his pre-war activism and as an interloper whose real home was in Brooklyn — a charge that was not entirely without merit — Holt lost the race to Republican Governor-Elect Hiram Bingham and was back on the lecture circuit when Bacheller's letter regarding the opening at Rollins arrived.

A CITIZEN OF the world who had counseled and cajoled U.S. presidents, Holt was not intimidated dealing with representatives from a shaky provincial college that surely needed him more than he needed it. In fact, some trustees speculated that Holt was "too big a man" to be truly interested in becoming a small-town college administrator, with its attendant paper-pushing and glad-handing. Yet he was very interested indeed — and likely relieved to learn that he had not pushed the trustees too far with his demands. "When I became president of Rollins College my viewpoint, naturally, was that of a layman," Holt recalled decades later as he prepared to retire. "But I knew very definitely what I did not want in the way of educational methods. I had suffered under the lecture and recitation system too long for too many years not to know how seriously [such a system] may handicap any real flowering of a student's mind; how eagerness may be replaced by indifference and finally boredom."

Holt's fascination with higher education was, of course, well established. In 1909 and 1910, *The Independent's* Edwin E. Slosson spent a week at each of 14 well-regarded and

---

round until their deaths in 1945 and 1968, respectively. Since 1970, Roseland Cottage — a National Historic Landmark — has been open to the public as a museum. Today, its grounds are also available to rent for weddings and private parties.

well-funded public and private institutions of higher learning — Yale and Columbia among them — and recorded his impressions in a series of journal essays that he later compiled in a book entitled *Great American Universities*, which he dedicated to Holt.[28] Little escaped Slosson's notice, and not every conclusion he drew was negative. However, he found teaching styles from institution to institution to be uniformly unsatisfactory. "In many cases it has seemed to me that the instructor has come into the room without the slightest idea of how he is to present his subject," wrote Slosson. "He rambles on in a more or less interesting manner, but without any apparent regard to the effect on his audience or the economy of their attention. The methods of instruction are much the same as those used by universities in the 13th century." That description sounded all too familiar to Holt, who in 1920 penned a manifesto entitled "The Ideal College President." The short essay, entirely hypothetical at the time, provided a preview of the Holt Era at Rollins:

> [The president] first decides how many students his kind of institution ought reasonably to have. Having made this decision, he gets it by the trustees. He then calculates how many dormitories, dining halls, stadiums, laboratories, etc. would be required to feed, exercise, and house the student body.
>
> He thereupon goes out and gets this necessary physical equipment, or as much of it as he did not already possess. Having got it, he inexorably stops all further expansion. He goes right on, however, raising all the money he can, putting every dollar of it into

---

28   In addition to Yale and Columbia, private colleges and universities visited by Slosson included Chicago, Cornell, Columbia, Harvard, Pennsylvania and Princeton.

professors' salaries.

When he has enough to pay his teaching force at least twice as much as they could get in any rival institution he discharges or pensions dead-wood professors, inviting the most eminent savants in the world to fill their places. Having the most attractive price to pay, he gets nine out of every ten he approaches.

He is now in a position to turn his full attention to the students. As his "star" faculty attracts many more than can possibly be accommodated, he naturally picks and chooses those he wants, refusing admittance to all undesirables of whatever kidney.

He can now, if he wants to, either expand again or merrily roll along ... conscious that he has eschewed the scandalous scramble for students so rife among other educational institutions, glad that he has not yielded to prevalent temptation of putting all his money into bricks and mortar, and proud that he leaves to his successor an institution with an unequalled grade of professors, an unequaled grade of students, a plant adequate for the needs of both.

Once installed in Winter Park, Holt began working through his to-do list. But success, he believed, would require that the community fully appreciate the value of Rollins as a regional asset. Before seeking money from outsiders, he felt it wise to demonstrate that locals shared his vision by raising $300,000 through the newly formed Orange County Development Fund.[29] That amount, he said, would cover the

---

29 In less than a week, $304,000 was pledged. But a calamitous hurricane devastated Miami and precipitated the collapse of the Florida land boom, rendering many pledges impossible to collect. Another local drive to raise $300,000 was announced in 1936, concurrent with the

college's annual operating expenses of $60,000 for the ensuing five years. The administration, relieved of day-to-day financial concerns, could then dedicate its time and energy to increasing the college's endowment to an astonishing $5 million, thereby ensuring the perennially struggling institution's permanent stability. Irving Bacheller was often at Holt's side during fundraising events, and rivaled the veteran orator with his impassioned pleas. At a 1926 dinner for local influencers at Orlando's Angebilt Hotel, Bacheller described the situation as dire: "The institution at Winter Park is under indictment. It is not fit for occupation. It has been a mendicant, living from hand to mouth!"

Holt, in speeches and a series of full-page newspaper advertisements placed by the trustees, laid out reasons why the college warranted financial backing in terms that any businessperson could understand and appreciate. A college, said Holt, "is without a doubt the most valuable asset that a community can possess." If Rollins were located elsewhere, he added, "Orange County would work incessantly and possibly raise several millions of dollars to get it." Luckily, he said, the college had been part of the community for 40 years "and is so familiar ... that perhaps few of you fully realize either what a priceless possession the county already has, or what a great future is in store for the college, if only its friends seize the opportunity beckoning for its development." Added Holt: "I venture therefore to present to you a plan by which, in my best judgement, Rollins College can become not only a cultural asset of increasing value to our county, but an institution that will reflect honor on the state and even the nation."

Holt declared that he would limit the student body to just

---

launch of the Adult Education Program, but only $50,000 was collected. The college's fundraising efforts fell victim to, in succession, the land bust, the Great Depression and the outbreak of World War II.

700 and recruit "golden personalities" as faculty members: "In almost every college there are at least one or two professors who not only know their subjects, they know how to impart what they know. These are the great teachers. As we add to our faculty, we shall invite only these rare souls to join our circle whose personalities appeal to young men and women. If they have superlative scholarship, good. If they can extend the borderland of knowledge, better. But they must have the gift of teaching and the nobility of character to inspire youth. I shall consider that I have failed as president of Rollins College if I cannot, as we develop, find these men and women and add them to our staff." Many, although certainly not all, of the golden personalities recruited by Holt possessed the attributes he described. Among the best was also the first: Edwin Osgood Grover, who would be instrumental in launching a precursor of the Adult Education Program — the Animated Magazine.

GROVER, WHO APPEARS dour in photographs, was described as formal and reserved by those who knew him. Yet, professorial as he seemed, he was an entrepreneur prior to becoming an academic. Like Holt, he understood — to use a now-tarnished phrase — the art of the deal. "Grover was an introvert and Holt was an extravert," said Grover's biographer, retired psychiatrist Eduard Gfeller.[30] "They worked well together.

---

30   Gfeller has made it a personal mission to rescue Grover from undeserved obscurity. He produced a documentary film, *Grover: America's First Professor of Books,* which debuted at Valencia College's Global Peace Film Festival in 2016. The following year he self-published a lively biography, *Edwin Osgood Grover: The Business of Making Good.* Gfeller also maintained a website dedicated to Grover, which has since been discontinued. In 1958, Rollins President Hugh McKean installed a stone honoring the 88-year-old Grover on the campus' Walk of Fame. The stone is, surprisingly, one of only a few Grover-related acknowledgments to be found in Winter Park. The others are Grover Avenue, near Mead Botan-

Grover spoke quietly. He was quite tall and tilted to one side in a way that made him seem to be floating as he walked." Born in Mantorville, Minnesota, in 1870, Grover was raised in Maine, New Hampshire and Vermont, where he wandered in the woods and developed a love for nature. While attending Dartmouth College, he worked as a reporter for the *Boston Globe* and edited the *Dartmouth Literary Monthly*.

After graduating in 1894 with a degree in literature, Grover enrolled in graduate school at Harvard University. However, instead of earning an advanced degree, he chose to visit Europe and the Middle East — an adventure he managed despite having only $300 to his name. Upon his return to the U.S. in 1900, Grover worked as a textbook salesman for Ginn and Company in the Midwest and shortly thereafter became chief editor of Rand McNally in Chicago. He formed his own publishing company in 1906 but sold his interest five years later to become president and majority owner of the Prang Company, a manufacturer of crayons, watercolors and school supplies.[31] After relocating the company from Manhattan to Chicago, he and his family moved to Highland Park and then to Western Springs, Illinois. Grover retired in 1925, at age 55, "after serving a sentence of 30 years in the publishing industry." His retirement, however, was short-lived.

In the late 1890s, Grover had penned "Because of Thee," a charmingly overwrought poem dedicated to his wife, Mertie,

---

ical Garden, and the Grover Trail, which runs through the garden along Howell Creek and is marked by a small sign.

31 Company founder Louis Prang, who began selling greeting cards in the U.S. in 1874, is sometimes known as "the Father of the American Christmas Card." Prang is also known for his efforts to improve art education in the U.S., publishing instructional books and creating a foundation to train art teachers. His early Christmas cards, prized by collectors for their elaborate beauty, were printed on high-quality paper using as many as 30 colors for a single image. Some cards were embossed, varnished and adorned with fringe, tassels and sprinkles.

and submitted it to *The Independent*,[32] where it was published in 1902, well before Holt's editorship. Although he did not submit additional poetry, Grover remained a fan of *The Independent* and contacted Holt during a 1912 business trip to New York. The two met for a convivial lunch at Coney Island and, not surprisingly considering their mutual publishing backgrounds, enjoyed one another's company. Surely neither man imagined that the meeting would have such profound implications for a small college in Florida.

After Holt was appointed to the Rollins presidency, Grover visited him again in Winter Park where the pair discussed, among other things, an observation by Ralph Waldo Emerson: Colleges, the Sage of Concord had noted, built impressive libraries, but inexplicably supplied no professors of books. "College education is the reading of certain books which the common sense of all scholars agrees will represent the science already accumulated," wrote Emerson in 1870. "If you know that — for instance, in geometry if you have read Euclid and Laplace — your opinion has some value; if you do not know these, you are not entitled to give any opinion on the subject. Whenever any skeptic or bigot claims to be heard on the questions of intellect and morals, we ask if he is familiar with the books of Plato, where all his pert objections have once and for all been disposed of. If not, he has no right to our

---

32   "No hint of bird songs in the hedge / Or from leaf-barren boughs, / Yet I can hark a silver throat / That lets my heart a-rouse, / 'Love! Love! Love!' it sings/and 'Love!' the live-long hours, / Till all my happy heart is brimmed / As beauty brims the flowers. / No glimpse of green upon the hills, / No promise in the sky, / Yet spring is buoyant in my heart / For love has loitered by. / 'Love! Love! Love!' it sings, / And 'Love!' throbs all my heart. / The lilacs bud in ecstasy, / And hark! The daisies start! / Chill doth blow the Winter's breath, / Bitter the biting cold, / Yet snug to leeward of wind and rain, / The balmy breezes hold. / Love, Love, Love, they bear. / Love-laden from Who knows? / No hand but thine, dear, sets the sails / From Southlands to my snows!"

time. Let him go and find himself answered there. Meantime the colleges, whilst they provide us with libraries, furnish no professor of books; and, I think, no chair is so much wanted."

A week later, Holt offered just such a post to Grover, and proclaimed with a publicist's flair that the poet-turned-publisher would be the first and only professor of books in the U.S. Although that contention was debatable, Grover's literary bent, combined with his technical knowledge of designing and printing books, made him an ideal selection. When some notable academicians sneered, Holt admitted that the professorship was "novel," but argued that Grover's position was far from frivolous. "His function is not so much to impart information as to inspire and direct enthusiasm," Holt told a reporter, distinguishing the function of a professor of books from that of a professor of literature.

In 1926, Grover moved his family to Winter Park, population 2,300. For his part, Grover was charmed by the city's ambiance and heartened by the fact that many of its founders and most prominent citizens were New Englanders. In his acceptance letter to Holt, Grover wrote that he hoped "to be able to interest a group of selected students in a wider and keener appreciation of books, and even in the making of beautiful books, until they agree that the companionship of a good book is better than the company of a thousand men."

Grover's bustling household included Mertie and his sister, Eulalie, the author of several series of bestselling children's books, including *The Sunbonnet Babies* and *The Overall Boys*.[33] Other residents at the Osceola Avenue home, locat-

---

33 *The Sunbonnet Babies Primer*, published in 1902, followed the adventures of Molly and May, two little girls whose faces were completely hidden by large sunbonnets. The primer was written using a 150-word vocabulary with later editions containing word lists to help teachers pick out key words and phrases for emphasis. In 1905 Eulalie Grover published a second series, *The Overall Boys*, which introduced lit-

ed within easy walking distance of Rollins, included Grover's sickly youngest sister, Nan, and his mother, Fanny. Daughters Frances and Hester were away at school, while an ill-fated son, Graham — who would take his own life in 1940, at age 25, by stepping in front of a speeding train — lived in the attic. Once the Grovers arrived, the ambitious little college, and the relatively refined community in which it was nestled, would never be the same.

Shortly after settling in, Mertie was joined by Lucy Vincent, wife of Clarence Vincent, minister of the First Congregational Church of Winter Park, in founding the Welbourne Avenue Nursery for children of African-American working mothers.[34] (The facility remains in operation today and serves a diverse population of local families.) Grover, meanwhile, embarked on a whirlwind of activities in addition to teaching three courses: "The History of the Book," "Literary Personalities" and "Recreational Reading." He provided startup capital for Winter Park's first bookstore, The Book-

---

tle boy characters, Jack and Joe. Grover's European travels provided themes for *Sunbonnet Babies in Holland, Sunbonnet Babies in Italy* and *Overall Boys in Switzerland,* which were used as geography textbooks for second- and third-grade children. Collectively the books are said to have sold more than 4 million copies worldwide.

34   Mertie Laura Graham Grover had a long history of working to improve educational opportunities for African-Americans. She and her future husband attended St. Johnsbury Academy in St. Johnsbury, Vermont, and graduated together in 1890. They were separated for a time when Mertie enrolled in Mount Holyoke Seminary and College — now Mount Holyoke College — in South Hadley, Massachusetts. She then attended Hartford Theological Seminary — now Hartford Seminary — in Hartford, Connecticut. Edwin, meanwhile, enrolled in Dartmouth College in Hanover, New Hampshire. Upon graduation, Mertie worked for the American Missionary Association, which was founded as an anti-slavery society in 1846. She taught literature at Tillotson College in Austin, Texas, and served as the principal at the Beach Institute in Savannah, Georgia. Both were colleges for African-Americans.

ery,[35] and launched a campus literary magazine, *The Flamingo*. His small press, Angel Alley, published faculty works and a student songbook.[36] "Mr. Grover stimulates and inspires student creativity, and is easily interrupted within the classroom and easily buttonholed without it," wrote student Stella Watson, an editor of *The Flamingo*. "He has spread his doctrine of book-love that not only the campus, but the entire community has become book-minded."[37]

Grover was soon appointed by Holt as vice president of the college and director of what was then the Carnegie Library, to which he added 14,000 volumes, some from his personal collection, over a three-year period. Grover mentored folklorist and erstwhile Eatonville resident Zora Neale Hurston, helping her to find a publisher for her first novel, *Jonah's*

---

35 The Bookery would remain in operation on Park Avenue until 1972, when owner Belle Autrey Thompson died.

36 Angel Alley's first book was *Psyche's Lamp*, a collection of poems by Rose Mills Powers published in 1927. Powers, wife of Hiram Powers, a professor of modern languages at the college, was a popular poet in the early 1900s and a founding member of Allied Arts, an organization of Winter Park-based authors. In 1912, she wrote the lyrics to the college's first alma mater: "Set like a gem amidst the waters blue, / where palms and pines their fragrance incense brew. / O Alma Mater as the swift year runs, / sing we thy praise, thy daughters and thy sons. / Sons who uphold thy fair unsullied fame, / daughters who love thine ancient honored name. / True to thy colors blazoned far on high, / gold of the sun and blue of blending sky. / Far from thy walls wherever we may go, / still with a heart where loyal memories glow, / still with a song for Rollins ringing clear, / guide of our youth O Alma Mater dear."

37 The centerpiece of Grover's classroom was a large oval table around which students sat to discuss their readings. The walls of the room were lined with bookshelves containing more than 1,000 volumes, and above the shelves were hung lithographs, block prints, images of writers and framed pages from old books. In 2016, thanks to a gift from David F. and Nancy Berto, the Edwin O. Grover Room was created on the ground floor of the Olin Library. David Berto, a 1956 graduate, was a student of Grover's, and the two continued to correspond until Grover's death in 1965. A highlight of the Grover Room is a ghostly, translucent image from 1926 of Grover and his students on the window glass.

Gourd Vine, and introducing her to Robert Wunsch, a young drama teacher who staged her play, *From Sun to Sun*, on the Rollins campus.[38] (Hurston was a frequent guest in the Grover home, a fact that raised eyebrows among white Winter Parkers.) He even recruited promising students, sometimes arranging personally for scholarships; and, not insignificantly, he persuaded the Congregational Board of Home Missions to forgive a $31,000 mortgage it held on the campus. Grover also co-founded the city's Mead Botanical Garden with former student Jack Connery, a protégé of Oviedo-based botanist Theodore Luqueer Mead.[39]

---

38 In 1933, when Wunsch sought to stage *From Sun to Sun* on campus, Holt agreed but did not think it wise, given prevailing racial attitudes in the community, to use the high-profile Annie Russell Theatre or to allow African-Americans to attend the performance. Wrote Holt to Wunsch: "I see no reason why you should not put on in the Recreation Hall the Negro folk evening under the inspiration of Zora Hurston, but I assume you will go over the thing enough to know that there will be nothing vulgar in it. Of course, we cannot have Negroes in the audience unless there is a separate place segregated for them, and I think that would be unwise. I do not think I would advertise it very much outside our own faculty and students, but I may be wrong about this." Holt's reservations aside, *From Sun to Sun* was well received. A short review in the *Orlando Morning Sentinel* noted that "an audience of invited guests showed its unmistakable approval by calling the performers back repeatedly for encores." *The Sandspur* also praised the production, calling it "one of the most effective productions given at the college this year."

39 A year after Mead's death in 1936, his protégé, Connery — who had inherited Mead's teeming greenhouses — approached Grover with the idea of creating a vast garden to memorialize the Oviedo-based botanist and to display his collection of amaryllis, hemerocallis, fancy-leaf caladiums and more than 1,000 orchids. Near the college was a low-lying area along Howell Creek that they thought would be perfect for the venture. At Grover's behest, owners of several tracts donated their holdings to Theodore L. Mead Botanical Garden Inc., a newly formed nonprofit. Four years later — aided by Works Progress Administration labor — Mead Botanical Garden opened with in a formal ceremony that included local dignitaries and elected officials. Grover, who presided over the festivities, laid out a grand vision of a garden that would encompass unspoiled natural areas, ornamental plots, greenhouses for exotic plants and even aquariums — which were never built. The garden did not become everything

Most notably, though, Grover and Holt concocted the Animated Magazine, which would later be packaged as a component of the college's original Adult Education Program. Although no physical magazine was produced, apart from a cursory printed program, Grover was called "publisher" and Holt was called "editor" of the Sunday afternoon event, during which prominent people from all professions — among them authors, actors, musicians, business executives and political leaders — lectured or read aloud from their works. The community was admitted free of charge, although donations for scholarships, library books, war relief and other good causes were accepted during the event's "advertising insert." Holt, ever the showman, sat onstage and wielded an oversized blue pencil — which he genially threatened to use if a speaker exceeded his or her allotted 15 minutes.

The first Animated Magazine — subtitled "Literary Vespers" because of the profusion of writers on the agenda — was held in February 1927 and drew about 2,500 people to the college's Recreation Hall. Among the contributors[40] were novelists Irving Bacheller, Rex Beach (*The Spoilers*) and Alice Hegan Rice (*Mrs. Wiggs of the Cabbage Patch*);

---

that Grover and Connery had envisioned. It is, however, one of the most beautiful urban greenspaces in Central Florida — a fitting tribute to the genius of Mead and the persistence of the unlikely pair who had implemented this far-fetched notion.

40   Some contributors did not have to travel far. Bacheller, of course, lived in Winter Park and was introduced as the city's "First Citizen." His upcoming novel, *Dawn, A Lost Romance of the Time of Christ*, was set to be released later that year and was favorably reviewed by essayist Corra Mae Harris during her presentation. Clinton Scollard and Jessie Belle Rittenhouse, a married couple, were also Winter Park residents who lectured on poetry at the college. The occasion was a homecoming for Rex Beach, a Rollins alumnus who was known as "The Victor Hugo of the North" for his formulaic adventure novels set in Alaska. Tennessee-born Opie Read presented a monologue evoking Southern dialect and stereotypes. Apparently, his presentation was so well received that he was invited back in subsequent years as the closing speaker.

poets Cale Young Rice, Jessie Belle Rittenhouse and Clinton Scollard; editors Ed W. Howe (*The Review of Reviews*) and Henry Goddard Leach (*The Forum*); humorist and publisher Opie Read (*The Arkansas Traveler*); and Georgia-born essayist Corra Mae Harris, whose work a seemingly smitten Holt had inexplicably published in *The Independent* despite its appalling racism.[41] Holt, who had been on the job for more than a year, would be formally inaugurated at convocation the following day. The event would highlight Founders' Week, which Holt — who reveled in academic pomp — decreed would be celebrated during the third week of each February.[42] He led off the inaugural Animated Magazine by reading aloud "The Ideal College President." Surely most in attendance, including many who had never before visited the campus, suspected that the sturdy, balding man over whom the newspapers had made such a fuss might be precisely that.

In 1935, Grover embarked on another adult education

---

41 In a short-lived, campus-based revival of *The Independent* in 2015, historian Jack Lane provided a fascinating analysis of the bizarre friendship between Holt and Harris. The Georgia-born Harris came to Holt's attention when she wrote him a letter in response to an article by editor William Hayes Ward that decried lynching. Holt wrote that he was "struck by [the letter's] sincerity, simplicity, and charm, the three graces of literary art, it evidenced, in its form and substance that something we call genius." Wrote Lane: "Employing racially charged language more often associated with the rantings of the KKK, [Harris] offered a passionate justification for the criminal Southern practice of lynching ... As managing editor of the nation's most progressive magazine with a long reputation for championing African-American rights, how could Holt express such enthusiasm for Harris's writing style while ignoring the letter's racist content and damaging language?" In fact, Lane added, Holt published subsequent articles by Harris that demeaned African-Americans. He awarded her an L.H.D. in 1927, during convocation, and in 1930 appointed her "Professor of Evil." Ultimately, Lane concluded, Holt's continued enthusiasm for Harris simply defied explanation.

42 In fact, Rollins was chartered in April 1885 and its first classes were held in November of that year. February has no special significance in the college's history.

adventure, founding a summer program in the Blue Ridge Mountains of North Carolina called the Banner Elk School of English. The operation moved the following year to a nearby hamlet and was renamed the Blowing Rock School of English, a joint venture with Duke University. At the school, professional writers could hone their craft and teachers of college and high school English could, according to an advertisement in *The English Journal*, "combine education with a real vacation 4,000 feet in the air!"

Margaret Mitchell, who had just published *Gone with the Wind*, was a Blowing Rock guest lecturer in 1936, as was Marjorie Kinnan Rawlings, who had just written *Golden Apples* and was working on a draft of *The Yearling*. Among the Rollins faculty members joining Grover that summer — and every summer until the school closed in 1940 — were Edwin Granberry, the Irving Bacheller Professor of Creative Writing; Fred Lewis Pattee, professor of American literature; and Willard A. Wattles, professor of English. Granberry, who reappears in this narrative, invited his friend Mitchell to Blowing Rock so that she could elude *Gone with the Wind* enthusiasts who recognized her in Atlanta, where she lived and wrote. Pattee, who spent 33 years at Pennsylvania State College (now Pennsylvania State University), retired to Florida in 1927 and began what would become a 22-year second career at Rollins. Wattles, who came to Holt's attention through submissions to *The Independent*, was an original golden personality with several published poetry collections to his credit. Grover's school, like many others in the 1930s, was modeled on the prestigious Bread Loaf Writers' Conference, a summer program sponsored since 1926 by Middlebury College in Vermont. While northern academicians flocked south during the winter, southern academicians often fled north during the summer. Many Rollins instructors, therefore, snared summer appointments at learning-oriented getaways while locals sweltered and swatted mosquitoes. Learning, it seemed, flourished wherever the weather was most temperate.

In balmy Winter Park, the Animated Magazine became so popular that it was soon moved from the Recreation Hall to the Sandspur Bowl (site of the present soccer field). The number of "subscribers," as Holt and Grover called attendees, sometimes topped 8,000, according to press reports. "Another Hamilton Holt brainchild has grown out of his swaddling clothes and now is approaching his teens," enthused the *Orlando Morning Sentinel*[43] in 1937. "[The Animated Magazine] is an institution within an institution that will outlive the youngest residents of today."

Contributors that year — during which unexpectedly rainy weather caused the event to be moved to the Annie Russell Theatre, necessitating multiple presentations — included John Erskine, a composer and educator whose general honors course at Columbia College had inspired the Great Books Movement; John Palmer Gavit, associate editor of *The Survey* magazine who had attended Holt's 1931 liberal arts colloquium; Cordell Hull, U.S. Secretary of State whose political career included 11 terms in the U.S. House of Representatives from Tennessee;[44] Fannie Hurst, a bestselling

---

43 The *Orlando Morning Sentinel* and the *Orlando Evening Star* merged into the *Orlando Sentinel-Star* in 1973. The newspaper has been the *Orlando Sentinel* since 1982. The Sunday paper had also long been called The *Orlando Sunday Sentinel-Star,* and for a time some regional editions were referred to as the *little sentinel*. For clarity, this work refers to all *Sentinel* references prior to 1983 as the *Orlando Morning Sentinel* and all those after 1983 as the *Orlando Sentinel*.

44 In 1943, Hull and his staff would draft the document that became the United Nations Charter. Hull, called "The Father of the United Nations" by President Roosevelt, would receive the Nobel Peace Prize in 1945 for his role in establishing the U.N.

novelist and social activist whose recent book *Imitation of Life* had just been adapted and released as a major motion picture starring Claudette Colbert and Louise Beavers; Nina Wilcox Putnam, a prolific writer whose short story had inspired the screenplay for the 1932 horror film *The Mummy*; Countess Alexandra Tolstoy, daughter and private secretary of Russian author Leo Tolstoy; and Thomas J. Watson, president of International Business Machines Corporation (which in 1933 had begun referring to itself as IBM). Journalist Ray Stannard Baker, who had been Woodrow Wilson's press secretary during negotiations for the Treaty of Versailles, and a pair of Holt favorites, Rex Beach and Corra Mae Harris, made return appearances.

Animated Magazine rosters through the years list many names that are no longer well-known alongside such storied figures as journalists Walter Cronkite and Edward R. Murrow; film stars James Cagney, Leo G. Carroll, Greer Garson, Edward Everett Horton, Mary Pickford and Basil Rathbone; FBI director J. Edgar Hoover; Major League Baseball manager Leo Durocher; inventor-engineer R. Buckminster Fuller; Maine U.S. Senator Margaret Chase Smith; civil rights leader Mary McLeod Bethune; social reformer Jane Addams; polar explorer Admiral Richard E. Byrd; poet Carl Sandburg; U.S. Army Generals Omar Bradley and Jonathan Wainwright; cartoonists Milton Caniff (*Steve Canyon*), Roy Crane (*Buz Sawyer*), and Walt Kelly (*Pogo*); and authors Willa Cather, Allen Drury and Marjorie Kinnan Rawlings.[45]

---

45 Rawlings, author of *Cross Creek* and *The Yearling*, received an L.H.D. from Rollins in 1939, and spoke at the Animated Magazine in 1934, 1937, 1938, 1941 and 1945. Rawlings and Holt corresponded over a 16-year span that ended only during Holt's final illness. "You are a very remarkable woman; I wish to know better what goes on in your head," Holt wrote Rawlings in 1938. Rawlings, referencing her books, replied: "Why, bless us, *South Moon Under* and *Golden Apples* and *The Year-*

The Animated Magazine was cancelled only once, in 1936, when the wives of both Holt and Grover died within 24 hours of one another. Alexena "Zenie" Crawford Smith Holt succumbed to bronchial pneumonia on February 20, followed a day later by Mertie Laura Graham Grover, who was struck by a car and killed when trying to cross Osceola Avenue.[46] Convocation went on as planned, however, with speakers Owen D. Young, founder of RCA and advisor to the Allied Reparations Commission regarding Germany's debt in the aftermath of World War I; and Frances Perkins, U.S. Secretary of Labor from 1933 to 1945 under President Franklin D. Roosevelt and the first woman to hold a Cabinet position.

---

ling are inside my head!" John "Jack" Rich, a Rollins student who later became the college's dean of admissions, served as an escort for Rawlings during her 1938 campus visit. In a 2005 oral history interview, Rich recalled Rawlings as "a delightful woman, and so interesting." He also remembered the delight Rawlings took in using bawdy language. "If she had as many as two cocktails, she started to swear like a trooper," Rich said. "Just for the fun of it! 'You bastard, you! So nice to see you!' Something like that. Of course, the students loved her." Rawlings had another Rollins connection: When Zelma Cason, a crotchety resident of Island Grove — a tiny hamlet near Cross Creek — sued the author for $100,000 over what she correctly believed to be an unflattering depiction in *Cross Creek*, Professor of History Alfred J. Hanna appeared as a witness for Rawlings, describing the 1942 bestseller as "of tremendous importance, in view of its honest and its true and its comprehensive description of an important section of Florida; it's an accurate delineation of characters, a sympathetic and truthful description in every way; one of compelling importance." Rawlings ultimately lost the case — which established that invasion of privacy by an author was actionable — but Cason was awarded only $1 plus court costs.

46 Zenie Holt had an elaborate service in Knowles Memorial Chapel while services for Mertie Grover were private. Her husband asked that, in lieu of flowers, donations be made in Mertie's memory to start the Hannibal Square Library for African-American children on the city's west side. He called it "the library that flowers built." Even in grief, Edwin Osgood Grover thought of others and emphasized to the *Orlando Morning Sentinel* that neither he nor his family held the driver responsible for an accident that they considered unavoidable.

ANIMATED MAGAZINE CONTRIBUTORS were asked to pay their own expenses but were feted in a manner that befitted guest celebrities — and sometimes were awarded honorary degrees at convocation the following day.[47] A gimmick, to be sure, but not without significance in many cases. For example, a measure of history was made in 1949 when Holt — who had announced his pending retirement and therefore felt unconstrained by pervasive racist sentiment — presented an L.H.D. to Mary McLeod Bethune, founder of what would become Bethune-Cookman University in Daytona Beach.[48] In doing so, Rollins became perhaps the first educational institution in the South to award an honorary degree to an African-American. Holt had wanted to honor Bethune in 1947 but the board of trustees, ostensibly over concerns for the safety of the college, said no.

Just three years earlier, the same trustees had insisted that Rollins forfeit its homecoming football game against Ohio Wesleyan University because the visiting team had an African-American, Kenneth Woodward, on its roster.[49] It was

---

47   In a 1977 edition of the *Rollins Alumni Record*, former college director of admissions Marita Stueve Stone Vandyck, who had been a member of the Class of 1938, recalled that Holt's delight with rituals and ceremonies was not necessarily shared by students: "[Holt] particularly enjoyed convocations, with the array of flags and the colorfully gowned procession moving sedately into the [Knowles Memorial Chapel] to 'Pomp and Circumstance.' It never occurred to him that the students grew tired of long citations and responses for honorary degrees, or that they thought six in one day were about four too many."

48   Other Animated Magazine participants receiving honorary degrees in 1949 were Serge Koussevitzky (L.H.D.), conductor of the Boston Symphony Orchestra; Edward R. Murrow (L.H.D.), radio (and later television) journalist; Albert J. McCartney (L.H.D.), theologian; and Karl T. Compton (LL.D.), president of MIT.

49   As a private institution, Rollins was not bound by a Florida law that mandated segregated public schools and colleges. Theory and practice, however, are entirely different matters. Holt, a founding member of the NAACP, was quite aware that even in relatively sophisticated

feared that violence would erupt at Orlando Stadium (now Camping World Stadium) if Woodward traveled with the team, and initially the Battling Bishops had agreed to leave the talented running back behind. But following the intervention of Major League Baseball manager and Ohio Wesleyan alumnus Branch Rickey — who had recently broken baseball's color barrier by signing Jackie Robinson to play first base for the Brooklyn Dodgers — the school's trustees reversed course and refused to authorize the team to head south without Woodward.

"Rollins College has no objection whatsoever to playing a game in which a negro participates," read a statement from the college released on behalf of the trustees. "However, a football game is a community affair and, after consultation with our leading community members, both white and colored, officials of the college have decided that in the best interest of racial relations, they are unwilling to take action which might interfere with the good progress now being made in Florida, and especially in the local community." Holt, who fumed that "the decision taken was not right," must have been humiliated by such national headlines as "Game Cancelled Because of Negro" and "Rollins Refuses to Play Against Negro Youth."

Four days later, though, he dutifully gathered Rollins

Winter Park, the presence of black students on campus would have been unacceptable to many locals. Still, the college considered itself racially progressive. Its active Inter-Faith and Race Relations Committee supported such institutions as Hungerford Preparatory High School (an all-black school for grades 6-12 in nearby Eatonville), the Winter Park Negro Grammar School and the Hannibal Square Library. In 1948, the college awarded its Decoration of Honor to Susan "Susie" Weasley, a housemaid at the college's Cloverleaf Cottage between 1924 and 1949. Weasley was the first African-American to receive the award, which was undoubtedly well intentioned but by today's standards appears paternalistic. The first black student at Rollins was a physician's son named John Mark Cox Jr., who enrolled in 1964. Still, there were only about 25 black students by 1969 and no black faculty members until 1971.

students and faculty in the Annie Russell Theatre and attempted to justify the trustees' stance: "May I say this to you students; you will probably have critical decisions like this to make as you go through life — decisions that whatever you do, you will be misinterpreted, misunderstood, and reviled," said Holt. "It seemed to all of us that our loyalties to Rollins and its ideals were not to precipitate a crisis that might, and probably would, promote bad race relations, but to work quietly for better race relations, hoping and believing that time would be on our side."

Did Holt believe any of this? Perhaps — but more outrage could reasonably have been expected from a man who had otherwise been so willing to champion unpopular causes.[50] In 1948, however, the old crusader reasserted himself with an act of defiance and courage — particularly at that place and time. "One of the highest privileges that has come to me as president of Rollins College is to do honor to you this morning," Holt said when awarding the degree to Bethune. "I am proud that Rollins is, I am told, the first *white college* [author's emphasis] in the South to bestow an honorary degree upon one of your race. You have, in your own person, once again demonstrated that from the humblest beginnings and through the most adverse circumstances it is still possible for one who has the will, the intelligence, the courage and the never-failing

---

50   Holt caused something of a scandal when he addressed a 1908 meeting of New York's Cosmopolitan Club where, according to press accounts, "white men and women sat elbow to elbow with colored men and women while they discussed social equality and cheered at the suggestion of intermarriage as a solution to the race problem." Holt later admitted that he had mentioned intermarriage in his speech but claimed that he had not endorsed it: "I said that intermarriage, if it were to be between white men and colored women and not between colored men and white women, would bleach the race, but I rejected this as a proper solution. I then laid stress on the education of the negro as the best means of dealing with the problem." Such an attitude hardly sounds enlightened today, but in 1908 the fact that Holt attended (and spoke at) an interracial gathering is worthy of note.

faith in God and in your fellow man to rise from the humblest cabin in the land to a place of honor and influence among the world's eminent. In paying honor to you, we show again our own faith in the land which made your career a reality."

THE ANIMATED MAGAZINE began to lose its luster following the retirements of its guiding lights Holt and then Grover, in 1949 and 1951 respectively. Less showy and more thematic editions were presented in the 1960s, now in the smaller Knowles Memorial Chapel. Once television became ubiquitous, the live event seemed more and more to be a quaint and quirky anachronism. The final Animated Magazine, held in 1969 with President Hugh F. McKean as editor and publisher, featured Wernher von Braun, aerospace engineer and first director of NASA; Al Capp, syndicated cartoonist and creator of *Li'l Abner*; and Peter Shaffer, playwright whose *Black Comedy* was staged during Founders' Week by the Rollins Players.

When the college celebrated its centennial in 1985, tradition-loving President Thaddeus Seymour dusted off the concept and presented a lineup that included sportscaster Red Barber, whose daughter was a college alumna; Barber's friend, NPR *Morning Edition* host Bob Edwards; and two Rollins parents, Orlando Mayor Bill Frederick and golfing legend Arnold Palmer, both of whom had daughters enrolled at the college. Non-speaker entertainment was provided by magician and humorist Jay Marshall, who appeared 14 times on the *Ed Sullivan Show*. Several students and faculty members read aloud original poems. Seymour — who in an homage to Holt toted an oversized blue pencil — sat on an outdoor platform along with the contributors. It was a laudable effort, but just 300 people gathered to listen. "It was a shadow of its old self," said Seymour in a 1980 interview with *Rollins* magazine. "But at least we re-created it." Those who did not attend, wrote *Orlando Sentinel* columnist Ed Hayes, missed "a two-hour blend of academe, nostalgia, poetry, science, humor and sheer entertainment."

In 2010 and 2011, the Winter Park Institute dubbed itself "The New Animated Magazine." The editor was the institute's distinguished senior fellow, former two-term U.S. Poet Laureate Billy Collins, who in 2010 welcomed Erik Calonius, journalist; Davey Johnson, former Major League Baseball player and manager; Scott Joseph, blogger and food critic; Jack C. Lane, professor of history emeritus and college historian; Mel Martinez, former U.S. Senator from Florida; N.Y. Nathiri, executive director of the Association to Preserve the Eatonville Community; Terry Teachout, drama critic for the *Wall Street Journal*; and James L. West, historian and biographer of novelist William Styron. In 2011, New Animated Magazine guests included Janice Aria, director of animal stewardship for Ringling Bros. and Barnum & Bailey Circus; Jim Evans, former Major League Baseball umpire; Porter Goss, first director of the Central Intelligence Agency; Randall B. Robertson, founder and executive director of GladdeningLight, a nonprofit based on the intersection of the arts and spirituality; and Christoph Wolff, a scholar of Bach.

In its heyday, the Animated Magazine drew upon Holt's vast network of contacts for talent. But not everyone was persuaded. "I can never be drawn into a show like your living magazine," wrote Robert Frost to Holt in 1936. Frost's first published poem, "My Butterfly: An Elegy," had appeared in *The Independent* in 1894. "My talents, such as they are, don't lend themselves to crowded programs. It is the rarest thing for anyone to ask me to speak or read in chorus. People have learned that my modest kind of entertainment is better when it has the occasion all to itself."[51] For Frost, then, the Animated Magazine was truly the road not taken.

---

51   It was not unreasonable for Holt to have invited a figure of Frost's stature, especially considering the poet's sentimental regard for *The Independent*. In addition, Frost had a winter home in Miami and had delivered a lecture the previous year at the University of Miami. It may be assumed, then, that Frost did not care for the carnival-like atmosphere surrounding the Animated Magazine and perhaps balked at sharing a stage with lesser lights. In any case, the event was cancelled that year following the deaths of Zenie Holt and Mertie Grover.

Chapter 2

THE FABIANS
AND HAMMER BOY

HAMILTON HOLT WAS cautious on race — a rare issue on which he behaved pragmatically, at least during his presidency — but did not hesitate to test the tolerance of conservative Winter Parkers by hiring intellectual eccentrics and placing them in the spotlight. More often than not, such characters won over the community despite their unorthodox views. That was certainly true of one golden personality who was crucial to the early Adult Education Program: the erudite John Martin, a dapper British-born socialist and self-styled authority on international affairs. Martin and his wife, Prestonia Mann Martin, moved to Winter Park from Staten Island in late 1929 at the behest of Holt, who had published Martin's editorials in *The Independent*.

Holt suggested that Martin, who was wealthy and not seeking permanent employment,[1] might enjoy conducting

---

1   In fact, the Martins' comfortable financial position was due in large part to Prestonia. She was the only child of John Preston Mann, a prominent New York surgeon who specialized in treating deformities, particularly

student seminars, perhaps at his home, and holding public lectures. "I am afraid I cannot offer you anything except the satisfaction of being 'noble' as I have exceeded my budget for instruction for this year," Holt wrote Martin in the summer of 1929. "But if you would care to give your services to the college this way, I am sure you would find yourself somewhat repaid in the inspiration you would give the young folks. I have found nothing more pleasant in my connection with Rollins College than the friendship I have formed with the coming generation."

Martin, whom Holt listed as a conference leader or a visiting lecturer and consultant on foreign affairs, was born in Lincoln, England, in 1864. After graduation from the University of London with a Bachelor of Science degree, he became a professor at East Lincoln Technical College. He also joined the London branch of the Fabian Society, an organization whose purpose was to advance the principles of socialism through gradual reform. (Essentially, then, Martin was ideologically akin to today's left-wing Democrats.) He lectured at the People's Palace in the East End of London, which offered an eclectic adult education program for working-class Londoners. And, accompanied by playwright and activist George Bernard Shaw, he attended an 1894 meeting in Brussels of the Second International, an organization of socialist parties and labor unions. Martin then crossed the pond for a lecture tour and decided to remain in New York, where he became a U.S. citizen in 1903. He subsequently directed the New York-based League for Political Education, an advocacy group for women's suffrage, and was appointed to the New York City Board of Education by Mayor George B. McClellan Jr. In addi-

---

club foot, and was unmarried when her parents died within a year of one another, enabling her to directly inherit the whole of her father's estate.

tion, Martin served on the City Housing Corporation, a private nonprofit that offered low-interest mortgages and promoted affordable housing, and later became vice president of the League of Nations Non-Partisan Association, which is almost certainly how he became acquainted with Holt.

Prestonia, born in New York in 1861, was a cousin of educational reformer Horace Mann and had an even more unorthodox background than that of her husband. Also a socialist, she had edited the *American Fabian* magazine and since 1895 had operated a rustic retreat in the Adirondacks called Summer Brook, which was modeled on Brook Farm — a short-lived utopian commune started in 1841 by transcendentalist George Ripley and his wife, Sophia, at the Ellis Farm in West Roxbury, Massachusetts.[2]

But while Brook Farm was intended to be a permanent self-sustaining settlement — hence its decline and dissolution — Summer Brook was intended for seasonal visitors only. "This experiment may fairly be deemed a success, although the critical mind, inclined to skepticism by a long line of failures, conjectures that one reason for the lasting power of the Adirondack scheme may be found in the short period of its

---

2 As a young woman Prestonia attended the Concord School of Philosophy, a lyceum-like series of summer lectures and discussions begun in 1879 by Amos Bronson Alcott and other transcendentalists in Concord, Massachusetts. At rustic Hillside Chapel, where sessions were held, Prestonia heard Ralph Waldo Emerson, de facto leader of the transcendentalist movement. The colorful and original Alcott — father of Louisa May Alcott (*Little Women*) — would certainly also have been one of the speakers. Prestonia might also have encountered Elizabeth Peabody, Julia Ward Howe, William Torrey Harris or Franklin Sanborn. "What is sought in the discussions at Concord is not an absolute unity of opinion, but a general agreement in the manner of viewing philosophic truth and applying it to the problems of life," said Alcott, who considered the school to be an adult education center and had hopes that it would evolve into a full-fledged college. Hillside Chapel still stands adjacent to the Orchard House, the Alcott family home. It is the site of an annual Summer Conversational Series and Teacher Institute.

annual endurance," opined a writer in *Munsey's Magazine*. "One can stand almost anything for a couple of months, and in the 10 months that elapse before the camp opens again, one has a chance to forget all but the pleasant features of the experience. But this is rank pessimism, induced, possibly, by contact with the optimism of the promoter and conductor of Summer Brook."

A 1900 edition of the *International Socialist Review* described Summer Brook as "a chalet built of picturesque spruce logs" where "sisters" and "brothers" shared chores during the day and, following an evening meal on a piazza overlooking mountainous terrain, enjoyed lectures, debates, poetry readings, dramatic presentations and musical performances. Prestonia, an accomplished pianist who had attended the New England Conservatory of Music in Boston, often played classical pieces or participated in reenactments of Greek tragedies, such as *Lysistrata*. "Here in the twilight, as the crimson glory of the sunset fades and the mist gathers on the dim mountains, the sisters and brothers come together in the great hall and discuss the serious problems of life, of labor, of love," rhapsodized writer Leonard Abbott, a frequent visitor.[3] "Some brother will give an informal lecture on a subject that is nearest to his heart. Or some sister — perhaps the hostess herself — will take her place at the piano, and strains from the splendid

---

3   The Liverpool-born Abbott was a member of the Socialist Party of America but was torn between anarchism and socialism. He was a founder of the Ferrer Modern School, which opened in Manhattan and later moved to rural New Jersey because of bomb threats. The school was named for Francisco Ferrer Guardia, a Spanish anarchist and free-thinker who established secular schools around Barcelona. Ferrer, who was executed in 1909 after being convicted of orchestrating an insurrection known as Barcelona's Tragic Week, was hailed as a martyr by anarchists and their sympathizers in the U.S., who established schools based upon a combination of Ferrer's pedagogy and emerging principles of progressive education. New Jersey's Ferrer Modern School closed in 1953.

operas of Wagner, or the somber sonatas of Beethoven, reecho through the hall and drift out over the valley."

A mural depicting men and women at labor topped the mantlepiece of the gathering area, while the walls were bedecked with portraits of such transcendentalist icons as the Ripleys, Ralph Waldo Emerson, Margaret Fuller and Henry David Thoreau alongside such political figures as Abraham Lincoln and George Washington. "As the summers come and go," added Abbott, "there meet in this earthly paradise among the mountains groups of kindred spirits — men and women whose lives are attuned to high ideals, whose efforts are pledged to the betterment of society."

H.G. Wells spent time at Summer Brook, as did Maxim Gorky and an array of lesser-known writers, academicians and social reformers. Martin, too, was often present at Summer Brook, where in 1900 he wed "America's greatest gift to me." The couple then bought a large home in the affluent Grymes Hill neighborhood on Staten Island, where they welcomed numerous prominent guests. One was Gorky, a Russian novelist and revolutionary who opposed the czarist autocracy and traveled to New York in April 1906 on a fundraising trip for the Bolshevik faction of the Marxist Russian Social Democratic Party. His visit had been organized by a group of anti-czarist writers that included Ernest Poole, William Dean Howells, Jack London, Mark Twain, Charles Beard and Upton Sinclair.[4] At the A-Club in Greenwich Village, Twain spoke at a dinner in Gorky's honor, proclaiming: "If we can build a republic in Russia to give the persecuted people of the czar's domain the same measure of freedom that we enjoy, then let

---

4   The Bolsheviks would eventually become the Communist Party of the Soviet Union. But in 1906, the Russian Revolution was viewed sympathetically by many Americans, who thought it akin in many ways to the American Revolution.

us do it. Anybody whose ancestors were in this country when they were trying to free themselves from oppression must sympathize with those who are now trying to do it in Russia."

Two days later, however, Joseph Pulitzer's *New York World* published the salacious news that Gorky was staying at Manhattan's luxurious Hotel Belleclaire with a Russian actress, Maria Andrieva, to whom he was not married.[5] Within hours, Gorky and Andrieva were ejected from the hotel and subsequently shunned by the literati who, in rapid succession, resigned from a committee formed to advance the revolutionary cause.[6] The Martins — to the horror of their neighbors — welcomed the couple, who stayed with their open-minded hosts for at least five weeks. Gorky wrote *Mother,* a novel about factory workers fomenting revolution, while on Staten Island and during forays to Summer Brook. Martin, who spoke Russian and enjoyed Gorky's company, told the *Orlando Morning Sentinel* decades later: "There was not a cultured family in Western Europe that would not have been honored to have them."

In 1916, the Martins collaborated on a book entitled *Feminism: Its Fallacies and Follies* with sections providing "The Man's Point of View" and "The Woman's Point of View" about topics ranging from "Women's Economic Value in the Home"

---

5   The *World* was motivated, in part, by revenge against Gorky, who had agreed to write exclusively for publishing rival William Randolph Hearst's newspaper chain.

6   Twain told the *New York Tribune*: "Gorky came to this country to lend the influence of his great name — and it is great in the things he has written — to the work of raising funds to carry on the revolution in Russia. By these disclosures he is disabled. It is unfortunate. I felt that he would be a prodigious power in helping the movement, but he is in a measure shorn of his strength. Such things as have been published relate to a condition that might be forgivable in Russia, but which offends against the customs in this country. I would not say that his usefulness has been destroyed, but his efficiency as a persuader is certainly impaired."

and "The Fading of the Maternal Instinct" (John Martin) to "Eugenics and Women" and "The Moral Uses of Husbands" (Prestonia Mann Martin). Feminism is generally a threat to the family unit, both argued, and men and women should embrace their traditional roles. "In their normal relations the special service which woman performs toward man is to *tame* him. The service he performs for her is to *steady* her. If it were not for woman's taming powers, we should lapse into savagery; if it were not for man's steadying power, society would approach Bedlam. It is true that a man engaged in correcting his wife presents a most odious appearance He is looked upon as a cad, and in general he feels himself to be one. Therefore men have withdrawn, more and more, from corrective functions. But just as almost all men are only half-tamed savages, so almost all women are potentially hysterics;" and just as it is true that the disciplined savage makes the strongest man, so the controlled hysteric gives the strongest, richest woman nature."

Prior to ratification of the 19th amendment in 1920, Prestonia became one of the most prominent anti-suffragettes in the U.S., contending that not only were women the weaker sex, they "lacked the aptitude either to make laws or ignore them." If women got the vote, she contended, then legislation should be passed allowing them to give proxies to their temperamentally better-equipped fathers or husbands. "The remedy for political ills is better men," she wrote. "Men are what women in the home have made them. There is where reform should begin."

Such views were not uncommon at the time and were espoused by women from both extremes of the ideological spectrum, albeit for different reasons. Anarchist Emma Goldman wrote in 1910 that "people of intellect ... [have] perceived that suffrage is an evil, that it has only helped to enslave people, that it has but closed their eyes that they may not see how craftily they were made to submit." Goldman, in other words, believed that women ought not to validate an inherently oppressive system by seeking more privileges within its confines. Could the Martins have accepted this rationale? If so, then why had John Martin worked for a pro-suffrage organization? The inscrutable tone of their writing — at turns both academic and outrageous — leads a modern reader to suspect that *Feminism: Its Fallacies and Follies* may have been intended as a parody. If so, only the Martins were in on the joke; newspapers reported their pronouncements in a straightforward manner — and feminists were not laughing.[7]

"It does seem to be a strange stance for them to take because in every way except suffrage, Prestonia was a feminist," said Enid Mastrianni, a historian of the Adirondacks who has researched the lives of the Martins.[8] "She and John were equal partners in their relationship. She had her own financial resources, which was very unusual at the time, and people in their circle would not have shared these views. Still, I think they meant what they said. Suffrage to them was a distraction from larger and more fundamental issues. Obviously, their language seems over the top to us today. But I will

---

7   Prestonia, when asked by the *Washington Herald* to comment on President Theodore Roosevelt's 1914 assertion that "no man is fit to be the free citizen of a free republic unless he is able to bear arms and serve with efficiency in the army," stated: "Aha! Mr. Roosevelt has inadvertently given away the case for women's suffrage, and since women are unable to bear arms and serve in the army, they are clearly unfit for citizenship." And while John did work for a suffrage organization, as a member of the New York City Board of Education he opposed paid maternity leave for teachers as elitist feminism.

8   Mastrianni, who lives in Glen Falls, New York, earned a BFA in photography from Pratt Institute and a master's degree in political science from the New School for Social Research, both in New York City. She has written articles and is working on a book about Prestonia Mann Martin.

say this: They didn't think women should vote, but once that changed, they wanted women to vote for socialists."

In late 1929, just months after the stock market crash that signaled the onset of the Great Depression, the Martins bought a lavish but unfinished Mediterranean-style home abutting Lake Virginia at 1000 Genius Drive, a road carved through then-remote grove land once owned by Charles Hosmer Morse.[9] There, at Holt's invitation, they planned to live during the winter months while maintaining their spacious home on Staten Island and their socialist retreat in upstate New York's Keene Valley, where in 1936 Prestonia's annual summer colloquium would welcome Holt and several faculty members as guest lecturers.[10] (The Martins spent their first season in Winter Park at the home of Rosalie Slaughter Morton, a pioneering surgeon and public-health advocate who owned what was then known as the Vans Agnew estate next door.)[11]

---

9   When John Martin willed the home to Rollins, the college used it to house the Conservatory of Music until 1976. It is today a private residence and has been extensively remodeled.

10   Those who were invited to Summer Brook received an invitation from the Martins that included an 1842 quote from transcendentalist educator Elizabeth Palmer Peabody: "Whoever is satisfied with society as it is, whose sense of justice is not wounded by its institutions and its spirit of commerce, has no business with this community. Neither has anyone who is willing to have other men give their best hours and strength to bodily labor in order to secure himself immunity therefrom. And whoever does not measure what society owes to its members ... by the needs of the individuals that compose it, has no lot in this new society. Whoever is willing to receive from his fellowmen that for which he gives no equivalent will stay away from its precincts forever."

11   Morton, a gynecologist, worked as a medic on the front lines during World War I and was one of the first female faculty members at the Polyclinic Hospital of New York and the College of Physicians and Surgeons at Columbia University. She was awarded an L.H.D. by Hamilton Holt in the summer of 1929 and published an autobiography, *A Woman Surgeon: The Life and Work of Rosalie Slaughter Morton,* in 1937.

The couple had barely unpacked their bags when John Martin began speaking to civic groups and participating in campus-sponsored symposia, including the second annual Institute on Statesmanship, which in January 1930 attracted more than 100 prominent figures in journalism and academia to discuss "The Formation of Public Opinion."[12] Martin's lecture series, which debuted in February 1931 at the Annie Russell Theatre, was open to the public and drew full houses with such topics as U.S. relations with India, China and the United Kingdom.

In April 1932, the lecturer was the victim of a brutal assault that left him in critical condition and attracted national newspaper coverage. Oliver Johnson Keyes, an unemployed 23-year-old college dropout, rode the train from Manhattan to Winter Park, where he purchased a hammer, tucked it into a briefcase and wandered through a driving rainstorm until he located the Martin home. Keyes, a would-be socialite whom the Martins had assisted financially when he briefly attended Hamilton College and Columbia University, was the son of Helen Johnson Keyes, the women's page editor at the *Christian Science Monitor*.

Keyes' maternal grandfather, prominent abolitionist Oliver Johnson, had been managing editor at Horace Greeley's *New York Tribune* before becoming an editor at *The Independent* from 1865 to 1870 — an irresistible coincidence that would nonetheless be overlooked by most reporters. It was later learned that Johnson and Prestonia's father, John Preston Mann, a prominent New York surgeon, had been friends. Although Johnson and Mann died before Keyes was born, their long-ago connection brought Keyes into the orbit

---

12   The Institute on Statesmanship was held for three consecutive years. Holt also initiated an annual Economic Conference that was held for 19 years.

of the childless Martins, who frequently mentored young people whom they deemed promising. Keyes even spent time at Summer Brook, he later told police, but felt abandoned by the Martins when they moved to Florida. He harbored a grudge against John Martin, more specifically, whom he had decided to kill because "I felt it was my duty." Martin, claimed Keyes, had spread rumors about him, which had resulted in his banishment from a prestigious Staten Island tennis club and had prevented him from finding employment.[13]

When the disheveled Keyes appeared unexpectedly, the Martins cautiously welcomed him and promised him food, rest and enough money to return to New York when he was ready. Keyes, who over the course of the afternoon "became more calm and gave up the idea [of killing Martin]," left after dinner but later returned and entered the unlocked home after the couple retired to their respective bedrooms. "The resentment and anger came back more strongly, and finally when I entered [Martin's] room I found him sitting up in bed reading," Keyes told the *Orlando Morning Sentinel* during a surreal interview from the Orange County Jail. "Some people might think it awful for a young man to attack someone Mr. Martin's age. But he is terribly strong and made such a vigorous effort to defend himself that I didn't feel any shame about attacking him. I would have felt forever a coward if I had not done so."

Keyes pummeled his erstwhile mentor with the hammer

---

13   The only time the name of Oliver Johnson Keyes could be found in a newspaper, other than in stories related to his crime, was in a 1930 edition of the *Baltimore Sun,* when his byline topped an article about the prospects of the American team to win the International Polo Cup at the Meadowbrook Polo Club on Long Island. Readers who are film fans will find Keyes uncomfortably reminiscent of the character Bruno Antony, played by Robert Walker in the 1951 Alfred Hitchcock thriller *Strangers on a Train.*

until Prestonia, hearing the melee, rushed to her husband's room and screamed at the bloody spectacle. She struggled with Keyes, twisting her ankle in the process, and begged him to stop. "Oliver, why are you doing this horrible thing?" she asked. "Don't you remember all that we have done for you?" Having been caught in the act, Keyes abruptly realized that Mrs. Martin, for whom he felt no ill will, would also have to be killed. Consequently he dropped the bludgeon and waited while Prestonia called the police. "I always liked her well enough," Keyes told Winter Park Police Chief A.A. Wesson, who arrived on the scene with two other officers. "It was because of her that I stopped. Really, she showed a lot of courage for a 70-year-old woman." Wesson arrested the nervous but entirely unrepentant Keyes, who matter-of-factly described what he had done and why he had done it. He was subsequently charged with assault with intent to commit premeditated murder, expressing regret only that he had apparently not succeeded. "This is the strangest crime ever to happen in Winter Park," Wesson later told reporters.

Martin, his skull fractured and barely clinging to life, was transported to the Florida Sanitarium, the precursor of AdventHealth Orlando,[14] where doctors doubted that he would live through the night. Keyes, meanwhile, dubbed "Hammer Boy" in the press, was adjudicated "hopelessly, dangerously and incurably insane" — paranoid dementia praecox was the diagnosis from a panel of doctors — and committed to Bellev-

---

14 Florida Sanitarium, owned by the Seventh-Day Adventist Church, opened in 1908 in what is now the College Park section of Orlando. The name was a holdover from the days when the institution treated primarily tuberculosis with a combination of rest, sunshine, fresh air, nutritious food, mild exercise and the "water cure" that consisted of hot baths during which patients breathed warm, moist air. But by 1932 it was as modern a hospital as could be found in Central Florida.

ue Hospital, a psychiatric facility in Manhattan.[15] He died in 1973 at the Harlem Valley Psychiatric Center in Wingdale, New York. Four months after the near-fatal attack, Martin, against all odds, had recovered sufficiently to discuss the redistribution of wealth at a meeting of the Florida Chapter of the League for Independent Political Action.[16]

But while John Martin drew large crowds for his talks, it was his wife who made national headlines with a policy proposal that caught the attention of Eleanor Roosevelt. In a 1933 pamphlet entitled "Prohibiting Poverty," Prestonia advocated conscription of everyone between ages 18 and 26 to produce the necessities of life, including food and clothing, which would then be distributed free of charge. Her "National Livelihood Plan" called for eight years of service as a "commoner" after which a newly minted "capital" would be guaranteed a basic level of subsistence permanently, even if he or she pursued a career and did not need assistance. Mrs. Roosevelt favorably referenced the program in a speech and even passed along the pamphlet to her husband, who dismissed its premise as simplistic and impractical.

Soon, though, President Franklin D. Roosevelt would introduce an alphabet soup of federal work programs, albeit less radical ones, to combat the Great Depression. "[Pres-

15   At a hearing before the county's "lunacy commission," Prestonia Mann Martin said that she and her husband tried to help Keyes because of the friendship between her father and his grandfather. However, she said, Keyes was unpopular because of his self-important attitude and "his apparent pleasure in annoyance of those about him."

16   The League for Independent Political Action was founded in 1928 by, among other prominent progressives, educational reformer John Dewey, who in 1931 chaired a colloquium on liberal arts education at Rollins. (See pages 77-81.) The league was intended to coordinate formation of a new political party uniting liberal and socialist groups. When Franklin D. Roosevelt defeated Herbert Hoover in the 1932 presidential election and began implementing New Deal programs, much of the impetus behind the league evaporated and it disbanded in 1933.

tonia Mann Martin's] ideas may seem visionary," said Walter Metcalf, senior minister of the First Congregational Church of Tampa during a public debate about relief and recovery methods. "But they have the explosive germs of a new civilization." Few reviewers, however, thought Prestonia's proposal feasible. Still, the very fact that "Prohibiting Poverty" was the subject of serious attention and contemplation is indicative of a growing sense of national desperation. It is no wonder that Holt gravitated toward the Martins, since such quixotic notions were reminiscent of his own fervor for world government.

By the mid-1930s, the John Martin Lecture Series encompassed nine talks on consecutive Thursday mornings from January through March. As audiences grew, the on-campus theater gave way to the larger First Congregational Church of Winter Park. When attendance began to top 1,000, only the auditorium at Winter Park High School (now the Winter Park Ninth Grade Center) could provide adequate seating capacity. Martin, described in the *Orlando Morning Sentinel* as "a penetrating analyst and a forceful speaker," always discussed issues of the day, encompassing domestic politics as well as U.S. relations with counties in Europe, Asia and Latin America. In 1935, he explored "Three Dictatorships (Russia, Italy, and Germany) and Three Democracies (France, Great Britain and the United States)," while in 1936 he expounded upon "The Policy of the United States Toward the War." Martin frequently posited ways in which the U.S. might avoid being drawn into the conflict raging throughout Europe and Asia. However, when the 1941 Japanese air attack on the naval base at Pearl Harbor negated neutrality, he explored the motivations of the combatants and in one lecture explained "Why War With Japan Was Inevitable."

Throughout World War II, at least one of the lectures in Martin's annual series was dedicated to what would today be called "breaking news." Many others, though, weighed potential scenarios for the war's aftermath. When in February 1943 Martin presented "Winning the War and Winning the Peace," city officials announced that the Winter Park Police Department would not enforce a federally mandated ban on pleasure driving for those who wished to attend.[17] In the lecture, Martin supported Holt's long-standing belief that only a world government that placed "irresistible might behind international law" could prevent future world wars. Martin's presentations, during which he spoke for about an hour, were free of charge; however, collections were taken to benefit scholarships, social welfare funds, war relief programs and Eatonville's Hungerford Vocational High School.

In 1944, Martin decided to retire — more or less. He delivered his final scheduled lecture, "A World Survey and the Position of the United States," before a full house at the First Congregational Church. Many Winter Park citizens, including Holt, rose to offer heartfelt tributes when the talk concluded. "Mr. Martin has probably done more for the education of this community than any one person," said Holt. "Now, are we going to *let* him retire? We are certainly not. We cannot spare him." A local physician, Eugene Shippen, then lauded Martin as "an internationalist whose loyal Americanism has never been questioned" and proposed a resolution that "put on record our sense of gratitude for the generous service this member of the Rollins faculty has rendered to the community without money and without price, our recognition of the scholarly research that has gone into the preparation of his lectures, our appreciation of the judicial and objective treatment of controversial issues and, not incidentally, the enjoy-

---

17   Although the *Orlando Morning Sentinel* dutifully reported this announcement from the college, it has a ring of hype to it since such driving bans were only sporadically enforced.

ment that has been ours in listening to the pure English and faultless diction of these discourses." The audience stood and cheered the 79-year-old socialist who, for perhaps the only time in his life, seemed all but speechless. "I can only say, my friends, that this need not be *absolutely* my last speech," he teased. "While I shall not announce any future complete winter course, I may at any time give an occasional address if circumstances warrant."

A program of presentations, renamed the John Martin Series of Lectures on International Affairs, continued with combinations of other speakers, including faculty members, winter visitors and the indefatigable Martin — who likely required little persuasion to return to the podium.[18] But few other presenters could match Martin's panache, and attendance began to dwindle. Royal W. France, an activist attorney and professor of economics who had chaired the Florida Socialist Party, was director of the series from 1945 until it ended in 1951. "A college professor with liberal views in a community like Winter Park was not all honey and roses," France would write in his 1957 autobiography, *My Native Grounds*. Indeed, Holt was often called upon to defend the hiring and retention of faculty members such as France and his colleague Edwin L. Clarke, a peace activist and professor of sociology who presented lectures in the community provocatively titled "Why I Am a Socialist."

Even Holt, well known as a progressive, was forced to tiptoe around the issue of socialism when quizzed about his own political views. "I am not a socialist," he wrote in a 1937 response to a now-lost query from his friend Irving Bacheller, who likely sought clarification because he found that whis-

---

18 Martin also celebrated the end of World War II as the college's commencement speaker in June 1945. His topic was "In Praise of General Eisenhower."

pers to the contrary had become a hinderance to fundraising. "Years ago, I gave up the idea that socialism would be my political philosophy. I felt as a young man, however, and I still feel, that as history is nothing more than the coming into his own of the common man, we shall have more rather than less democracy in the future, and therefore more collective thought and action. Whether this will be one of the hundred definitions of socialism, I cannot say." Martin's politics, however, were entirely beside the point. The nuances of difference between socialists and Fabians would have mattered little to conservative Winter Parkers, who were disinclined to embrace either political theory. Martin had managed to successfully positioned himself as an analyst, not an advocate, and was embraced for his colorful personality and good humor (to say nothing of his impeccable elocution).

Prestonia Mann Martin, who also presented lectures on campus, remained active in civic organizations but fell ill and died at age 83 on Easter Sunday in 1945. Her death came just weeks after she delivered the closing address at the Animated Magazine entitled "The Medicine Man," described as "a comical tale concerning the difficulties of a sheriff in a small town under prohibition." She was eulogized in *Winter Park Topics,* a seasonal weekly, as "original, independent and witty" and "one of Winter Park's best known and most beloved women." In his remaining years, the robust John Martin, dubbed by a reporter the "Genial Genius of Genius Drive," lectured occasionally, hosted friends constantly and enjoyed long walks along the tree-shaded streets surrounding Lake Virginia. During the 1953 edition of the Animated Magazine, he read aloud "Grandma's Declaration of Independence," a humorously defiant poem about aging written by his late wife.

On his 90th birthday, Martin complained (not so genially) to the *Orlando Morning Sentinel* that "Winter Park has

changed almost beyond recognition — and not for the better!"
When he died in 1956 at age 92, Martin willed his body to
medicine and his home to Rollins. "[John Martin] was a great
humanist," said William A. Constable, an associate professor of English, during a public service at Knowles Memorial Chapel. "He was devoted to other peoples and such social
reforms as would alleviate the lot of the poor and needy. ... But
unlike others with similar ideals, he was never intolerant. He
was always willing to learn and alter his opinions if he thought
that facts warranted the change. He never allowed his mind
to become closed. Indeed, he dreaded the possibility that he
might become what he called 'an old fossil.'"

Was Martin more an expert on international relations,
or more a suave spellbinder with an authoritative accent? No
recordings of his lectures are known to exist, and contem-
poraneous news accounts reveal mainly the topics, not the
substance, of his talks. His published scholarship is minimal
and his best-known book, *Feminism: Its Fallacies and Follies,*
has not (at the risk of understatement) held up well. However,
even if Martin's appeal was attributable in large measure to
showmanship, his popularity reinforced the college's cachet
among lifelong learners. Yes, crowds were impressive at
the Animated Magazine, thanks to savvy marketing and an
eclectic roster of celebrities (and semi-celebrities.) But the
fact that discourses on international affairs drew upwards of
1,000 listeners must have confirmed to Holt that the community wanted more of what the college had to offer.

"[Students] do not come very much as auditors or spectators to our chapel, our theater or our lectures," Holt noted
in a 1936 talk at Knowles Memorial Chapel. "It is the public
that largely fills our halls and supports our programs. Even in
our athletic contests it is difficult to get students on the sidelines except in football, and even then community spectators

are overwhelmingly in the majority. ... I will have to confess it is difficult for me to keep my internal equanimity when we have a college assembly under the cypresses on the lakeside to hear a distinguished visitor deliver a worthwhile message, and I see a couple of students walk to within 50 yards of the assembly, sit down under a tree, light cigarettes and vegetate."

Chapter 3

————

MORE THAN
MERE AMUSEMENT

JOHN MARTIN CLEARLY exuded star quality, but the Rollins College faculty included many subject-matter experts who could, and often did, speak with authority before adult audiences. Likewise, the so-called "winter faculty" — visiting scholars who gladly lectured gratis at Holt's request — enabled the college to offer a smorgasbord of diversions for dilettantes. Indeed, beginning in the late 1920s the college aggressively publicized its winter term as a kind of high-minded holiday for scholarly snowbirds. A December 1929 story in the *Orlando Morning Sentinel* read: "Winter school, corresponding in content and purpose to summer school conducted by colleges and universities in the north, will be held at Rollins College from January 6 to March 22, President Hamilton Holt has announced. As usual, college officials are expecting a large number of 'specials' who are being attracted by pleasant climate conditions in the winter term. A distinguished faculty, including a number of guest members of the staff, will conduct courses."

Guest lecturers in the winter of 1930 included Holt acquaintances such as Sir Herbert B. Ames, Canadian philanthropist and former finance director for the League of Nations; Robert Welch Herrick, novelist and professor of literature at the University of Chicago; Frederick Lynch, theologian and secretary of the Church Peace Union; and William English Walling, social reformer and founding member of the NAACP. John Martin would also be in residence, as would Animated Magazine veterans Corra Mae Harris and Jessie Belle Rittenhouse. Combine the intellectual talent readily available (and already on salary) with an all-star slate of visiting lecturers and the usual campus cultural offerings — such as plays, recitals, concerts and, of course, the Animated Magazine — and it became clear that an adult education program had, in fact, been in existence for several years; the college had simply not packaged it as such. Holt, a brilliant marketer, knew that the unveiling of yet another innovative initiative at Rollins would garner national publicity and began plotting a grandiose rollout.

Genteel Winter Park, populated by more than its fair share of intellectuals and achievers, was certainly fertile ground for such a venture. Holt's perplexing friend Harris made the case through "The Town that Became a University," a 1929 essay for the *Jacksonville Times-Union*. Harris' ode to the accomplishments of her erstwhile editor, with an introduction by Edwin Osgood Grover, was reprinted in pamphlet form and was for years distributed by the college. "Another boom, educational this time and as yet no larger than a man's hand, has started in Florida, where the trustees went crazy four years ago and elected Hamilton Holt president of the college," Harris wrote. She recounted Holt's "provocative" undergraduate academic reforms, then turned her attention to Winter Park, which she described as "a University at Large:"

By entering [Winter Park] you automatically matriculate at Rollins College, or as a winter colonist at one of the fine hotels, or as a citizen entitled to vote in the next election. You may be called upon to vote yea or nay on the Einstein theory or on the merits of a hog epic written by Carl Sandburg.[1] At the present moment, the voting privileges of every man and woman in Winter Park are practically unlimited. Whether he is a millionaire or poor man he can "make a motion" or express his opinion on the simplest or most abstruse subject that pertains to art, culture, philosophy or science.

Sensing an opportunity, and despite harsh economic conditions at home and growing turmoil abroad, Holt and Dean Winslow S. Anderson[2] conceptualized the official Adult Education Program in late 1935 and announced it in early January 1936 — just in time for registration. The compressed planning period was possible because administrators likely did little more than order brochures that bundled previously planned activities. "Winter residents have a new vista of enjoyment opened before them by the new policy of Rollins College effective next week to conduct extensive courses for adult education," reported *Winter Park Topics*. "While there have been several courses in past sessions, such as that of Dr. John

---

1 Harris appears to have been referencing Sandburg's 1913 poem "Chicago," in which he refers to the city as "Hog Butcher for the World."

2 In 1944, Anderson would become the sixth president of Whitman College in Walla Walla, Washington. Prior to Anderson's departure, Holt awarded him an L.H.D., saying that he had "complete confidence you will rise to higher and even higher achievements, both professionally and personally throughout the unfolding years." Anderson, who died suddenly in 1944, did indeed have a successful if abbreviated presidency at Whitman.

Martin on International Relations open to the general public under the auspices of the college, the new plan contemplates a further development in the field and will involve registration and regular attendance for some of the subjects taught." Such an effort would be welcome, the article continued, because "Winter Park is already known far and wide as one of the few Southern winter resorts where culture is more eagerly sought and more highly valued than mere amusement."

Holt, as was his wont, described the (not-so) new program in terms both prosaic and profound. "Adult education is nothing more than teaching an old dog new tricks," he told *Winter Park Topics*. "Scientists now know that an old dog learns more easily than a younger dog, all things being equal. Young people do not know enough to take full advantage of their college opportunities; in this new Adult Education Program, the college is offering older people the opportunity of making up what they missed in youth."

He went on to describe "four stages of man."[3] The first stage, he said, was from birth to about 15, when "predigested knowledge is imposed on young people while they are learning to be individuals." The second stage, he added, was from 15 to 25, when "youth reaches physical maturity but not intellectual or moral maturity." The third stage, Holt said, was from 25 to 45, which he described as "the serious period of a man's life, when he becomes interested in civics, politics, marriage

---

3   Holt appears to have borrowed this concept from a 1932 paper called "New Aims for Our New Adult Education" in *The Journal of Educational Sociology*, by A. Caswell Ellis, director of Cleveland College — an institution exclusively serving working adults — and former director of the University of Texas Division of Extension Program. In that paper, Ellis described four "mental youths" through which people pass regardless of chronological age; "Each of these periods brings to the mind new interests, aptitudes, and capacities which hitherto had been absent or only slightly manifested." Ellis had attended Holt's 1930 colloquium, "The Curriculum for the Liberal Arts College" (see pages 77-83).

and establishing a family, a home and finding his place in society." The fourth stage, Holt concluded, 45 and up, "is spent perfecting the third stage. Knowledge plus experience turns to wisdom. It is a philosophic stage; one is not so elated by success nor let down by failure. Life has achieved a balance and proportion." It was for the fourth-stagers that Rollins opened its campus for new adventures in learning. Smugness of *Winter Park Topics* notwithstanding, there would, in fact, be some "mere amusement" on the roster.

IN HOLT'S ARCHIVAL files is an undated, one-page report from an unnamed phrenologist who had examined Holt's facial features and the contours of his skull using a photograph. Almost certainly, given that phrenology had fallen out of favor in the late 19th century, no one at Rollins had solicited the practitioner's suspiciously spot-on report. Still, few could have disagreed with the description of Holt as a man who "would be modern and up to date in whatever line of endeavor he will pursue" and who possessed "an inborn ability to manage big things." He was, according to his cranium, "a good talker and a good listener" who was ambitious, "but not in a personal way; instead for the benefit of many." Holt also had "a keen sense of humor" and was "an entertaining and instructive speaker." While Holt was "broad-minded and willing to consider other opinions," he was determined to have his way once his mind was made up. Above all, he was "a born educator, pioneer and philosopher." All of that, without question, was true. But despite Holt's name being attached to an adult education program, his most significant pioneering and philosophizing concerned improving the experience of traditional fresh-from-high-school undergraduates.

Adult education in some form or another had existed for generations. Its roots could be traced to the lyceum movement, which was popular following the Civil War, and the Chautauqua movement, which was popular in the late 19th and early 20th centuries.[4] While these programs could certainly be educational, they drew crowds with a mixture of entertainment and intellectual content (not unlike the Animated Magazine). Holt did *not* propose a liberal arts degree program for working adults. In fact, adult education as we now know it was in its infancy in the 1920s. The University of Wisconsin-Madison began its New School for Social Research, an adult education program, in 1919, while Cleveland College, founded by Western Reserve University and Case School of Applied Science, followed in 1925. Many land-grant universities offered extension programs, but most were related to vocations, agriculture or home economics. There were few other options until the conclusion of World War II and subsequent passage of the Servicemen's Readjustment Act of 1944 — better known as the G.I. Bill — which offered educational benefits for returning service members. Rollins, in Holt's era, engaged adults in ways more suited to its time and to its mission — through a cornucopia of noncredit offerings burnished with a quasi-academic sheen.

Which is not to say that interest in a more formal

---

4   The lyceum movement in the U.S., which consisted of public education and entertainment programs, lasted through the mid-19th century and was especially popular in the Northeast and Midwest. After the Civil War, lyceums were more often vaudeville and minstrel shows, although many public figures still gave lectures, including Susan B. Anthony, Elizabeth Cady Stanton, Victoria Woodhull, Anna Dickinson, Mark Twain and William Lloyd Garrison. The Chautauqua movement, arguably the successor to the lyceum movement, was organized in 1874 as the Chautauqua Assembly by Methodist minister John Heyl Vincent and businessperson Lewis Miller at a campsite on the shores of New York's Chautauqua Lake. At the peak of the movement, several hundred independent Chautauquas operated in semi-permanent locations around the country, while independent Chautauquas staged tented events from town to town. Chautauquas remained popular in rural areas through the 1920s.

approach was lacking. In the December 1929 edition of the *Rollins Alumni Record*, a recent graduate named E.A. Upmeyer Jr. penned a prescient guest column beseeching Holt to start an adult education program in response to "a new ideal that is taking its place among ... the graduates of our colleges and universities, a new hope that education need not cease altogether at commencement. In greater numbers people are becoming interested in a continuing education, in an education that truly commences at commencement." Upmeyer, then secretary of the alumni association, lamented the fact that most graduates of Rollins — indeed, most graduates of colleges everywhere — remained connected to their schools primarily through ongoing requests for donations.

Upmeyer concluded: "We sense a growing sentiment that before long the alumni, fully appreciative of all that their alma maters have done for them and entirely willing to continue their support, will nevertheless seek from and ask of these same institutions help and guidance in the realization of fuller intellectual attainments after graduation. They will call upon the colleges and universities for this guidance. They will do so insistently and expectantly. We, representing the alumni, foresee this and are getting our organizational house in order. But we cannot and should not proceed alone. We need the help and cooperation and sympathy of the institutions and their faculties. It is something which they should foresee and be proud to meet."

HOLT'S TOP PRIORITIES, however, were to make certain that Rollins earned accreditation from the Southern Association of Colleges and Schools — a seal of approval would come in 1929 — and to restructure the undergraduate academic program. He accomplished the latter through the two-hour conference plan, developed over the summer of 1926 and implemented just days before classes began in September. The plan established a four-period day, with two-hour classes meeting three times weekly. The fourth period would be dedicated to such supervised activities as recreation, field trips and laboratory work. Noted the quotable Holt: "Far from being a radical movement, the plan simply goes back to Socrates and puts that noble Athenian on an eight-hour day." The longer class sessions, according to the college catalog, would facilitate "the free exchange of thought between pupil and teacher in personal conference during which the student is helped over difficulties, shown how to study and given an illustration of a scholarly attitude for knowledge." Further, Holt hoped, the conference system would condemn the lecture system — "probably the worst scheme ever devised for imparting knowledge," he often said — to the dustbin of educational history.

In a letter to *The Sandspur*, Dean George Carrothers explained that the new approach "may mean individual or group discussion; it may mean students working in the library while others are working in the classroom; it may mean a complete break in the continuity of all group and individual activity and sending the entire class to the open air for relaxation; it may mean leaving breaks and study time to the discretion of the individual students." In an October 1930 edition of *The Nation*, Holt wrote that the conference plan "assumes an approximation of college life to normal living as well as a correlation of subjects to be studied. On this premise, we have shifted our emphasis and our forms of responsibility from the faculty and administration to the students. We find that because young people really accept responsibility willingly and carry it well because they like being treated as adult, reasonable beings [and] seem to lose, if they have it on entrance, the average student's resistance to things academic. They learn to recognize education for the thing we believe it should be: a joint adventure and a joint quest."[5]

What, then, should be taught during those two-hour blocks? Holt sought direction in January 1931 with a high-profile campus colloquium, "The Curriculum for the Liberal Arts College," led by educational reformer John Dewey, professor of philosophy at Columbia University, founder of the University of Chicago Laboratory Schools and co-founder of the New School of Social Research in New York.[6] Dewey, one of the most important thinkers of the 20th century, believed that a democratic society functioned best when populated by informed and engaged citizens. Therefore, he also wrote hundreds of commentaries on social issues for such popular publications as *The New Republic,* and was a celebrity intellectual whose participation ensured that the colloquium would attract national attention. Other participants included two college presidents: Arthur E. Morgan of Antioch College; and Constance Warren of Sarah Lawrence College — both "experimental" institutions that emphasized individually tailored programs and small seminar-style classes.

Also attending were Henry Turner Bailey, director of the Cleveland School of Art and lecturer at the Cleveland

---

5   The article was originally a speech entitled "The Rollins Idea." It was reprinted in several education magazines and earned the college significant publicity in the mainstream press.

6   Dewey, whose work had been almost entirely focused on elementary and secondary education, told attendees that he had little expertise in undergraduate education — but added that his lack of experience might give him "the degree of ignorance necessary to make me a suitable chairman of this meeting." He noted that his own children were in college and were offered "a deadly scheme" of six courses, two hours at a time, as freshmen. Dewey said he told his children that he "didn't care about their slighting some courses, but I did hope they would find some one thing they were interested in to which they could really devote their thoughts and mental operations." Dewey was a Fabian and a friend of John Martin and Prestonia Mann Martin.

Art Museum; Wilder D. Bancroft, professor of chemistry at Cornell University; Joseph K. Hart, professor of education at Vanderbilt University; James H. Robinson, former professor of history at Columbia University and co-founder (with Dewey) of the New School for Social Research; and Goodwin Watson, professor of educational psychology at Teachers College at Columbia University.[7]

All were ardent progressives; Watson had, in fact, spoken at Rollins the previous April and declared to an audience of students and faculty members that most introductory and prerequisite courses were wastes of time. "There is about as much difference between the civics books I have read and the actual methods of government in New York City as there is between the beatitudes of the Marines and their activities in Central America,"[8] he said. "Life is too short to be crowded with unimportant and irrelevant material." Watson called upon colleges to replace standard academic departments with "functional" departments based on life and work, including health, vocation, leisure, citizenship and home participation. A journalist had also been invited to the colloquium: John Palmer Gavit, associate editor of *The Survey* magazine, who had recently visited more than 30 campuses in preparation of

---

7   In 1964, Watson and Antioch College President James P. Dixon would co-found the Union for Research and Experimentation in Higher Education, a consortium of small progressive colleges that included Antioch, Sarah Lawrence College, Goddard College, Hofstra University and Bard College. This was the genesis of Union Institute and University, based in Cincinnati, which offers accredited distance-learning degree programs for nontraditional students.

8   Watson seems to have been referring to the so-called Banana Wars, which were police actions by the U.S. government, usually carried out by the Marines, in Central America and the Caribbean between the end of the Spanish-American War in 1898 and the inception of President Franklin D. Roosevelt's noninterventionist Good Neighbor Policy in 1934.

an article on higher education.[9]

However, only one recognized expert on adult education was on the roster: the irascible A. Caswell Ellis, director of Cleveland College — an institution exclusively serving working adults — and former director of the University of Texas Division of Extension Program.[10] Ellis' presence indicated that Holt may have considered devoting a session to adult education, but the topic was never addressed during the colloquium's public sessions. It is likely, however, that Holt had read a widely circulated transcript of Ellis' incisive 1927 speech, "Adult Education: Its Role in Our Educational System and a Few of its Problems," originally delivered at an Association of Urban Universities conference in Pittsburgh. In typical forthright fashion, Ellis pointed out the "educational folly" of trying to teach everything worth knowing in the years that span first grade through college.

"The processes of civilization have become so complex, and new knowledge is being added so rapidly each year in every field, that is imperative for education to continue

---

9 Gavit had in 1909 complied the first journalist's stylebook — a precursor to the *A.P. Stylebook* dubbed *The Reporter's Manual: A Handbook for Newspaper Men.* The manual offers dictionary-style entries on what topics journalists should and should not cover, why and how as well as practical advice. Correspondents should have a notebook, Gavit wrote, with the names of "local officers, justice of the peace, coroner, postmaster, station agent, ministers, lawyers, undertakers, doctors, teachers and others upon whom you may call in a pinch." This list is like a "mine of diamonds. ... The man or woman whom you met two years ago and forgot, but whose name is in your book, may be the very one who will save the day [with] first-class scoops." The only two golden rules in Gavit's manual: "Never betray a confidence" and "never deliberately pervert or misrepresent facts."

10 Under Ellis' leadership, Cleveland College grew from 1,400 students in 1926 to nearly 7,000 in 1941, when he resigned and returned to Texas. There he was appointed adult-education counselor for the University of Texas in 1942 and became director of the University Evening College in 1946.

throughout life," Ellis insisted. "Even the college graduate has acquired a fair knowledge of only the one or two fields in which he specialized, with overpowering ignorance of nearly everything else. And 10 years after graduation, if he has not kept up with his studies, he is out of date even in his specialty." More than vocational training, Ellis added, adults needed "culture courses" that would help them better enjoy their leisure time and mitigate "the great danger that life may lose its zest" in middle age. He lambasted many nascent adult education programs as "intellectual vaudevilles" begun as business enterprises to support struggling day colleges. Five decades later, some would repeat that very criticism about the Rollins program.

Ellis could have contributed much to any discussion about adult education, particularly in the company of like-minded reformers. But his concluding remarks at the colloquium did not mention adult education at all. In a talk he labeled "Required Courses and Minimal Essentials," Ellis voiced support for the goal of a flexible, student-centered undergraduate curriculum: "It seems reasonable to say that there must be some irreducible minimum somewhere in college education, but the more I have studied the facts the more doubtful I have become that anybody knows what that minimum is, or even that there is a single irreducible minimum best for all students."

Yes, Ellis conceded, required courses might rid some students of "warped, stupid views and distorted, ephemeral, destructive interests." But in most cases, he insisted, "the effect of a mere requirement is just the opposite, building up a distaste that may spread over the entire college course. In the rare cases in which good results follow a requirement, [the good results] have been brought about not by the mere requirement, but by other factors present that might function even better without the requirement ...We should recognize that, in so far as we resort to compulsion, we are depriving the students of the opportunity of gaining mastery of themselves through considering values intelligently and making their own choices. To the extent that compulsion is found necessary, it should be regarded as a confession of failure."

Opinions expressed during the five-day event, which consisted of open-to-the-public panel discussions at the Masonic Temple on Comstock Avenue,[11] were lively and varied. Cornell's Bancroft, playing devil's advocate, offered perhaps the most entertaining observation: "If we consider Rollins as an experiment, then it is a grand experiment, but so is Prohibition — and some of us don't like it." A young woman told the educators that she and her friends had determined that they would take no courses that might qualify them to teach. "Not that we do not regard teaching as an honorable profession," she said. "We just want to do something else. If we take these subjects, we're afraid we might be induced to teach later."

Ultimately, the conferees validated what Holt had called "a common-sense approach" to higher education and endorsed such progressive principles as individualization and the collaborative quality of the student-teacher relationship. In a February 1931 letter to Holt, which included a typewritten copy of his remarks, Ellis noted that "Dewey seemed to think this was so good that it should be put into the minutes and [he] asked me to write it out. Morgan and Gavit both said that it jarred them pretty much loose from their former adherence to required courses." In his reply, Holt agreed that Ellis had "provided the best summary ... that I have yet seen" and had "forever disposed" of the debate over required courses. In fact, required courses were

---

11   The building still stands and was, as of 2019, home to the college's office of marketing and public relations.

not abolished — at least not entirely — but profound change greeted the freshman class of 1931.

Using the colloquium's final report as a guide, the college adopted a new program that reflected what Holt called "individualization in education." The process started with admissions, where personal characteristics — not the number of credits completed — became determinative. "Personally, I would admit to Rollins any student above the intelligence of a moron and mature enough to carry out college work, provided only he shows capacity for improvement," wrote Holt in a 1932 edition of *American Scholar*. "It ought not to be vital to success in college ... whether one improves slowly or quickly. We all have to start at some particular time and place and do the best we can with the faculties God has given us. He who keeps improving will surely amount to something, and he is worth educating." Upper and lower divisions were created, replacing the designations of freshman, sophomore, junior and senior. "New methods of evaluating a student's work have evolved, grades and credits have been abandoned, rigid course requirements have been abolished and the time element in getting a degree has been eliminated," Holt continued. "The work of the student has been placed on an 'accomplishment' basis rather than on a specified term of residence and the passing of a heterogeneous group of unrelated courses."

There were, in fact, some required courses in the lower division, but with the help of a faculty advisor even recently admitted students could pursue individual areas of interest. "The plan calls for no required courses [in the upper division] but prescribes definite accomplishments for each student," wrote Holt. "The college will offer — and probably the majority of students will take — courses in which they will acquire the materials necessary for the satisfaction of requirements; but there is nothing to prevent a student from satisfying the requirements purely by independent work or by work carried on under the informal guidance of a member of the faculty." No grades? No credits? Few required courses? This was indeed a leading-edge approach. Although the curriculum would change over time — major revisions, always guided by progressive principles, would occur every several decades — the adoption of "individualism in education" exemplified a willingness to challenge academic orthodoxy that would become permanently embedded in campus culture.

"An immediate benefit of the new curriculum ... was the intellectual ferment that engulfed the campus during the early thirties," wrote college historian Jack C. Lane. "The entire college community was involved for over a year in an intensive debate over educational ideas. This discourse itself was a significant learning experience at Rollins, and as it turned out, it precipitated an academic dialogue that would become a lasting part of the Rollins tradition."

WHEN THE FIRST specifically branded adult education classes began in January 1936, none of the reforms related to the conference plan or the curriculum colloquium were applicable to locals and winter visitors for whom "culture is more eagerly sought and more highly valued than mere amusement." No one was seeking a degree — the program did not offer one — and no one was interested in an outcome beyond personal enrichment. Few who registered knew that the college, often described in press reports as "swanky" or "ritzy," was on the brink of financial collapse. Money problems were due in part to Holt's Depression-be-damned building spree, which was dotting the lakeside campus with finely wrought Mediterranean-style structures. The cohesive architecture, Holt believed, served as both an homage to the college's subtropical location and a symbol of its unified academic purpose.[12]

But faculty salaries were cut by 30 percent in 1933, prompting the American Association of University Professors to complain that the ambitious construction program was essentially being financed by faculty members who could ill afford to do so. Further, a new method of calculating tuition called the "unit cost plan" — which divided the college's operating budget by the estimated number of students, thus producing a per-student unit cost — was implemented in 1934 and resulted in ill-timed out-of-pocket increases. Although endowment funds were used for financial aid, hopefully cushioning the impact on students not from wealthy families, enrollment in 1936 dropped by 25 percent, to about 470.

Adult education was not, of course, meant to erase operating deficits since many of the classes and lectures were free of charge and others carried only modest fees. Holt hoped that the program would encourage philanthropic support from well-to-do enrollees who, through their participation, would feel warmly toward the college and vested in its success. But the effort had an altruistic purpose as well. In a 1936 brochure that listed winter offerings, Holt dusted off a quote from one of the first speeches he delivered after his appointment as president: "My ideal of a college is based on service. First, of course, to the students who have paid their tuition and gathered on this campus to continue their search for Truth. Second, to the community in which the college is located, and third, so far as resources permit, to the general public. We are all debtors to the world. We owe everything we have in life. We know we can never pay this debt, but the only real happiness in life is trying to pay it."

12 The architect for Holt's first buildings — Rollins Hall, Mayflower Hall and Pugsley Hall — was Richard Kiehnel of Miami. By the time he retired in 1949, Holt had added 32 new buildings to the campus, including Knowles Memorial Chapel and the Annie Russell Theatre.

The first season was marred by tragedy, when the wives of both Holt and Grover died within 24 hours of one another and the Animated Magazine was, for the first and only time in its history, cancelled. But other offerings were presented as scheduled, including the always-popular John Martin Lecture Series as well as nine talks by Thomas Chalmers, a winter visitor and professor of history at Boston University, who spoke Monday mornings at the Annie Russell Theatre on the general theme of "Tragedies in Diplomatic History." His topics ranged from "The Sad Blunders of July 1914," about the international crisis that began with the assassination of Archduke Franz Ferdinand in Sarajevo and culminated in the British declaration of war on Germany, to "America at Versailles: The Wilson-Lodge Conflict," about the rejection in the U.S. Senate of the League of Nations. Chalmers also addressed the ascension to power of Hitler and Mussolini in "The Failure of Communism: The Restless Sweep of the Dictators."[13] Other lecture series for which no registration was required were presented by Harve Clemens, director of the Conservatory of Music ("Music Appreciation"); Virginia Robie, assistant professor of art ("Great Personalities in Art"); and by four members of the English faculty, including Richard E. Burton and Fred Lewis Pattee, professors of American literature; Jessie Belle Rittenhouse, poet and visiting lecturer; and Bertha Wright, exchange professor from University College of the Southwest at Exeter, England, who joined forces for "Excursions in English and American Literature."

Registrants were also invited to audit selected regular college courses, including astronomy with Phyllis H. Hutch-

---

13 It would be interesting to read a transcript of this lecture, since Chalmers was later criticized for alleged anti-Semitism and advocated a "hands-off" stance regarding criticism of Hitler and Nazi Germany in the mid-1930s.

ings, associate professor of astronomy; sculpture and drawing with Marjorie D. Holmes and Hugh F. McKean (who would become president of the college in 1951), assistant professors of art; and art history and interior decoration with the art department's versatile Robie, who for several years arranged tours of Winter Park's most impressive homes for her students.[14] Lecture series were most often free, although a silver collection was taken. A few cost $5 for the series or 60 cents for a single lecture. The cost to audit a regular college course ranged from $25 to $37.50 and, although credit could be arranged through the registrar's office, it seems unlikely that many chose to view the Adult Education Program as an academic endeavor.

In addition, private music lessons were offered by conservatory faculty members, while the Rollins Players mounted several productions at the Annie Russell Theatre, including Lewis Beach's holiday-themed comedy *The Goose Hangs High* and Martin Flavin's romantic drama *Children of the Moon*. Irish-born stage actress Annie Russell, the venue's namesake, had been in failing health and died at age 72 just as the season opened.[15] So the plays were directed by Dorothy Lock-

---

14   Robie, who trained at the School of Decorative Design at the Boston Museum of Fine Arts and the School of Decorative Design and Applied Ornament at the Art Institute in Chicago, was an editor of home design magazines and the author of many books about art and architecture. In addition, she wrote fairy tales, children's plays, book reviews and articles for such publications as *Country Life*, *Century Magazine*, *International Studio*, *House and Garden*, *Ladies' Home Journal*, the *World Book Encyclopedia* and *Légion d'honneur*. After joining Rollins in 1928 as an assistant professor of art, Holt asked her to become the college's official interior decorator.

15   Russell's Olde English Comedy Company, which occupied the intimate 299-seat Princess Theatre in New York, attracted a variety of patrons, but none more important in Russell's life than Mary Louise Curtis, daughter of publishing magnate Cyrus H. K. Curtis, founder of Curtis Publishing Company. Curtis saw Russell in *The Stronger Sex* and was mesmerized. She later met the actress through her fiancé, Edward W.

hart Smith, also an actress and the wife of Assistant Professor of History Rhea Marsh Smith.[16] In addition, the theater sponsored a professional artists' series that featured a performance by legendary dancer and choreographer Martha Graham. The Symphony Orchestra of Central Florida, founded by local patron of the arts Mary L. Leonard[17] and conducted by Professor of Music Alexander Bloch, presented Thursday evening concerts at the Recreation Hall.

A speakers' bureau was organized and offered the services of faculty members and students of speech and debate for presentations at local high schools. One of the more intriguing lecturers was student Anny Rutz, the only woman to have played the role of the Virgin Mary twice in the 300-year history of the passion play at Oberammergau in the Bavarian Alps. Holt, who saw Rutz perform in 1934, was so moved that he encouraged her to relocate to the U.S. and offered her a schol-

---

Bok, editor-in-chief of her father's flagship magazine, *Ladies' Home Journal*. For the rest of her life, Russell would regard the meeting as "the beginning of the dearest friendship I have ever established." It was Bok who gifted Rollins the funds to build the Annie Russell Theatre, which opened in 1933. Russell was awarded an L.H.D. from Rollins that same year.

16   Dorothy Lockhart, a Baltimore native, worked as an actress in the U.S., England and Ireland. She held a theater promotion job in Cambridge until 1932, when she visited her friend Annie Russell as the opening of the Annie Russell Theatre neared. She intended to remain in Winter Park only three weeks and then resume her career in New York but met Smith and married him just months after. She later described Smith, who also did some acting, as "one of those many young men who sat at the feet of Miss Russell." She added that he was "a delightful creature."

17   Leonard, who trained as a pianist, formed the orchestra in 1927 as the Winter Park Symphony and recruited players mostly from the Rollins Conservatory of Music faculty. Charles Sturgis Andrews, then director of the conservatory, was the first conductor. Later, violinist and conductor Alexander Bloch joined the faculty and wielded the baton for what had become the Symphony Orchestra of Central Florida. In 1933, Leonard was given a D.Mus. degree from Rollins.

arship.[18] Rutz's presentation, "Behind the Scenes at Oberammergau," was accompanied by more than 100 slides and was apparently so well received that she left Rollins to tour the U.S. as a lecturer.

Capping off a successful program launch, just days after the winter term ended (and less than a month following the death of Zenie Holt), President Franklin D. Roosevelt — whom Holt had met nearly two decades before, through the Woodrow Wilson Foundation — was on campus to receive an L.H.D. in ceremonies at Knowles Memorial Chapel.[19] (Eleanor Roosevelt received the Algernon Sydney Sullivan Award, prompting her husband to remark that it was the first time he had seen his "better half" in a cap and gown.)[20] The Roosevelts

---

18   Rutz portrayed the Virgin Mary at Oberammergau two more times, in 1940 and 1950, but townspeople opposed allowing her to reprise the role in 1960 because she was by then divorced.

19   In John "Jack" Rich's 2005 oral history interview, he recalled the reaction of Rollins benefactor Frances Knowles Warren to the Roosevelts' visit: "The residents of Winter Park were very conservative, dyed-in-the-wool Republicans ... who hated the name Roosevelt. So when [Holt] finally worked out the date for the Roosevelts to come... [he] thought it would be a polite gesture to let Mrs. Warren know. ... She said, "Hamilton, if you're about to tell me that the Roosevelts have accepted an invitation to come here, and that you want to have the convocation in the chapel, don't forget I gave that chapel to the college not with any strings attached. It's for you to use as you see fit. So, if that's the purpose of all this, you're wasting your time." And she said, "I just have one request. Don't ask me to be in town when those people are here, because I will not be here when they're in town."

20   The genesis of the Algernon Sydney Sullivan Award was a friendship between Holt and George Sullivan, son of Algernon Sydney Sullivan and Mary Mildred Sullivan. The elder Sullivan was a civic-minded trial lawyer and philanthropist in New York, while his Virginia-born wife was active in the Southern Relief Association following the Civil War and later managed the New York Nursery and Child's Hospital. George Sullivan and the New York Southern Society — a social organization founded by his father — began the awards program in 1927 to recognize outstanding community service by undergraduates. Rollins, however, presented the award to notable nonstudents as well. In 1930, George Sullivan created the Algernon Sydney Sullivan Foundation and in 1936

had originally scheduled their trip to coincide with Founders' Week, but when they were delayed the college pulled together a special convocation at which FDR heaped praise upon his host. "[Holt's] old friends were not at all surprised when he substituted new ideas in education for old practices," Roosevelt said. "These changes at Rollins are bearing fruit. They are being watched by educators and laymen. The fact that in some respects they break away from the old academic moorings should not startle us. In education, as in politics and economics and social relationships, we hold fast to the old ideas and only change our method of approach to the attainment of the ideals. Stagnation follows standing still. Continued growth is the only evidence of life."

Despite its financial travails, there had certainly been no stagnation at Rollins in 1936. Many hundreds of locals and winter visitors availed themselves of one or more adult education opportunities. The following season, the program was expanded to include more regular college classes available to audit. And the Bach Festival of Winter Park, launched the previous year by artist and educator Isabelle Sprague-Smith and conducted by new conservatory director Christopher O. Honaas, was added to the roster of cultural attractions. Chalmers, a popular speaker from the inaugural season, was back with a nine-lecture series on "Critical Hours in the History of the World," in which he expounded upon "moments of hesitation and ill-considered decisions equally fatal." His topics ranged from "Catherine de' Medici and the Night of St. Bartholomew," about the 1572 St. Bartholomew's Day Massacre during which more than 10,000 French Huguenots were killed, to "The English Marriage Crisis," about the tumult

---

began the Algernon Sydney Sullivan Scholars Program. As of 2019, more than 60 campuses participated in the scholarship program.

following the 1936 engagement of twice-divorced American socialite Wallis Simpson and King Edward VIII of England.

On a lighter note, a new lecture series was offered by Evelyn Newman, professor of English literature, who discussed her travels to literary sites and such topics as "Current Plays on Broadway," "Recent English Novels" and "Streamlining Shakespeare for the World." In addition to lectures, in the late 1930s still more regular courses were opened for auditing, including language, religion and psychology. No wonder the Adult Education Program was so successful, wrote University of Florida President John James Tigert in a 1940 letter solicited by the college to use for fundraising: "First of all there is the inescapable influence of a great personality as president, surrounded by a whole host of literary and intellectual personages who live in and around Winter Park. During recent years the difficult conditions do not appear to have impeded the progress of Rollins."

Or so it seemed. By the early 1940s, the Adult Education Program had grown to include courses on etchings, the study of antiques, conversational Spanish and creative writing. The writing course was offered by Edwin Granberry, author of three novels — *The Ancient Hunger* (1927), *Strangers and Lovers* (1928), and *The Erl King* (1930) — as well as an acclaimed 1932 short story, *A Trip to Czardis,* which won the 1932 O. Henry Memorial Award and was anthologized more than 40 times.[21] Granberry, the college's Irving Bach-

---

21 *A Trip to Czardis*, set in the Florida backwoods, supposedly near Orlando, is about a woman — her two unwitting sons in tow — traveling to visit her condemned husband for the last time. The story was adapted into a radio play broadcast over the CBS Radio Network in 1939. *A Trip to Czardis* made its television debut on NBC's *Colgate Theater* in 1949. Another teleplay was produced in 1956 by writer Robert Herridge as part of a dramatic anthology series called *The Robert Herridge Theater*. The series, rejected as too highbrow by CBS, ran in syndication on educational television stations during the 1960 season. Granberry

eller Professor of Creative Writing, also reviewed books for *The New York Sun* and was among the first to praise Margaret Mitchell's *Gone With the Wind*,[22] which the native Mississippian particularly appreciated for its sympathetic portrayal of idealized Southern culture. But those who signed up for Granberry's adult education creative writing class likely knew him best as the writer of *Buz Sawyer*, a popular syndicated comic strip about the adventures of a raffish naval aviator drawn by fellow Winter Parker Roy Crane. For a $50 fee, Granberry — whose admirers included Mitchell, Thornton Wilder and Sinclair Lewis[23] — not only provided written critiques of student submissions but also shared his expertise on navigating the world of marketing and publishing works of fiction. A

---

expanded *A Trip to Czardis* into a novel in 1966 and wrote an unproduced screenplay.

22 Wrote Granberry in the *New York Sun*: "We are ready to stand or fall by the assertion that this novel has the strongest claim of any novel on the American scene to be bracketed with the work of the greats from abroad — Tolstoy, Hardy, Dickens and the modern [Sigrid] Undset [a Norwegian novelist who won the Nobel Prize for Literature in 1928]. We have had more beautiful prose from American writers; and we have had those who excel in this or that branch of the novelist's art. But we can think of no single American novelist who has combined as has Mitchell all the talents that go into the making of the great panoramic novel such as the English and Russians and the Scandinavians have known how to produce."

23 When Lewis was awarded the Nobel Prize for Literature in 1930 – the first American to be so honored — his acceptance speech offered a harsh critique of the literary establishment in his home country, particularly the American Academy of Arts and Letters. But Lewis singled out Rollins for praise: "No, I am not attacking — I am reluctantly considering the [American Academy of Arts and Letters] because it is so perfect an example of the divorce in America of intellectual life from all authentic standards of importance and reality. Our universities and colleges, or gymnasia, most of them, exhibit the same unfortunate divorce. I can think of four of them, Rollins College in Florida, Middlebury College in Vermont, the University of Michigan and the University of Chicago — which has had on its roll so excellent a novelist as Robert Herrick, so courageous a critic as Robert Morss Lovett — which have shown an authentic interest in contemporary creative literature. Just four."

popular program — and a particularly quaint one, in this age of instant streaming entertainment — was "Listening Hour," during which student proctors played phonograph records of classical music at the Dyer Memorial Building, now the Faculty Club. There was also an "astronomical open house," during which visitors could peer through the college's telescope and have the constellations explained by a college instructor.

"In town and gown there seems to be someone who is an expert about every vital human interest," wrote Holt in a 1941 edition of *Winter Park Topics.* "These we are lucky enough to have ever with us, but in addition we hope to have distinguished visitors here who can help us interpret the rights and duties of the hour, and Rollins College will certainly do its part both in our college courses and in our Adult Education Program, primarily for the benefit of the community, to explain what is explainable in the great new problems confronting all good Americans." That year's roster did indeed seem to have something to interest just about everyone.

Boston University's Chalmers, around whom the lecture program had been designed, had died in 1940, but other guest speakers filled the void. Notable among them was Alonzo L. Baker, field secretary of the Race Betterment Association, a group that advocated for improvement of the human species through eugenics, a term coined in 1883 by English scientist Francis Galton, a cousin of Charles Darwin. Eugenics promoted the perfecting of humankind by encouraging the procreation of the fit and discouraging, or prohibiting, procreation of the unfit, sometimes using moral or racial criteria to identify undesirables. The concept fell into universal disrepute when it was appropriated by the Nazis to justify atrocities but was accepted as reasonable by some social reformers prior to World War II. "Needed: Better People for a Better World" was Baker's topic. Other lecturers included Hayne Davis, an author and activist who attended the second peace conference at The Hague with Holt and wrote about it for *The Independent*, and the dashing Count Jehan de Noue, who fought in the British Expeditionary Force and told stories from the front lines in World War II.[24]

As the war dragged on, the Animated Magazine and such recurring programs as the Annie Russell Theatre plays, the Bach Festival and recitals from members of the conservatory faculty continued unabated. Permanent faculty, however, lectured more often than out-of-town academicians due to travel restrictions. In 1944, for example, Edwin Osgood Grover presented a 10-lecture series called "Romance of the Book," during which he discussed rare books and the history of printing and shared such artifacts as a Babylonian clay tablet and a single leaf from a Guttenberg Bible. Kathryn Abbey Hanna, wife of Professor of History Alfred H. Hanna and former chair of the Department of History at Florida State University, presented a 10-lecture series called "The National State System of Hispanic America," during which she discussed challenges facing Mexico, Central America, South America and the Caribbean.[25]

Grover, Hanna and the ubiquitous John Martin were the only lecturers in 1944, although an expanded roster of regular college classes were available for auditing. Generally, though, adult education offerings were categorized as "lecture courses," for which no registration was required;

---

24 The count, who would later become chief of protocol to the United Nations, joined the faculty in the fall term and taught courses in French and French civilization. When he left in 1948 for the U.N. job he was replaced by another titled instructor, the Baroness Colette Van Boecop.

25 Hanna's most enduring legacy is as an environmentalist. She was a member and chairwoman of the Florida Board of State Parks from 1953 to 1963 and lobbied for the protection of the state's natural resources. A city park in Jacksonville is named in her honor.

"study courses" and "college courses," for which registration was required; and "entertainment programs," such as plays, concerts and the Animated Magazine along with other Founders' Week activities. Private music lessons were always on the schedule as well.

Holt, meanwhile, redoubled his world government activities when atomic bombs devastated Hiroshima and Nagasaki in August 1945 and the war ended with Japan's surrender later that month. Holt got an opportunity to deliver what he called "an open sermon" to President Harry S. Truman in February 1946, when the steely Missourian who had deployed nuclear weapons made a whirlwind trip to Central Florida and stopped by the college to receive an L.L.H. during convocation at Knowles Memorial Chapel.[26] His Founders' Week appearance coincided with the Soviet Union's blockade of Berlin, which marked the first major skirmish of the Cold War. "We are working for peace," vowed Truman, who likely anticipated, and just as likely did not wish to hear, an admonition from Holt. "We want peace. We pray for peace all the time in the world. And to attain that peace we must all learn how to live together peaceably and to do to our neighbors as we would have our neighbors do to us. Then we will have a happy world. And that is what we all want."

Holt, in turn, repeated much of his now-familiar stump

---

26 Truman was the third sitting president to visit Rollins. Holt had to promise President Calvin Coolidge that he would not be required to speak or to accept an honorary degree when he visited in 1930. The Coolidges attended a musical program in the college's Recreation Hall but "Silent Cal" did not address the crowd of 2,000. Holt thanked Coolidge for his role in steering about $50,000 to the college from the estate of flashlight manufacturer Conrad Hubert, who had stipulated in his will that two-thirds of his $8 million fortune be administered jointly by a Protestant, a Catholic and a Jew, and distributed to organizations that "served the public welfare." Coolidge, Alfred E. Smith and Julius Rosenwald decided how the money would be allocated.

speech and argued that Truman's military buildup was as likely to cause conflict as to preserve peace. "The fact is there is no such thing as absolute preparedness," he said. "That is why the generals and admirals are never satisfied." Yes, Holt acknowledged, the Soviet Union almost certainly intended to "extend her political ideologies to the outside world and thus eventually abolish capitalism, if not democracy." But the answer was not "feverishly to arm ourselves against an impending World War III." Truman should instead call for the United Nations to revise its charter and reconstitute itself as a "world government with direct power to tax, conscript and otherwise make and enforce laws."

Holt claimed not to know what the domestic political ramifications of such a stance would be for Truman. He insisted, however, that in the grand scheme of things it hardly mattered: "If you are reelected you will have four more years to carry out your great design. If, however, you are defeated, you will still have the acclaim of millions of mankind as well as the personal satisfaction of having done more than any living man to put this great ideal into the minds and hearts of your fellow men." How would this organization deal with a recalcitrant Soviet Union? "We might have to set [world government] up without Russia and her satellites," Holt conceded. "But sooner or later, all the outside nations will come in." Holt, although he tempered his remarks during convocation, had previously opined that any nation rejecting United Nations control over atomic energy "should be wiped off the face of the earth with atomic bombs." Geopolitical realities had shaken his view that every civilized nation, based upon self-interest, would sooner or later decide to become "federated in a brotherhood of universal peace." Some nations, it now appeared, might require more persuasion.

Holt, whose activism never waned, convened the Rollins

College Conference on World Government in March 1946, inviting 40 like-minded luminaries — 25 of whom attended — representing academia, industry, politics and the clergy.[27] After several days of discussion, the group, chaired by historian Carl van Doren, adopted an "Appeal to the Peoples of the World." The three-page document, which mirrored Holt's convocation speech, called for creation of a world government "to which shall be delegated the powers necessary to maintain the general peace of the world based on law and justice." Conferees agreed that the United Nations, toothless in its present form, at least provided a ready framework — much as the League of Nations had more than 25 years before — and could be reconstituted as a legislative body that would regulate the use of atomic energy, impose civil and criminal sanctions against violators of international law and, if necessary, launch military action against malefactors.

Although practical detail, as usual, was lacking, the appeal was signed by 80 prominent individuals. Theoretical physicist Albert Einstein, whose warning to President Roosevelt about Germany's atomic research had spurred the Manhattan Project, was among the absentee signatories. Holt, who declared the committee's proposal to be "the soundest, most advanced

---

27   Other than Einstein, few of the signatories are familiar names today. Exceptions are Justice William O. Douglas of the U.S. Supreme Court (1939-1975); Florida U.S. Senator Claude Pepper (1936-1951), who later served in the U.S. House of Representatives; and California U.S. Representative H. Jerry Voorhis (1937-1947), who is remembered for losing his seat to a Red-baiting novice named Richard M. Nixon. Holt's son, George, who had graduated from Rollins and was now its director of admissions, chaired the conference. Also in attendance was Edwin E. Slosson, Holt's colleague from *The Independent* who had written *Great American Universities*, and Ray Stannard Baker, a muckraking journalist whose eight-volume *Woodrow Wilson: Life and Letters (1927–1939)*, won the Pulitzer Prize for Biography or Autobiography in 1940. Baker's 1908 book *Following the Color Line: An Account of Negro Citizenship in the American Democracy*, was among the first to seriously examine the racial divide in the U.S.

and most statesmanlike yet issued to the world by men of high distinction and responsibility," also announced that the college would launch an Institute for World Government led by 25-year-old Rudolph von Abele, an assistant professor of English who had been active in the world peace movement during graduate school at Columbia University.[28] When von Abele did not return to the college in 1947, the fledgling operation, which promoted internationalist ideals, was placed under the supervision of George Sauté, an assistant professor of mathematics who would later direct the college's reconstituted adult education program.

Holt headed the executive committee, which also included E.T. Brown, college treasurer; Edwin L. Clarke, professor of sociology; Royal W. France, professor of economics; Nathan C. Starr, professor of English; and Mary Upthegrove, a student active on the Inter-Racial Committee and the Pan-American League. The executive council included students Weston Emery, Eleanor Holdt, Marcia Huntoon, Tony Ransdell and Phyllis Starobin. Wendell C. Stone, the college's dean, Horace A. Tollefson, the college's librarian, and Alex Waite, professor of psychology, also served.

In the meantime, Holt was consumed with fundraising. The Victory Expansion Program, the most recent in an endless parade of capital campaigns, enabled the college to claim a $500,000 matching grant from the Davella Mills Foundation for construction of the Mills Memorial Library. The campaign also saw the addition of two dormitories, Corrin Hall and Orlando Hall, as well as the Warren Administration Building. Enrollment had jumped 28 percent, to 511, from its

---

28 Von Abele, who had just published a well-received biography of Alexander H. Stephens, vice president of the Confederacy, parlayed acclaim for the book into a more remunerative career as a professor of English literature at American University in Washington, D.C.

prewar nadir. But because of a dormitory shortage, returning veterans sometimes found themselves billeted in the Hamilton Hotel (now the Park Plaza Hotel on Park Avenue) or the on-campus Fred Stone Theater. After years of too few students, there were now too many.

And Prexy — the affectionate nickname that students and faculty members often used for Holt — had worn himself out chasing money, a task that left him drained physically and emotionally. In a 1977 edition of the *Rollins Alumni Update*, Marita Stueve Stone Vandyck, college director of admissions who had been a member of the Class of 1938, recalled driving Holt to Sarasota to meet with a potential donor, possibly Edith Conway Ringling, wife of circus magnate Charles Ringling and a Rollins trustee from 1934 to 1947. "As we pulled up in front of her villa, Dr. Holt said, 'We are too early. Drive around the block a time or two — we can't be early,'" recalled Vandyck. "Later, on our way home, he confessed that we had not been early but that he had stalled because 'I was nervous. I hated to go in.'"

In May 1947, following the groundbreaking for Orlando Hall, Holt was hospitalized following an emergency appendectomy and spent much of the summer recovering at his home in Woodstock. "No one will ever know how hard [Holt] and his assistants worked during the late stages of the drive," reported the *Rollins Alumni Record*. "This tremendous effort drained his physical strength and undoubtedly contributed to his illness. He personally wrote hundreds of letters, sent innumerable telegrams and made countless long-distance telephone calls in his appeal for funds. [He] felt there was nothing else to do but put his whole strength into the undertaking or he would probably not reach his goal — and he says that he would do it again."

In his politics, Holt was no less dogged. Whether his ideas

were popular or not, he felt a moral responsibility to push for them. But the twin responsibilities of saving a college and saving a planet weighed on Holt's health and surely on his psyche. "During a crisis I feel like a man battling a current," he reflected in 1949, as he prepared to retire. "I see a bend in the river and try to tell myself that if I reach the turn, the water will be calm. But I know that is not so. When a problem is solved there are others to take its place."

Chapter 4

THE MATHEMATICIAN
AND THE BOY WONDER

GEORGE SAUTÉ MUST have been puzzled by several questions on his faculty application for Rollins College when he filled it out in the summer of 1943. It appeared that Holt, whom Sauté had never met but whom he admired as an innovative reformer, was looking to weed out troublemakers. In addition to the usual questions about academic qualifications, the application asked: "Can you be counted upon for undeviating loyalty to the administration; or, in the event of disagreement, for frank and full discussion of the differences with the administration?" Answered Sauté: "Yes, indeed." The application asked: "What importance does character assume in your conception of an educational program?" Answered Sauté: "Primary." The application asked: "In your attitude and participation in political, ethic, religious, educational, etc., questions, is your general approach that of a reactionary, conservative, liberal or radical?" Answered Sauté: "Somewhere between conservative and liberal; a little to the latter." The application asked: "Rollins, while not sectarian, is a

Christian college in origin, also by purpose and intent. Are you in hearty and active sympathy with the character-forming ideals of such an institution, including cooperation with the chapel program?" Answered Sauté, judiciously: "Yes."

The questions may have seemed at best out-of-the-ordinary and at worst intrusive and inappropriate. But Holt had been more careful about faculty hiring since 1932, when he made a spur-of-the-moment decision to offer the iconoclastic John A. Rice a position as professor of classical studies. Rice, whom Holt fired to great upheaval just a year later, was accused of everything from parading about in public clad only in a jock strap (which he denied) to insulting religion and alienating members of the local clergy (which he did not deny).[1] But the impact of Rice's dismissal on Rollins was significant, causing the college to be censured by the American Association of University Professors over its malleable tenure policy and leading to an exodus of eight highly regarded faculty members who formed the experimental Black Mountain College in North Carolina.[2] Rice, who elevated insubor-

---

1 Not long after Rice's arrival, during a conference dubbed "The Place of the Church in the Modern World," Rice questioned the place of the church in Winter Park, specifically. Addressing a roomful of clergymen, he asked what the impact might be if all the houses of worship along Interlachen Avenue vanished and were replaced by open space. "What difference would it make," he asked, "and to whom?" Rice offended many others, most notably Frances "Fannie" Knowles Warren, donor of the Knowles Memorial Chapel, by describing the chapel's inaugural Christmas service as "obscene" within earshot of one of the college's most generous benefactors.

2 The best account of the Rice Affair can be found in Jack C. Lane's *Rollins College Centennial History: A Story of Perseverance, 1885-1985*. An interesting account of Black Mountain College can be found in Helen Molesworth's *Leap Before You Look: Black Mountain College 1933–1957* (Yale University Press, 2015). Black Mountain College, in brief, was based on John Dewey's progressive education principles and owned and operated by the faculty. It was committed to democratic governance and to the idea that the arts were central to all learning. All members of the college community participated in its operation, including farm work,

dination to an art form, exposed Holt's autocratic streak and demonstrated that even the proud progressive had his limits. "Someone, Emerson I think, said that every institution was the lengthened shadow of a man," wrote Rice in his 1942 memoir, *I Came Out of the Eighteenth Century* (reprinted in 2014 by the University of South Carolina Press). "He might as well have said a cloak to wear, a decoration, to catch the eye and keep it from the wearer; bootstraps for increasing one's height; a screen to hide the thing he was; a dream and a hope, dim, but still hope — hope for his own salvation. Rollins was all of these, and Rollins was Holt and Holt was Rollins."

Holt, who did indeed cast a lengthy shadow, need not have been concerned about the easy-going Sauté — a brilliant mathematician with an eagerness to please and, apparently unknown to Holt, a shared passion for world government. Much of Sauté's previous experience was related to adult education. He came to Rollins from Cleveland College, founded in 1925 by Western Reserve University and the Case School of Applied Science for adult learners.[3] The college offered both degree and nondegree programs in credit and noncredit classes. An early catalog stated the pioneering school's philosophy: "Education has, in truth, become a lifelong process. The individual or the community that fails to recognize this fact will not only lose much of the richness, beauty, and joy of life, but will also fall hopelessly behind in the economic struggle."

---

construction projects, and kitchen duty. Ironically, Rice was too disagreeable even for the college he helped to found and was asked by other faculty members to leave in 1940. The college closed in 1957.

3 Cleveland College was founded after Newton D. Baker, secretary of war under President Woodrow Wilson, persuaded the Cleveland Foundation, a community-based charitable organization, to support creation of a college for adults, primarily service members whose educations had been interrupted due to service in World War I. Baker later co-founded the law firm Baker & Hostetler, now BakerHostetler, which has a large Orlando branch.

The director of Cleveland College was A. Caswell Ellis, a veteran of the 1931 colloquium on liberal arts education, who wrote Holt that Sauté was "well-liked by both his students and his colleagues; his scholarship, character and native ability are all of a very high order." Sauté's wife, Marie-Louise,[4] was a vivacious woman who had studied acting at the Leland Powers School of the Theater in Boston, and the couple had three young children: 11-year-old George DeWitt[5] and 7-year-old twin girls, Louise and Marie, all of whom would eventually attend Rollins but graduate elsewhere.

Sauté, who was born in Belgium in 1903 but moved with his family to Rhode Island when he was a child, earned his bachelor's and master's degrees in mathematics from Brown University and completed coursework for a Ph.D. from Harvard University, although he failed to complete his thesis. He considered teaching in California, as his wife would have preferred, but instead took a job in 1930 as associate professor of mathematics at Cleveland College, where he also taught physics, trigonometry, analytical geometry and advanced calculus. Sauté had been hired by Holt as an assistant professor of mathematics, in part, to teach physics and mathematics for the Army's Specialized Training and Reassignment (STAR) program, through which enlisted personnel were

---

4   Marie-Louise Sauté would later lead an annual Christmas Community Sing under the sponsorship of the Winter Park Garden Club. The event, held in front of City Hall, grew to attract more than 1,000 participants. Wrote the *Orlando Morning Sentinel* in 1949: "So impressive were the features of the program, and so widespread the evident goodwill of the assemblage, that many have voiced the thought that through programs such as this, bringing together all nationalities and creeds, might come a sound basis for world peace."

5   George DeWitt Sauté was a standout student at Rollins, editing *The Sandspur*, participating on the debate team and acting in dramatic productions. He later became a psychologist for the Wisconsin State Department of Public Welfare, but sadly took his own life in 1966.

offered brief refresher courses, primarily in the sciences and languages, before transferring to larger state universities and completing 36-week terms in those subjects.

At Rollins, as many as 50 uniformed service members at a time lived in the men's dormitories, marching together to class and standing at attention along the so-called horseshoe — the walkway surrounding the campus green — at 5 p.m. when the flag was lowered. "To teach physics, I had to study a lot myself," said Sauté in an oral history interview conducted in 1969. "I became interested in the atom and atomic energy. The year before [the atomic bomb was dropped on] Hiroshima, I foresaw some activity in that direction. That led Dr. Holt to ask me to lecture on atomic energy. He took a fancy to me because I knew my stuff pretty well."

Sauté believed that mathematics, or at least the thought processes required to master mathematics, could make a difference in society. In 1942, he wrote an article for *The American Mathematical Monthly* called "Mathematics and the War Effort," quoting at length a statement from Admiral Chester W. Nimitz, commander in chief of the Pacific Fleet. According to Nimitz, most college freshmen could not pass a basic mathematics skills test required for acceptance into the Naval Reserve Officer Training Corps. While this was obviously a problem for the war effort, Sauté wrote, mathematics had nontechnical applications that few seemed to appreciate. Algebra and trigonometry, for example, could foster logical thinking about social and political issues.

"For several months at Cleveland College, we have been giving intensive six-week courses, one on algebra and one on plane trigonometry," Sauté continued. "For the most part, the students who take them are college graduates who have never taken college mathematics. Through these courses they improve their speed and accuracy of computation using tables, set up problems in mathematical form, and learn enough of the technical side of the subject to solve those problems. But perhaps most important is the self-confidence these men acquire when they realize how much common sense pervades a subject which, to them, has always [seemed] so abstruse ... There are other values besides the ones tied up with military problems to be derived from a knowledge of mathematics. It is not likely that human engineering or sociology will become less complex after the war. Scientific methods of solving those problems will go further and be more reliable than rule-of-thumb methods."

Enlightenment through algebra? It is not an argument that would have occurred to Holt, who looked to writers, historians and political scientists as his most likely academic allies. But following the departure of Rudolph von Abele, he asked Sauté to head the college's nascent Institute for World Government. In addition, Holt sent Sauté to the 1947 Convention of the United World Federalists held in St. Louis and asked him to determine how the college could participate locally. The movement was, in fact, enjoying a brief resurgence in the years between the end of World War II and the start of the Korean War. Gallup Polls in 1946, 1947 and 1948 asked: "Do you think the U.N. should be strengthened to make it a world government with the power to control the armed forces of all nations, including the U.S.?" In each of those three years, around 55 percent answered yes. The number began dropping in 1949 and bottomed out at 40 percent in the mid-1950s. Still, it is inaccurate to contend that the concept of world government was never broadly popular — after two world wars in 20 years, many in the late 1940s were at least willing to listen.

In 1947, following a meeting of internationalist groups in Montreux, Switzerland, a global coalition called the World Federalist Movement was formed and quickly claimed 56 member-groups in 22 countries with some 156,000 members. The Montreux Declaration declared that "the peoples [of the world] suffer from lack of shelter, food and clothing, while the nations waste their substance in preparing to destroy each other. The second attempt to preserve peace by means of a world organization, the United Nations, is powerless, as at present constituted, to stop the drift of war. We world federalists are convinced that the establishment of a world federal government is the crucial problem of our time. Until it is solved, all other issues, whether national or international, will remain unsettled. It is not between free enterprise and planned economy, nor between capitalism and communism that the choice lies, but between federalism and power politics. Federalism alone can assure the survival of man."

In the U.S., the Asheville, North Carolina-based United World Federalists (later renamed the World Federalist Association, then Citizens for Global Solutions) was growing and claimed membership of 20,000 throughout hundreds of local chapters. President Truman, at the 1948 dedication of a war memorial monument in Nebraska, did not endorse world government — he was speaking in general of arbitration — but sounded very much like Hamilton Holt when he declared that disputes between nations should be solved in the same way as disputes between states within nations: "When Kansas and Colorado fall out over the waters in the Arkansas River, they don't go to war over it; they go to the Supreme Court of the United States, and the matter is settled in a just and honorable way. There is not a difficulty in the whole world that cannot be settled in exactly the same way in a world court."

Sauté was energized by the meeting in St. Louis. "This crusade is not one to join, talk about, go home and forget," he reported to Holt upon his return. "It is a crusade that will continue until a rule of law is established for the settlement of international disputes; then and only then can we enjoy lasting peace." Clearly Sauté was preaching to the choir with Holt, who was nonetheless pleased to have found a faculty surrogate with whom to share the burden of advocacy. And share it they would. Sauté possessed the physical endurance that Holt, now past 70, found it more difficult to muster. Over the next several years, scarcely a civic group in Central Florida — indeed, scarcely a civic group in the state — did not hear an address on world government from the indefatigable mathematician. One headline announcing a Sauté presentation at a Florida church most accurately described his ambitious objective: "Sauté Charts Course Needed to Save World."

In addition, Sauté became a prolific writer of letters to the editor, and while his missives lacked Holt's literary flair, they were effective in their forthright fashion. "Some people say we cannot hope to have a world government until nations understand each other better and are willing to cooperate," he penned in a 1948 edition of the *Winter Park Herald*. "They add that you should have peace at home, in your community and in your country before you talk about world peace. Why do some think that the protection of law is all right up to the level of nations but shrink from the idea of extending it to the international level? There is nothing whatsoever that we are advocating ... that denies the necessity of our country's keeping a strong military until world government is established. Our strong contention is that we will not prevent war by preparing for it and doing nothing else."

Sauté helped organize local United World Federalist chapters on campus and in Winter Park. He even launched a weekly radio program, "World Government and You," on Orlando station WORZ-AM, and was interviewed over Voice of America radio speaking entirely in French. Yet Sauté seemed an unlikely crusader, according to a profile in *The Corner*

Cupboard, a local weekly newspaper: "A man with an enviable philosophy of life is George Sauté. He lives life as it comes, day by day, with a deep conviction in the power of prayer to set things right. In his own affairs, Prof. Sauté takes a middle-of-the-road position. He is not one to have more courage than wisdom. Rather, his is a moral courage that has the patience and the self-control to await the outcome of events." Soon Sauté's patience and self-control would be tested in ways that he could not have imagined.

HOLT, NOTING THAT "it is better to quit when they want you to stay than to stay when they want you to quit," submitted his resignation in early 1948 but agreed to remain until his successor was chosen the following year. The man selected to become the college's ninth president, 32-year-old Paul A. Wagner, arrived to great fanfare in 1949 but departed in 1951 following a bitter brouhaha that roiled the campus and the community and permanently soured friendships of long standing. Of course, controversial characters had come and gone with some regularity at the college. But never had one person, not even John A. Rice, wreaked such utter havoc. The so-called Wagner Affair, in retrospect, seems preternatural, as though it might have been written by Rod Serling or Gabriel García Márquez. Only one conclusion can surely be drawn: Paul Wagner, at least in the beginning, could sell anything to anyone.[6]

---

6 Wagner's charisma is apparent from this breathless description from the *Miami News* of a November 1949 presentation he gave to the Florida Conference of Parents and Teachers, a consortium of PTAs: "A packed house at last night's session heard the star performer, Paul A. Wagner, president of Rollins College, who lived up to his reputation as a speaker with a challenge. Dr. Wagner, developing the convention theme, used a large amount of personal magnetism, a pair of very expressive hands, a voice that is as resonate as that of Orson Welles, and a number of visual aids, in which he believes as a master of educational methods."

Wagner and Holt had known one another casually, although the circumstances of their original meeting are unclear. Holt later said that he had "discovered" Wagner through Louis Lochner, a peace activist prior to World War I and a journalist during World War II who had won a 1939 Pulitzer Prize for Correspondence. Lochner also lectured about the dangers of fascism and translated diaries by Nazi propaganda chief Joseph Goebbels, which were published and found some commercial success. However, there are no obvious connections between Lochner and Wagner.

In any case, Wagner was subsequently described in college press releases as having completed a four-year course of study at the University of Chicago in three years, earning his undergraduate degree at the age of 19. Impressive, but not quite true. Wagner, who was born in September 1917, did indeed graduate from the University of Chicago, where he was a protégé of its respected chancellor, Robert M. Hutchins. But he graduated in August 1938, just prior to his 21st birthday, taking the standard length of time to earn an undergraduate degree in education. Wagner was a popular student who acted in dramatic productions and served as the official college videographer through a club he founded called Campus Newsreel. Following graduation, he taught high school at the University of Chicago Laboratory Schools, founded by John Dewey, where he was lauded for his innovative use of audiovisual technology. Then after earning a master's degree in English at Yale, which he attended under a Carnegie Fellowship, he returned to Chicago and joined the faculty at his alma mater. Shortly thereafter, he was off to New York for an instructor stint at Teachers College, Columbia University.

With the outbreak of World War II, Wagner became a civilian consultant to the Great Lakes Naval Training Station near Chicago, where he introduced the use of audiovisual aids in training recruits. In 1942, the Department of the Navy offered him a lieutenant's commission to continue his work at the Naval War College in Newport, Rhode Island, where he developed training materials and made hundreds of films to support the college's evolving curriculum. After the war, Wagner joined American Type Founders, a manufacturer of foundry type and printing presses, as assistant to the president. He then worked as a counselor to the Committee on Economic Development, a private consortium of executives formed to promote the free enterprise system. (The Washington, D.C.–based CED remains a potent advocacy group today.) In 1947, Wagner landed an ideal position at Bell & Howell, a leading manufacturer of motion-picture equipment, where he was first vice president reporting directly to another wunderkind, 29-year-old company president Charles H. Percy, who would later be elected to the U.S. Senate from Illinois.[7] While at Bell & Howell, Wagner was involved in the making of promotional films — including one that featured Eddie Albert, who would later portray gentleman farmer Oliver Wendell Douglas on the sitcom *Green Acres*[8] — and gave hundreds of presentations throughout the U.S., Mexico and Canada on the promise of technology in the classroom.

In May of 1949, when Wagner learned that Rollins was looking for a new president, he jetted to Florida and dazzled

---

7   In 1966, Percy was elected to the U.S. Senate from Illinois as a Republican. He served for three terms before being defeated in 1985 by Paul Simon, a bowtie-wearing Democrat who was briefly a frontrunner for his party's presidential nomination in 1988.

8   The film with Albert was likely an episode of *Action Autographs*, a short-lived TV series that ran on ABC during the 1949-50 season. The 15-minute shows, sponsored by Bell & Howell, were essentially infomercials for the company's 16-millimeter cameras. The first episode featured Albert and singer Burl Ives hunting for gold in Mexico. Albert also had a company, Eddie Albert Productions, that made 16-millimeter industrial and educational films.

Holt and the search committee with his energy and intellect. In June — following equally compelling performances before faculty committees, student groups and the board of trustees —he was named Holt's successor, effective in September. "I was impressed, as other people were, that [Wagner] was a go-getter and had all this energy and initiative," recalled Sauté two years later in a deposition related to libel and slander lawsuits brought by Wagner against the college and a group of trustees. "His answer to one question impressed me about raising money for a small college. He said, 'Oh, that's nothing at all. I've been working for Bell & Howell and they have a $20 million budget. So your $500,000 budget is not anything to phase us.' He was the only one of the fellows we interviewed who wasn't worried about the money."

Holt, who had advocated for Wagner, was optimistic that "the greatness of Rollins" would be preserved and enhanced under the charismatic upstart's leadership. In a farewell address during June commencement ceremonies, 76-year old Prexy — who feigned surprise when he was awarded the Algernon Sydney Sullivan Award — said: "I will not worry very much if Rollins changes in the future its classroom techniques, its extracurricular activities or its campus customs. I know the gap between age and youth cannot be completely bridged. But if you lose the friendly feeling on the campus that now prevails between faculty and students, if the faculty reverts to the lecture-and-recitation system with its inevitable grades, marks and examination, all of which make the professor a detective and the student a bluffer, then you may hear that creaking sound as I turn over in my grave."

The guest speaker at Wagner's formal inauguration, held at convocation during Founders' Week in February 1950, was the University of Chicago's Hutchings. "Paul Wagner is a stalwart and original young man," Hutchings said. "I do not know what course he will take. But I predict that you will have an exciting and rewarding time, and that Rollins is entering a stirring and significant phase of its distinguished career." The descriptors "stirring and significant" would prove to be accurate — just not in the way Hutchings had intended. The transition began peacefully enough when Wagner "edited" his first Animated Magazine. The lead speaker was Holt, now a winter visitor, whose topic, "The Hydrogen Bomb," mattered less to attendees than the fact of his reassuring presence. The failing firebrand, whose retirement title was "honorary president," awkwardly hobbled about due a wooden prosthesis — his right leg had been amputated the previous September due to complications from diabetes — but he was in good spirits and was welcomed with nostalgic affection. Contributions collected during the event's "advertising insert," which were matched dollar for dollar by an anonymous donor, helped seed a newly launched Hamilton Holt Loan and Scholarship Fund.

Among the 14 other Animated Magazine speakers in 1950 were Ogden Nash, a popular writer of humorous verse,[9] and Edward Everett Horton, a character actor whose voice would become iconic to baby boomers as narrator of "Fractured Fairy Tales" in *The Rocky and Bullwinkle Show*. Also of note during Founders' Week was the premier of an original play by Edwin Granberry, *The Falcon,* which was staged at the Annie Russell Theatre, and the final John Martin Lecture Series, during which the semi-retired Martin commandeered his familiar pulpit at the First Congregational Church

---

9   Nash was best known for pun-like rhymes, sometimes with words deliberately misspelled for comic effect, as in his response to Dorothy Parker's "Men seldom make passes / At girls who wear glasses." Nash's version was: "A girl who's bespectacled/ May not get her nectacled." Nash, whose 1938 best-seller was *I'm a Stranger Here Myself,* made guest appearances on comedy and radio shows and toured the U.S. and the U.K. giving lectures at colleges and universities.

to ask, "Can Democracy Cover and Save the World?" There appeared to be little additional adult education activity that year except a concert by the Rollins Chamber Orchestra and special exhibits at the Beal-Maltbie Shell Museum and at Casa Iberia, which housed the Central Florida Hispanic Institute. The robust assortment of events, lectures, noncredit courses and for-credit courses that comprised the adult education program prior to World War II had sadly dwindled.

Wagner, though, was getting plenty of attention. *Colliers* dubbed him "education's new boy wonder." *Newsweek* also wrote a flattering story about the youthful dynamo, who seemed so full of novel ideas on how to prepare the college, and higher education in general, for a new era in which multiple modes of teaching would be available. An Associated Press story quoted the "broad-shouldered, square-jawed" Wagner as saying that he hoped graduates would be "generalists" who liked football as well as poetry, insisting that "such men will be the next leaders." Wagner also rebuked colleges for eschewing sex education. "Now think of this," Wagner told the AP reporter. "We spend about two thirds of our lives living with the opposite sex — and these schools practically ignore the subject." Wagner, pacing and pontificating while chewing on the earpiece of his glasses, made it clear during the interview that he wanted students to be challenged: "Today, facts are flooding in upon us," he said. "The students are becoming mere walking catalogs of facts. But there's the crux of it: Do students know what these facts *mean*?" Warming to the subject, Wagner elaborated on the importance of critical thinking in ways that were strikingly prescient, considering the state of American political discourse in 2019: "In totalitarian states, only a few people have to know the significance of facts. Here in America, everyone has to know what facts *mean*."

If the college community was entranced by Wagner, they

were also charmed by his attractive family, including his wife, Paula ("a slim, pretty blonde," according to a newspaper account), and their 3-year-old son Paul A. (The "A" stood for nothing; it was chosen by the Wagners so their son would not be "Paul Jr." and could select his own middle name when he grew older.) One clearly not entranced was Marie-Louise Sauté, who found Wagner to be phony and pompous. During the 1951 deposition given by her husband, she related a revealing anecdote to attorney Howard C. Hadden: "We entertained Paul Wagner at our house in January. ... I introduced him as 'Paul Wagner' because I introduce all people by their first names, and we were having a very informal party. When I introduced him as 'Paul Wagner' he gave me a dirty look. So, I then introduced him as 'President Wagner,' and that seemed to please him. I think the man lacks, and never has had, a sense of humor." Marie-Louise said she warned her husband that Wagner "is not sincere; he can sell something because he has great power of persuasion without believing it himself. From the beginning, personally, I have never completely trusted him. It may be womanly intuition, but I said it on different occasions to different members of the faculty."

At first, it appeared that the new president's "great power of persuasion" would enable him to act first and explain later with impunity. For example, prior to the 1950 season he abolished the football program, which he said operated at a $57,000 deficit. During a meeting at the Annie Russell Theatre, using a plethora of slides and charts, he made a persuasive case that the college would be better served by increasing the emphasis on less costly sports, such as basketball, baseball, tennis and golf. "The history of Rollins can be summed up in four words," said Wagner. "Constant lack of funds." An editorial in *The Sandspur* described the decision as "a bitter pill," but one worth swallowing for the college's fiscal health. Charlie

Wadsworth, featured columnist for the *Orlando Morning Sentinel*, reflected that "Rollins will get along just as well or better without football. It won't be the same, but the school will get along."[10]

Wagner, however, faced financial hurdles that the abolition of football alone could not mitigate. First, most World War II veterans who used the G.I. Bill to attend college had completed their educations by 1951 and the post-war enrollment surge had receded considerably. Second, the impact of the Korean War on college enrollment remained unknown. Although student deferments were available, Wagner had been warned during a recent trip to Washington, D.C., that all 18-year-olds might be declared draft-eligible following the November presidential election. Those factors, plus the college's debt of a quarter-million dollars, led Wagner to conclude that decisive action was required to ward off fiscal disaster.

At the February 1951 board of trustees meeting, Wagner, employing dramatic language and a daunting deluge of charts and graphs, presented a budget that anticipated just 449 students in the coming year — a drop of 200 students, or nearly 30 percent. At that level, tuition revenue would drop by as much as $150,000. And since the budget anticipated no other sources of income, then cost reductions at least equal to $150,000 would be required to avoid an operating deficit. Vice President and Treasurer John Tiedtke, who had already identified $77,000 in nonfaculty cuts, followed and confirmed Wagner's generally pessimistic outlook. But he reminded the trustees that Rollins offered a premium product: "We have a Cadillac assembly line, and we cannot turn out Cadil-

---

10 The football team had been .500 since 1946 and played mostly other small schools. As recently as 1956, however, it had played an away game at University of Florida, losing to the scout team 41-12. Its fiercest rivalry was with nearby Stetson University in DeLand.

lacs without fenders or radiators or wheels; nor can we turn out Fords, for we are not built that way." Tiedtke, who had not been present during Wagner's trademark tour de force, drew a vivid analogy regarding the impact of draconian cuts: "I look at this very much like a cancer. To save your life you may have to amputate your hand, but it is a serious matter to amputate your hand."[11] Appointed by Holt as interim treasurer in 1948, the no-nonsense Tiedtke had already saved the college from financial collapse once by postponing his honeymoon to accompany Holt to New York, where with the help of several trustees they had negotiated a $500,000 loan from Connecticut Mutual Life Insurance Company. And while the amputation argument was well-phrased, it was the treasurer's seeming validation of the college's grim financial situation that packed more punch.

The trustees, therefore, authorized Wagner to slash faculty positions based upon what they were told was a logical formula that would consider seniority and exempt "the only one in a division qualified to teach a particular subject that is considered essential." The governing panel even awarded the president a $2,000 raise, an unseemly decision under the circumstances, and promised him an additional $500 annu-

---

11 Wagner soon found himself very much at odds with Tiedtke, who shortly thereafter told student groups and members of the press that Wagner had presented an incomplete picture of the college's financial situation. Wagner had not, Tiedtke said, mentioned that gifts totaling $100,000 had been committed and were anticipated. Conflicting and confusing accounts about what the trustees were told or not told emerged in the furor to come. This is puzzling because Wagner had, after all, predicated that only tuition, not gifts, be used in estimating the college's income. The argument, it seems, ought to have been whether this was a reasonable premise on which to base a budget. Right or wrong, the assumptions used in the planning process were known. Perhaps Wagner's presentation style — to overwhelm listeners with data and deliver his conclusions with absolute certitude — contributed to the confusion.

al increase until his salary reached $15,000. To insulate him from backlash, Wagner was extended a five-year contract and, through a split-decision bylaw change, was given "the sole power to hire and discharge employees and to fix administrative and educational policies of the college subject to the veto of the board of trustees."

According to John "Jack" Rich, an alumnus who was then the college's dean of admissions, Wagner was the wronged party in the furor soon to follow: "[The trustees] all were very loyal to Hamilton Holt, but sick and tired of seeing him go year after year with such terrible deficits, appealing to people, down on his knees. [They] said, 'This can't go on indefinitely,' and they were right about that. So they brought in Wagner with the understanding that one of his first assignments would be to reduce the faculty." Rich spoke at length about the Wagner Affair during a 2005 oral history interview. Although some of what Rich contended could not be corroborated, the passion with which he recounted his version of events is indicative of the decades-long rancor engendered by the Wagner Affair.

On February 23, Wagner edited his second Animated Magazine. It was the first without Holt and his oversized blue pencil, although Prexy telephoned long distance and his familiar voice was amplified for the audience. Speakers included Wagner's former boss, Percy, as well as retired Air Force Lieutenant General George H. Brett, cartoonist Roy Crane (*Buz Sawyer*), U.S. Senator Paul Douglas of Illinois, Major League Baseball manager Leo Durocher, *Time* magazine editor Thomas Stanley "T.S." Matthews and actor Basil Rathbone. Then on March 8, believing that the trustees would supply cover, Wagner fired 19 full-time and four part-time faculty members — one-third of the entire teaching staff — many of whom had earned tenure. Wagner had warned of retrenchment and some dismissals had been expected, but nothing of this magnitude. Among those informed that their jobs would vanish in August was Sauté who, like many of his peers, had believed himself to be safe. After all, he had earned tenure and taught courses that were required for most science majors, including those in pre-medicine and pre-engineering. There was also a mathematics major, in which Sauté taught both introductory and advanced courses. "Nobody expected it to be in such a knot," recalled Rich. "The faculty had been prepared for it, but the students hadn't been prepared for it. I mean, the students during the day were in the classrooms with these men and women they admired so much. How can you prepare [them] for something like that?"

On March 5, Wagner had written Holt in an effort to explain his actions. Perhaps he also hoped to enlist his predecessor's support — or to at least head off his opposition — during the anticipated upheaval. With higher costs and lower tuition, Wagner explained to Holt, he had no choice but to act: "This is the first time we have had to cut faculty personnel and although it is a terrible emotional experience I would not care to repeat, I am very much afraid it was an imperative one. ... But despite this fact I know that there will be a tidal wave of resentment toward the youngster you picked as your successor. I am prepared for this eventuality, but I must admit that I would have given a great deal to have enjoyed a honeymoon period for at least three years." If Wagner thought that Holt would offer sympathy, however, he was mistaken. After all, Wagner claimed that the college's desperate circumstances were precipitated in part by Prexy's longstanding negligence — a stance that was unlikely to earn an ally in Woodstock.

In the chaotic several months that followed, students went on strike and *The Sandspur* published an issue in which every article excoriated Wagner, who in turn threatened to suspend the entire editorial staff unless a retraction was forthcoming. "We stand behind all the material presented," said editor Betsy Fletcher, who promised a special edition "in elaboration of the first one."[12] There were mass meetings, both spontaneous and planned, at which animosity was aggravated by the seemingly random nature of the firings and the president's imperious (and at times petulant) attitude toward those who questioned his wisdom. "I will be the most hated college president in America," Wagner claimed he had told the trustees before launching his austerity campaign. "Now I'm afraid that has come to pass." As the situation deteriorated, a three-member trustee committee was appointed by Winthrop Bancroft, a Jacksonville attorney who chaired the board of trustees, to investigate the agitation.[13] Committee members included fellow trustees H. George Carrison, also an attorney, Milton Warner, a retired railroad executive (and Holt's roommate at Yale), and Eldridge Haynes, a magazine publisher and international business consultant.[14]

On campus the mood grew increasingly edgy, with charges and counter-charges hurled. Sauté told an assembly

---

12   Fletcher was not to be trifled with. Born in West Virginia, she contracted polio as a child and gradually recovered after undergoing a controversial treatment regimen at the Sister Kenny Institute in Minneapolis. Elizabeth Kenny was an Australia-born nurse and physical therapist who treated the disease with movement and heat packs instead of splints and braces. Fletcher graduated from Rollins and, although it was thought she could never have children, she married and gave birth to three girls.

13   A fascinating account of the committee's investigation can be found in Jack C. Lane's *Rollins College Centennial History: A Story of Perseverance, 1885-1985.*

14   In 1940, Haynes founded *Modern Industry* magazine, which he published until 1953, when it was sold to Dun & Bradstreet. The following year he founded Business International Corporation, a consultancy with an impressive roster of clients. Future President Barack Obama worked as a research associate at Business International Corporation in 1983. In 1986, the company was acquired by The Economist Group in London.

of students that Wagner had, in fact, devised a "mathematical formula" to guide faculty dismissals but had "twisted the formula" and instead conducted a purge. Later the besieged president fired back, reading from a memorandum written by Sauté that contained obsequious praise: "I admire you more every time I meet with you, Paul, and sympathize with you on the problems you have to face." Wagner, waving the document above his head, seemed incredulous: "Just a very few days after [Sauté] wrote this, he was accusing a man whom he had admired of twisting the formula to suit another end." Sauté, in turn, revealed that the correspondence had been written in November — not "a very few days" but exactly 122 days before dismissal notices were issued. The otherwise agreeable mathematician further accused Wagner of "violating a confidence" by making portions of the communication public. "Then as now, I place my personal integrity of character first," he said. "In accord with that, I do not propose here or in any public meeting to reveal matters written by me or received by me in the same spirit."

In his 1951 deposition, Sauté offered more detail about the memorandum, explaining that in the early days of his administration Wagner had met in his office with a group of several faculty members regarding "a tough decision" pending in the science department. Wagner had asked for additional thoughts in writing, and Sauté had responded accordingly. "The essence of [the memorandum] was, if the man had integrity, he should be kept; if he lacked integrity, he should be fired," Sauté recalled. "I felt pretty good. I praised [Wagner] because I thought he was doing it the right way." He further told attorney Hadden that Wagner had offered no explanation for his firing when the two met privately. Yes, Sauté insisted, he had pressed the president for specifics, but no, he had not elicited an answer other than "it had to be done."

Marie-Louise — whose "womanly intuition," it appeared, should be overlooked at one's peril — interjected that Wagner's animus for her husband may have been the result of yet another petty personal slight during a farewell gathering at the president's residence in Holt's honor. "We felt very close to Dr. Holt," she told Hadden. "I just loved Dr. Holt as though he were a father. I went over and kissed him and said, 'You'll always be president to us.' That was in Mr. and Mrs. Wagner's presence. She gave me a dirty look. And I think Mr. Wagner had a feeling of jealousy." Marie-Louise had managed during two social occasions to elicit dirty looks from both Paul and Paula Wagner. One can imagine — perhaps even understand — the incoming president's pique over Marie-Louise's passive-aggressive disrespect. But was spousal tactlessness a firing offense? In Wagner's world, it seemed possible.

Holt, quizzed by reporters in Woodstock about turbulence at the college, at first cautiously defended Wagner, whom he described ambiguously to a UPI reporter as "a very remarkable man." He said that although the dismissals were "a very regrettable thing," he was certain that the trustees must have given the matter careful consideration before authorizing such a drastic measure. Still, the old crusader averred, he was retired and did not know enough about the situation to offer further comments. In fact he knew plenty, having been in constant touch with troubled trustees and furious faculty members. Almost certainly Holt was reminded of 1932, when another powerful personality — John A. Rice — had won his confidence only to wreak havoc once unleashed. On April 10, Holt wrote Wagner a letter calling upon him "with reluctance and grief" to resign before he was ousted. "You must see that if you are not dismissed [by the trustees] that you will still lose out for you have lost the confidence, to say the least, of an overwhelming majority of faculty, students and alumni in addition to a strong possibility of a majority of the trustees." Even if a bare majority of trustees stuck with him, Holt warned, the atmosphere was too toxic to deal with the challenges Wagner faced: "Such a convulsion would follow your retention that you and the trustees loyal to you cannot possibly surmount the difficulties confronting you."

On April 11, via telephone, Holt expressed the same opinion to the New York Chapter of the Rollins College Alumni Association. The group, which also heard from others, including Eugene R. Smith,[15] a member of the executive committee who supported Wagner, voted 55-2 in favor of a resolution calling for the president's immediate resignation.[16] Holt then issued a statement to the *Orlando Morning Sentinel* that read, in part: "I doubt if there is a living man who can succeed in leading Rollins College through the staggering problems ahead without the good will and cooperative support of all elements interested in its future. I therefore appeal to President Wagner to resign immediately. If he resigns now, he may save himself and the college. If he does not resign, he may ruin the college and himself." Holt's statement also outlined ways in which the crisis might have been averted, including an expanded adult education program and a temporary across-the-board salary reduction such as he had implemented in 1933. "In regard to the methods, manners and morals of the way in which the dismissals were made, all I wish to say is that the things that make a college great are the quality of those

---

15 Smith, who had been the college's commencement speaker in 1950, was a progressive educator who founded and served as headmaster of several innovative day schools in Baltimore and Chestnut Hills, Massachusetts, before retiring to Winter Park in 1943. He donated his collection of more than 1,200 watch keys to the college in 1965.

16 On the call with Holt and Smith was Dean of Women Marian Cleveland and Alumni Association President Howard Showalter Jr., both of whom opposed Wagner.

who teach and of those who are taught," Prexy wrote. "All else, however important, is secondary."

Holt, a seeker of peace, finally found it on April 26, 1951. His health had been in precipitous decline since his leg amputation, and he died at home of a heart attack at age 79.[17] The Wagner Affair, although it remained unresolved, was careening toward a messy conclusion. In the meantime, the campus response to Holt's passing must surely have weighed on Wagner; flags were flown at half-mast, classes were dismissed and a play at the Annie Russell Theatre, Shakespeare's *Much Ado About Nothing*, went on that evening only because the cast decided that "the grand old trouper" would have wanted it that way. Holt's last public act, after all, had been to try and save his beloved college from Wagner, now viewed as a reckless man-child who appeared in every way to be the anti-Holt with his boardroom prattle about running the college as a business, his obsession with obtuse charts and graphs and, most egregious on a campus where democratic governance was espoused — if not always practiced — his authoritarianism.

The Sandspur rushed to produce a commemorative edition in which every Holt tribute, some composed by faculty members who would soon be unemployed, seemed by implication to be a condemnation of Wagner. "I believe [Holt] was the greatest man I ever had the privilege of knowing," wrote Rhea Marsh Smith, a professor of history whose job had been spared. "He is responsible for making Rollins a college of distinction. He built the spirit of the Rollins family." Nathan C. Starr, a popular professor of English who had been dismissed, added: "All of [Holt's] achievements were

---

17   Among Holt's files of correspondence in the Olin Library's Department of Archives and Special Collections is a get-well message from lecturer John Martin that reads: "You're a better man with one leg than most are with two."

less than the man himself. Those of us who were close to him were truly uplifted by his greatness of spirit, and our hearts were warmed by his humanity. He was a man of humility in the deepest sense of the word, a man who looked at the foibles and perplexities of the world with a tolerant eye. His tolerance and his sense of proportion lay behind the waggish sense of humor, which he had in abundance."

Sauté recalled an incident from Holt's final visit to Winter Park "that illustrated how much he taught by his example." Despite difficulty walking because of his wooden leg, Holt had insisted upon honoring a commitment to speak before a small civic group in Volusia County. "He could reasonably have asked to be excused," wrote Sauté. "But he said he would go. Mrs. Sauté and I took him in our own car. At the meeting he spoke with his usual eloquence for over an hour, as if there had been thousands in the audience. During the question period, a frustrated old man monopolized the time with pointed, unfair questions, which Dr. Holt answered generously. Afterward, when asked how he could be so tolerant with a heckler, he answered simply, 'Everyone has a right to speak.'" As Holt became larger in death, Wagner seemed to become smaller in life.

A CADRE OF TRUSTEES, some now claiming that they had been bamboozled, finally acted to quell the outrage. At an April 27 meeting in New York, 11 members — 10, including college attorney Raymer F. Maguire Jr., did not attend — agreed to ask Wagner to resign and, as a face-saving measure, to offer him chairmanship of a nebulous commission to study the financial problems of liberal arts colleges. He would be given a deadline of May 3 to accept or reject the offer, but either way Hugh F. McKean, professor of art, would then be named acting president. By the time the clock ran out, however,

Wagner had rejected alternatives, refuted the legality of the out-of-state meeting and refused to vacate his office.

Behind-the-scenes wrangling continued until May 13, when the exasperated trustees publicly announced that Wagner had been dismissed "because his services on behalf of the college have not contributed to the best interests of the institution." Wagner, in turn, announced that he was still president and would report to his office the following morning as usual. "I am still president of the college and will remain so unless legally removed by the board of trustees," Wagner said. "I will be in the president's office as usual. The basic story is simple. I was given orders by the board of trustees. I carried out those orders, and now some of the individuals who gave me those orders do not have the moral courage to face the consequences of their own actions."

"It is of no material consequence where Mr. Wagner chooses to sit," McKean told the *Orlando Morning Sentinel* on May 15 from his own office at the Morse Gallery of Art, which had now been recognized by the college's deans as the official seat of campus authority. "Rollins College has returned to life. Classes are meeting in a happy atmosphere and all other college activities are humming along. This is no tribute to any individuals. It is simply a release of our vitality and energy and a demonstration of the loyalty of us all to our college." Just two days earlier, after the vote to dismiss Wagner was announced, at least some of that vitality and energy had been released on Horace A. Tollefson, the college librarian whom Wagner had appointed as a special assistant. Tollefson reported to police that a pair of professors — James Russell, professor of psychology, and U.T. Bradley, professor of history and government and coach of the crew team — had roughed him up and kidnapped him as he was moving files from his beleaguered boss's office. The alleged assailants replied they had simply escorted Tollefson away from a threatening gathering of students and perhaps, quite by accident, injured his arm in the process.

Part of that story was true; Wagner and his wife also ventured onto the campus that night to find the administration building surrounded by students, faculty members and curious onlookers. Police escorted the couple safely through the throng, which remained strangely silent. Among the students milling about would have been one Fred McFeely Rogers, a talented music composition major from Latrobe, Pennsylvania, who was by all accounts every bit as sweet-natured then as he appeared to be in adulthood, when he created the now-iconic PBS series *Mister Rogers' Neighborhood.* Even the young man who would later profess to like everyone "just the way you are" disliked Wagner and agitated for his removal.[18]

McKean's sanguine pronouncements notwithstanding, the battle raged on. A never-say-die group called "Citizens Committee for Rollins College" placed a series of full-page ads in the *Orlando Morning Sentinel* that sought to rally locals around Wagner. Winter Park Mayor William H. McCauley scheduled — and then abruptly cancelled — a public hearing at which he promised "the nature of the true issues of the

---

18   Fred Rogers — Mister Rogers to generations of television viewers — was born in Latrobe, Pennsylvania. But Winter Park claims him as one of its own, in part because he graduated from Rollins in 1951. It was at Rollins where he met his future wife, Joanne Byrd, and participated in an array of campus activities, serving on the chapel staff and as a member of the Community Service Club, the Student Music Guild, the French Club, the Welcoming Committee, the After Chapel Club and the Alpha Phi Lambda fraternity. He formed enduring friendships in Winter Park and was a frequent visitor. Rogers, who died in 2003, was inspired by the "Life Is for Service" motto he saw engraved on a wall near Strong Hall and carried a photograph of the plaque in his wallet for years. It was finally framed and prominently placed on his desk. Rogers' nephew, composer Daniel Crozier, has continued the legacy as a professor of music theory at the college.

conflict" would be revealed. McCauley apparently believed that college's tax-exempt status somehow brought its personnel matters within the purview of municipal government.[19] But, in an unexpected twist, it was the State Legislature that gave Wagner reason for hope. On May 24, a bill offered by Representatives Edward R. Kirkland and Charles O. Andrews was passed that would have ousted most out-of-state trustees and replaced them with a slate of pre-selected local appointees. "I was entirely unaware of this," a straight-faced Wagner told reporters.

The bill — a local measure of little if any interest to most who blithely voted for it — was introduced at the behest of the citizens committee, whose members persuaded Kirkland and Andrews, both from Orange County, that only legislative intervention could save the college from collapse. However, faced with a furious backlash, the lawmakers decided on May 28 that the entire effort "had been a mistake." Among those who weighed in was Ralph Himstead, secretary of the American Association of University Professors, who warned that legislative meddling could endanger the college's accreditation. Added McKean: "This unwarranted interference in the private affairs of Rollins College ... is a gross misappropriation and misuse of political power and has done a terrible wrong to the college." The House and Senate, after initially refusing to reconsider passage, backpedaled and voted to recall the bill from Governor Fuller Warren. Kirkland told a contingent of more than 200 students who had descended upon Tallahassee to protest the measure that the missing-in-action Andrews was so upset by the whole matter that he had taken to his bed.[20]

---

19   After McCauley announced the public hearing, the city commission issued a statement confirming its neutrality and distancing itself from McCauley's efforts on Wagner's behalf.

20   On May 24, the *Sanford Herald* published one of the more powerful

On May 30, four trustees resigned and a reconfigured panel meeting on campus upheld Wagner's dismissal. McKean, in turn, named Tiedtke and Alfred J. Hanna, professor of history, as executive assistants.[21] And although McKean did not revive football, he did immediately reinstate the fired faculty. On June 8, Wagner finally surrendered his keys "under protest" and vacated his office and the president's residence. In March 1952, Wagner dropped his $500,000 libel and slander suit against the 11 trustees who had engineered

---

editorials on the so-called "Rollins Bill." The commentary, headlined "In Ignorance and Haste," read, in part: "The Legislature has in effect said, 'We know the students of Rollins do not want this man as their president. We know that the alumni do not want him. We know that a majority of the board of trustees voted to fire him. But whether you want him or not, you have got to have him as your president.' Hamilton Holt was not a resident of this state when he became president of Rollins. Neither was Paul Wagner. Many of the students attending Rollins and other colleges in Florida are from outside the state. Can Florida invite students to come here from all over the nation while maintaining that only Florida residents may be trustees? Central Floridians have contributed generously to Rollins, but most of the money that has gone into its fine library, its beautiful theater and chapel and its many attractive dormitories has been provided by people who live outside this state. To say that they should have no voice in the operation of the college smacks of ignorance and prejudice unworthy of the great State of Florida and detrimental to her future welfare."

21 McKean later said that if "an artist, a historian and a farmer" could straighten out the college's problems, then finding a qualified president should not be all that difficult. While the artist and historian references are obvious, McKean's reference to the versatile Tiedtke as a farmer was an exercise in whimsical understatement. It was technically true; Tiedtke owned 2,000 acres of sugar, citrus and corn farms near Lake Okeechobee and was already a wealthy philanthropist and patron of the arts during the Wagner Affair. When Bach Festival of Winter Park founder Isabelle Sprague-Smith died in 1950, he took over as president of the nonprofit and would remain in that position — often funding deficits from his own pocket — for 54 years until his death at age 97. In 1950, Tiedtke and several local businesspeople, including former Orlando Mayor Robert Carr, formed the Central Florida Symphony Society, which founded the Central Florida Symphony Orchestra, which debuted in 1951. The name was changed to the Florida Symphony Orchestra the following year.

his dismissal. An additional $100,000 suit against the college was settled for $50,000 because, according to joint statement from the litigants' attorneys, "it was thought by the contending parties to be in the best interest of Rollins College, in which everyone concerned maintains a sincere interest."[22]

Wagner, however, ignored the paragraph of the settlement that stipulated "neither of the parties will ... attempt to publicize or issue statements to the press with respect to the matters heretofore in controversy." In April 1952, he gave a talk at Roosevelt College[23] in Chicago entitled "Academic Lynchings," which prompted the *Orlando Morning Sentinel* to editorialize that "this new activity makes [Wagner] a poor sport, at least." The speech was less about Rollins — although Wagner included numerous references to his mistreatment

---

22   The statement made it clear that neither the college nor Wagner was satisfied with the outcome: "There are still honest differences of opinion with respect to the matters in dispute. In view of the many unfortunate implications and inferences which were drawn from the actions of the two parties, it was almost inevitable that strong feelings would be aroused, and strong opinions held on both sides. It is, however, the opinion of everyone that both sides were honestly endeavoring to work for what they considered to be the best interests of the institution. ... This settlement is made by the college and concurred in by Dr. Wagner in the honest belief that thereby the best interests of Rollins College will be served. It is also intended thereby to indicate that both sides have made considerable concessions from what they maintain to be their rights in the matter, but in the spirit of compromise and with a view toward a common objective of the general good of the community and of the institution, these concessions are made with wholeheartedness and accord."

23   Roosevelt College, now Roosevelt University, is a private institution with a social justice mission. It was founded in 1945 by Edward J. Sparling, previously president of Central YMCA College in Chicago, after a dispute with his board of trustees. Sparling refused to provide the board with demographic data regarding the student body, fearing the data would be used to develop a quota system to limit the number of African Americans, Jews, immigrants and women admitted. As a result, Sparling resigned under protest and took with him many faculty and students to start the new college. It was initially called Thomas Jefferson College but was renamed for President Franklin D. Roosevelt shortly after Roosevelt's death.

in Winter Park — and more about ways in which college presidents in general are wronged by faculty organizations, boards of trustees, alumni associations, newspaper reporters and members of communities at large. "Many men [have become college presidents] because they think it is a glamorous thing," Wagner lamented. "Many of them take it because they think they will be thought leaders. ... What happens to the college president? This is the college president — spread eagle all over, crucified on the cross of his own convictions." Trustees should grant college presidents permanent tenure, Wagner said, so they could be free to take unpopular but necessary actions.

The *Lakeland Ledger* waggishly wondered what sort of person could survive a Rollins presidency: "The best we figure it, he should be a tightrope-walker, a financier, a scholar, a regular fellow, an acrobat, a teacher, a student, a juggler, a diplomat, a disciplinarian, an optimist, a pessimist, an actor, a politician, a pragmatist, an idealist, a charitable humanitarian, a fire-eater, a quarterback, a preacher, a wrestler, an orator, a writer, a flatterer, an alarmist, a man of deep serenity, a poet, a philosopher and a contortionist. If he has all these qualifications, he may gradually adjust himself to the hazardous occupation of college president and go along for three or four years before faculty, students, alumni and townspeople begin calling him a liar, a thief and maybe a backslidden Democrat."

Still, not surprisingly for a man of Wagner's undeniable gifts, he bounced back. The deposed president went on to become founding executive director of the Chicago-based Film Council of America, funded by the Ford Foundation, then vice president of the New York-based public relations firm Hill & Knowlton in Manhattan. In 1958 he divorced Paula, and in 1965 remarried Jeanette Sarkisian, who later became vice president of the Estee Lauder Companies. Sarkisian's stature was such that she was invited to lecture at the college's Roy E. Crummer Graduate School of Business in the late 1980s. Apparently, no one at the college realized that Sarkisian's husband had once been the institution's president. Then-President Thaddeus Seymour got wind of the visit and invited Wagner, who had accompanied his wife, to tour the campus with him. The very sight of the one-time wunderkind, now in his 70s, shocked those who remembered the crisis and amused the mischievous Seymour, who had located Wagner several years before and struck up a social relationship.

"By the time Polly (Seymour's wife) and I arrived in 1978, Paul Wagner's name was never mentioned, and there was no visible indication that he had ever served as president," Seymour wrote in the spring 2017 issue of *Winter Park Magazine*. "There was no portrait of him hanging on a wall, and no mention of his name in catalogs or handbooks. When I asked, no one seemed to know what had become of him. For the heck of it, one day on a trip to New York, I picked up the phone book and looked up 'Wagner, Paul A.' Then I dialed the number. 'I'm sorry to bother you,' I said, 'but I'm trying to locate the Paul Wagner who was president of Rollins College.' Pause. 'Yes?' We met in the Metropolitan Club for a drink and a cordial visit, and I began a mission to bring him back into the Rollins family."

The task was not an easy one, Seymour wrote, because feelings about the Wagner Affair remained raw. One major donor threatened to discontinue his substantial financial support "if I let the SOB back on the campus," recalled Seymour, who persuaded Wagner to send a photograph of himself for display in the administration building. Seymour had it framed and hung only to have it vanish within a week. "At my awkward request, he sent another one, and we used bolts to hang it," Seymour wrote. "We kept in touch, usually via

Christmas cards, over the years. One summer about 10 years ago we were visiting our son and his family on Shelter Island, a small community at the end of Long Island. On the map, I discovered that it was next to Sag Harbor and I remembered that the Wagners had a summer home there. One phone call and we were together again for lunch. We continued to stay in contact, including occasional luncheons when we were visiting Long Island. We'll miss those congenial gatherings and conversations, which covered a range of interesting subjects. But the one topic [Wagner] would never discuss was his brief tenure as president of Rollins College."

Writes college historian Jack C. Lane: "Paul Wagner's demise was tragic in the sense that his good intentions were doomed by the man's own hubris. He brought plight on an institution he was trying to guide into a new era of educational change. His downfall left the college with a deep sense of what might have been. He deprived Rollins of his exceptional insight into the future of higher education and the opportunity of placing itself in the forefront of the coming 21st century technological innovations in higher education."

Said Sauté in an oral history interview conducted in 1969: "Things got pretty sticky here around 1950 and 1951 with the Wagner explosion. When Wagner was through, and McKean, Tiedtke and Hanna formed kind of a triumvirate to get the college going again, I volunteered to help the cause by setting up some evening courses, which I thought would be good public relations. The community was split right down the middle after that affair. But as a result, I had some of the best students I've ever had in my career."

Chapter 5

MAKING FAST FRIENDS

THOSE WHO MET Hugh Ferguson McKean, the 10th president of Rollins College (1951-69), likely remember him as a dashing older man with a shock of wavy white hair, a twinkle in his eye and a square jaw indicative of the matinee-idol good looks that he enjoyed in his youth. They recall his wry humor, his courtly manner and his cultural pursuits, usually those aimed at making art more accessible to people not generally inclined to visit museums. McKean's endearing quirks are usually prominent in any conversation about him.[1] Although

---

1 One of McKean's more enduring but undoubtedly quirky legacies remains Fox Day, an all-campus holiday declared each spring at the president's discretion. Holt had received two donations of statues — a fox and a cat — from DeLand lawyer Murray Sams. Although they were intended to be displayed, a student prank destroyed the cat and the fox went into storage. A year after he became president, McKean retrieved the fox and placed it on the library lawn, announcing that it had reappeared to announce a spontaneous holiday during which all classes were cancelled, and students were asked to spend the day "doing things for the college." In 1963, McKean began writing whimsical and poetic proclamations to mark Fox Day, the culmination of which was an all-campus gathering (for the first several years a luau) followed by a special service

he was not an eccentric — that descriptor generally denotes episodes of bizarre behavior — he was undeniably quirky, in a visionary sort of way. In 1967, for example, he submitted to the board of trustees an annual report that was hand lettered and illustrated with whimsical cartoons. And in his post-presidential years, he began salvaging and restoring commercial signs — particularly garish neon ones — including two from notorious local strip clubs.

McKean and his wife, Jeannette Morse Genius McKean, brought the first peacocks to Winter Park and opened the grounds surrounding their sprawling estate, Wind Song, so the public could see the noisy peafowl strut and preen. Today, a peacock is emblazoned on the city's official logo. Had he not become engulfed by the responsibilities of being Hugh McKean, he might have become as well known for his paintings as for his projects, the scope of which relegated his art to something considerably more than a hobby, but something considerably less than a profession. Still, for as long as he lived, and despite constant demands for his time and attention, McKean continued to paint. Ensconced in an apartment above the Winter Park Land Company overlooking Park Avenue, which he dubbed his "scriptorium," he surrounded himself with canvases, brushes and tubes of oils.[2] He delighted in producing pictures that reflected his (sometimes puzzling) vision of humanity in general and Florida in particular.

---

in Knowles Memorial Chapel. Fox Day was eliminated in 1970 by President Jack Critchfield — it seemed frivolous during the Vietnam era — but restored in 1986 by President Thaddeus Seymour and continued through subsequent presidents. However, there is no longer an evening communal activity.

2   Scriptorium is a Latin word meaning "place for writing," and is commonly used to refer to rooms in medieval European monasteries where scribes copied and illustrated manuscripts.

Born in Beaver Falls, Pennsylvania, in 1908, McKean was the son of Arthur McKean, an attorney who served for a brief time in the Pennsylvania legislature. His mother, Eleanor Ferguson, was a homemaker. Arthur McKean was a man of many interests. In addition to careers in politics and the law, he roamed the sidelines for five seasons as head football coach at his alma mater, Geneva College, which his wife had also attended.[3] The McKeans were not wealthy but they were well-connected, socially prominent and solidly upper middle class. In 1920, the family — which included brothers Keith and Vance — moved to Orlando, where they lived in an impressive home, since demolished, on Hillcrest Street near East Colonial Drive. According to U.S. Census records, the home was then valued at $40,000 (the equivalent of nearly $600,000 today). McKean graduated from Orlando High School in 1926 before enrolling at Rollins, where he majored in English and creative writing. His father had insisted that he earn an undergraduate degree in a subject other than art.

That same year, McKean met a young woman who would become his lifelong creative and intellectual soulmate: 17-year-old Jeannette, a Chicago resident who had vacationed in Winter Park since childhood and was now taking summer classes at Rollins. Her maternal grandfather was Charles Hosmer Morse, the Windy City industrialist who shaped modern Winter Park and is remembered today as the city's most important benefactor. A serious artist, Jeannette — who would become a Rollins trustee at age 27 — had attended exclusive private schools and, like her future husband, would later study in New York at the Grand Central School of Art and the Art Students League. These two kindred spirits,

---

3   In 1930, Arthur McKean ran unsuccessfully for mayor of Orlando while serving as a municipal judge.

who would together and separately dedicate their talent and treasure to energizing Winter Park's cultural life, struck up a romance that blossomed like a Tiffany daffodil.

Although he did not major in art, McKean spent the summer following his sophomore year in France, studying at L'École de Beaux-Arts in Fontainebleau. And while still a senior he was named assistant instructor in landscape painting in the art department at Rollins. He graduated in 1930, having followed his father's wishes — at least nominally — by earning an academic degree. Arthur, perhaps resigned to having an artist in the family, then submitted two of his son's paintings to the jury of the Tiffany Foundation. One of those paintings, *Ruins of Old Florida Mission, New Smyrna*, earned McKean a Tiffany Fellowship, which allowed him to spend two heady months at Laurelton Hall, the Oyster Bay estate of artist Louis Comfort Tiffany, designer of ceramics, enamels, jewelry, metalwork, glass mosaics, blown glass and, most notably, decorative stained-glass lamps and windows.

At 82 and in declining health, Tiffany had created a surreal summer camp where aspiring artists could live and work in an unstructured but inspirational setting. It was certainly inspirational to McKean, who later described the 84-room home and the 580 acres surrounding it as "a three-dimensional work of art, fabricated of marble, wood, plaster, winds, glass, copper, rains, light, sound, sunlight, flower gardens, running water, terraces, woods, hills." The magnificent home was itself a work of art, combining art nouveau and Islamic motifs. "My Lord, the windows, this was the thing that really turned me on about Laurelton Hall," McKean remembered in a 1992 interview with the *Fort Lauderdale Sun-Sentinel*. "Light didn't just fall on them, no, the glass actually radiated light, like trays of jewels in a jewelry store, like something alive." The McKeans would return more than 25 years after Hugh McKean's apprenticeship and rescue truckloads of Tiffany's creations — by then so maligned by the art world's cognoscenti that they were considered virtually worthless.[4] The price tag for the haul, McKean later recalled, was about $10,000.

In the busy summer of 1930, McKean also studied at the Art Students League in New York, learning anatomy and figure drawing from George B. Bridgman, whose book *Bridgman's Complete Guide to Drawing from Life* remains a classic in art instruction. While in Manhattan McKean somehow found the time for additional courses at the Grand Central School of Art, run by the Painters and Sculptors Gallery Association, a collective formed by painters Edmund Greacen, Walter Leighton Clark and John Singer Sargent. Greacen, under whom McKean studied, was a notable impressionist. The following summer, McKean won a Carnegie Foundation scholarship to attend a series of art-appreciation lectures at Harvard University's Fogg Museum. There he was exposed to

---

4   After the Laurelton Hall fire, the McKeans were asked by a Tiffany daughter to try and rescue what they believed to be important from the ruins. The couple hurried to Oyster Bay, where they were shocked and saddened at what they found. "I shook something against a tree," McKean wrote in his book *The Lost Treasures of Louis Comfort Tiffany* (Doubleday, 1980). "It rattled. The head of the wrecking company waiting to clear the property was with us. I asked him what it was. 'That's one of the old man's windows,' he replied." And not just any window. It was one of the *Four Seasons* windows, created in 1900 for the Exposition Universelle in Paris. Seeing this quartet of magnificent, fully restored panels today, it is almost beyond comprehension that they were once regarded as little more than trash. "It's virtually impossible to put a value on the collection because so many pieces are one of a kind," says Harold Ward III, whose law firm, Winderweedle, Haines, Ward & Woodman, manages the Charles Hosmer Morse Foundation. The foundation was set up by the McKeans in 1959 to fund the Charles Hosmer Morse Museum of American Art, which McKean directed after leaving Rollins. In 1996, McKean was posthumously named Floridian of the Year by the *Orlando Sentinel* because "he believed passionately that art and culture should be part of everyone's everyday life — regardless of age. He felt that the soul and intellect would flourish when exposed to beauty and knowledge. To that, he devoted his life."

the facility's vast collection of sculpture, photographs, prints, drawings and paintings. Back at Rollins, McKean became a full-fledged art instructor. He returned to New York briefly in 1935 for a one-man show at Delphic Studios, a gallery established by a bohemian journalist, pacifist and patron of the arts named Alma Marie Sullivan Reed.[5]

In 1937, McKean was named assistant to William H. Fox, chairman of the Rollins art department. Fox, previously director of the world-renowned Brooklyn Museum, undoubtedly shared a wealth of knowledge about collecting and exhibiting art. In 1939, McKean enrolled in a one-year master's program at Williams College in Williamstown, Massachusetts, where he earned his graduate degree in art history. His thesis was entitled *American Patterns of Thinking as Reflected in American Painting.* Finally, he had a credential with "art" in the title. McKean returned to Rollins, and shortly thereafter was elevated to art department chairman — a position he presumably would have happily occupied for the remainder of his career.

Jeannette decided in the late 1930s to fund construction of a facility on the Rollins campus that she would call the Morse Gallery of Art in honor of her grandmother. Fortunately, she knew someone who would be an ideal candidate to run the gallery, which opened in 1942 on the site of the current Cornell Fine Arts Museum. McKean, who shared Jeannette's enthusiasm for collecting and sharing art with the community, unsurprisingly won the director's job. Jeannette's stature as both an artist and an heiress was undeniably a bonus for all involved; the gallery's holdings quickly grew to encom-

---

5   Reed, a former journalist for the *San Francisco Call* and *The New York Times*, rented a portion of the top floor of a building on East 57th Street and established Delphic Studios, at which she promoted many Mexican artists. Some of her reporting assignments were in Mexico and she was in a romantic relationship with Mexican muralist José Clemente Orozco.

pass an intriguing assortment of American and European fine art. Surely by now the couple was engaged, implicitly if not formally. But marriage would have to wait; McKean, a lieutenant, junior grade, in the U.S. Navy Reserve, served three years in World War II, attaining the rank of lieutenant commander and spending at least a portion of his stint as an instructor at the Advanced Naval Intelligence School in New York. The intelligence assignment was likely a result of his travel abroad; he and boyhood friend John Tiedtke had traipsed across Europe together in 1936, ostensibly to tour the continent's great museums and concert halls. The Navy's intelligence units were actively seeking Americans who had spent time overseas.

When McKean returned to Winter Park in 1945, he and Jeannette were finally wed. He was 37, she was 36, and their courtship — if such a prosaic descriptor is applicable — had spanned 18 years. The couple, who would have no children, lavished attention on their hometown instead. "Jeannette brought this huge fortune to the marriage, and Hugh brought all this knowledge," recalled Keith McKean in a 1995 *Orlando Sentinel* obituary written about his brother. "So she learned more about art from him, and he and she together found ways to spend this fortune ... They were wonderfully generous to the community."

Although an art professor with limited administrative experience might have been an unconventional choice, McKean appears to have been a perfect fit for Rollins at that moment in its history. College historian Jack C. Lane noted that McKean's unpretentious demeanor helped mitigate the turmoil of the previous spring and summer: "A soft-spoken, artistic man with a penchant for philosophizing on any subject from the art of fishing to the meaning of art, McKean, with a gentle, unassuming manner, seemed an especially appropriate leader for the college in the post-Wagner years. There was a certain romantic appeal to this picture of an uncomplicated man, happily teaching art and suddenly propelled into the presidency with an urgent mission to wrest his alma mater from the throes of deep crisis."

The enrollment apocalypse predicted by Wagner never materialized; student deferments remained in effect based upon class standing and performance on a standardized test. Still, McKean hoped to solidify the college's finances and sought new sources of income. While the G.I. Bill had run its course, he found that opportunities remained to supply educational services for the military. One such opportunity was Operation Bootstrap, started nationally in 1949, which allowed U.S. Air Force personnel to take college courses with the government paying two-thirds of the tuition.[6] Most were young enlistees taking college courses for the first time, while others had interrupted their college careers to join the Air Force during World War II.

Some, though, were approaching completion of 20-year hitches and were preparing for post-retirement second careers outside the military. When a service member was within six months of completing a degree, he (or, very rarely, she) could then select a school and take a paid leave of absence to finish. Assistant Professor of History Rhea Marsh Smith,[7] the college's military liaison, coordinated the local launch of

---

6   Operation Bootstrap was revamped in 2002 and, as of 2019, was called the Air Force Educational Leave of Absence program.

7   Smith had taken a leave of absence during World War II to join the U.S. Army Signal Corps in Washington, D.C. He entered the service in 1942 as a captain but returned to Rollins in 1946 as a colonel. In addition to serving as a military instructor stateside, Smith had spent a year in France on the faculty of Biarritz American University, one of several temporary universities operated by the U.S. Army's Information and Educational Branch for demobilized service members.

Operation Bootstrap during the last week of July 1951. Smith had also designed a course for undergraduates — Orientation for the Armed Forces — which would elicit mixed responses from students when it was offered in the fall.[8]

THE COLLEGE'S FIRST Operation Bootstrap classes were offered only at Patrick Air Force Base in Brevard County and attracted 168 students for seven courses that included English composition, business law, elementary Spanish, principles of accounting, social psychology, algebra and trigonometry, and geometry and calculus.[9] The program consisted of two 16-week terms and one eight-week summer term, with classes meeting once weekly for three-hour sessions. Initially all the instructors were college faculty members, who commuted to the base near Cocoa Beach and earned 50 percent of the tuition or $320 per course, whichever was greater.

In the fall of 1951, Operation Bootstrap outposts were also established at Naval Air Station Sanford (now Orlan-

---

8   The course, which enrolled 27 students, was meant to prepare young men for military service. It was designed by Smith in consultation with officers from various branches. "On the whole, despite a certain public apathy and the resistance of students to military affairs, the course seems to have attained its objective," Smith reported to McKean. Although Smith described the course as "pioneering," it was not offered again.

9   In 1961, after formation of the School of General Studies, the Rollins College Patrick Air Force Base Branch, directed by General George F. Schlatter, began granting degrees. In 1981, following a sweeping reorganization under President Thaddeus Seymour, the branch became relatively autonomous and was placed under the supervision of a resident dean, first Robert E. Lee and then Richard Miller. In 1988, the college opened a separate campus in Rockledge and later West Melbourne and called it Rollins Brevard. However, enrollment declined due to competition from the University of Central Florida, which offered upper-level courses at considerably lower tuition at Brevard Community College. In 1998, Patricia Lancaster became dean of both the Holt School and Rollins Brevard in what was described as a merger between the two programs. The Brevard campus, however, was closed over a two-year period ending in 2003.

do Sanford International Airport), Pinecastle Air Force Base (later McCoy Air Force Base and now Orlando International Airport) and Orlando Air Force Base (later Naval Training Center Orlando and now the Baldwin Park master-planned community). The accelerated programs in Orlando and Sanford were offered in three eight-week semesters and met twice weekly for three-hour sessions. Classes, held both on campus and at the bases, were open to civilians as well as service members. The program netted just $5,940 for the college in its first two terms, reported Smith, but was growing as the new bases came on line. Plus, Smith was also pursing — ultimately in vain — the more lucrative establishment of an ROTC unit on campus.

The college, wishing to extend a personal welcome to its uniformed undergraduates, invited Bootstrappers to an open house and dance on the campus in early November 1952. McKean, however, wanted to make certain that attendees understood the rules of proper conduct. "There is always the possibility of friction between all groups and, of course, between servicemen and non-servicemen," McKean wrote in a memorandum to Rhea Marsh Smith. "This fact must be faced and accepted by all of us and, of course, we must all see that there is no cause for friction. Rollins College has certain customs which are important, and which should be respected and observed. One of these is that there is no cutting at dances. Service men, like other Rollins students, should ask for introductions. If they care to ask some young lady who has no previous engagement to accompany them to the dance, they should also have a proper introduction. This visit is intended to introduce the non-Rollins students at the air bases to Rollins College and give them an opportunity to make acquaintances with other members of the Rollins community. It is not to be treated as a lark in any sense of the word and careful decorum must be maintained." There is no indication that anyone behaved in an untoward manner. And the fact that 15 service members brought their wives reduced the possibility that any young ladies might experience unwanted advances.

Sauté's daughter Marie met her husband-to-be in one of her father's Operation Bootstrap mathematics classes at Patrick Air Force Base. Thanks in part to the program, Donald Lee Scharfetter, an airman first class, later entered Carnegie Mellon University in Pittsburgh, where he set a record at the institution by earning his bachelor's degree in 1960, his master's degree in 1961 and his Ph.D. in 1962. He went on to become a professor of electrical engineering at Carnegie Mellon and to have a successful career as top executive with Bell Laboratories, Xerox Corporation and Intel Corporation.

Of course, Scharfetter's story was not typical. But Operation Bootstrap, which eventually encompassed more than 200 college affiliates, allowed many service members to eventually earn degrees and helped to mitigate a worsening retention problem for the Air Force. "Education and professionalism go together to produce top-quality people," wrote Chief of Staff Curtis E. LeMay in 1960.[10] "Without question, one of the most critical problems posed to the Air Force today is in the officer career field. In general, our aim is to encourage those officers on active duty who do not have a baccalaureate degree to take advantage of the programs in existence — such as the Air Force Institute of Technology[11] and Operation Bootstrap. The Air

---

10 LeMay may be best remembered as former Alabama Governor George Wallace's vice presidential running mate when Wallace mounted a third-party bid for the presidency in 1968.

11 The Air Force Institute of Technology, located at Wright-Patterson Air Force Base in Ohio, is the graduate school of the U.S. Air Force. It offered advanced technical training since its founding in 1919 but did not confer degrees until 1956. The school's undergraduate equivalent is the U.S. Air Force Academy.

Hamilton Holt, president of Rollins from 1925 to 1949, bundled the college's abundance of cultural offerings into a catch-all adult education program that he described as "merely teaching an old dog new tricks." The program debuted in the winter term of 1936. (Unless otherwise noted, photos in this section are courtesy of the Department of Archives and Special Collections, Olin Library.)

Top: John Martin, a lecturer on foreign affairs, and his wife, Prestonia Mann Martin, an author who owned a socialist retreat in the Adirondacks, held unorthodox views but were nonetheless revered by locals.

Center and bottom: Edwin Osgood Grover, a retired publisher, became the college's professor of books and taught undergraduates in a cozy classroom featuring a rectangular table. Grover also helped Holt found the Animated Magazine, which drew huge crowds to campus and presaged the adult education program.

George Sauté, an assistant professor of mathematics, was the first director of Courses for the Community, which was reconstituted in 1960 as the degree-granting Institute for General Studies. Many iterations of the night school, which changed its name and its direction with regularity, were still to come.

Top: Operation Bootstrap, an early component of the night school, was offered for U.S. Air Force personnel beginning in 1951.

Left: Assistant Professor of Music Alphonse "Phonsie" Carlo taught violin through Community Courses for Young People and later helped found the Florida Symphony Youth Orchestra.

Bottom left: Pianist Marion Marwick was the first director of the School of Creative Arts, which subsumed the children's program in 1962.

Bottom right: Paul Wagner, 32, was named president when Holt retired in 1949. His tumultuous tenure may have hastened formalization of the adult education program, which was leveraged to improve the college's image following the so-called Wagner Affair.

Top: Thaddeus Seymour, Sr., who was president of the college from 1978 to 1990, believed that the School of Continuing Education had strayed too far afield from the liberal arts and sought major changes in its structure and curriculum.

Left: Daniel F. Riva, dean of the night school when Seymour arrived, had built a financially successful program in part by offering such grant-supported majors as criminal justice and fire safety administration.

Top: In addition to Holt and Seymour, other college presidents — Hugh McKean, Jack Critchfield, Rita Bornstein and Lewis Duncan — influenced the night school's direction.

Right: The College Planning Committee recommended sweeping changes for the School of Continuing Education. Daniel R. DeNicola, an associate professor of philosophy, chaired the committee. He is shown with Seymour, Marsha L. Clore, committee secretary, and Connie Riggs, assistant to the president.

Bottom: Seymour and Robert A. Miller, newly appointed dean of the Division of Continuing Education, are shown at a special 1987 commencement announcing that the night school had been renamed the Hamilton Holt School. Seymour holds a bust of the college's eighth president.

Top: In a Holt School class, Jie Yu, associate professor of education, shows future teachers how to use manipulatives, which are objects designed to demonstrate mathematical concepts in the classroom.

Bottom: Holt School graduations are always emotional affairs, especially for the families of nontraditional students who earn degrees while juggling an array of other responsibilities. (Photos by Scott Cook, courtesy of the Hamilton Holt School.)

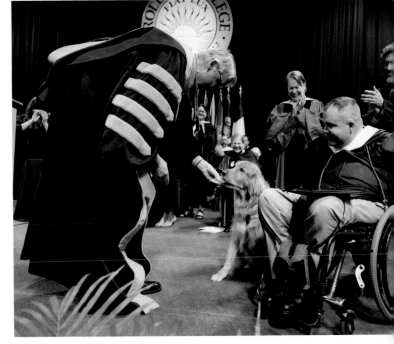

Top: President Grant Cornwell presents the Outstanding Senior Award to Doragnes Bradshaw, who overcame several serious personal challenges to complete her undergraduate degree in communication studies. "Live with meaningful purpose and your heart will be full of love and your mind will be full of wisdom," Bradshaw told the 2018 graduating class.

Right: Cornwell congratulates Tom Jacobson, who in 2019 earned a Master of Arts in Counseling, and gets a nuzzle from Jacobson's service dog, Palmer. (Photos by Scott Cook, courtesy of the Hamilton Holt School.)

Force is a professional force — from top to bottom. There is no place today or in the future for those who do not approach their specialties and jobs in a professional manner and with the intent of constant learning and personal improvement."

Just as Operation Bootstrap got underway, McKean also launched "Courses for the Community," slated to begin in the fall term, which he envisioned as encompassing Holt-style lectures for cultural enrichment, a grab bag of noncredit courses, a handful of for-credit courses and a sizable selection of arts-oriented activities for children. McKean dropped the term "adult education" and appointed Sauté, who had lobbied for the position, to be the new program's director. An indicator of the urgency McKean felt to quickly generate positive news from the college is the fact that he announced Courses for the Community in the *Orlando Morning Sentinel* a week prior to the program's first organizational meeting and less than three months before classes were slated to begin.

"We wish to take the best of our extension courses from the past and enlarge and improve them with careful selection of new courses to the point where Rollins will be of even more direct service to the educational desires of the community," McKean declared in a July 8, 1951, story headlined "College to Give Community Try at Courses." Sauté, quoted in the same story, added that the curriculum would be "vocational, cultural, recreational and civic; as far as possible we want to open up the facilities of the college to the community." There were no specifics reported because the college had none to share.

Sauté insisted nearly two decades later that Courses for the Community was introduced primarily to heal the public-image wounds inflicted by the Wagner Affair. Whatever the impetus, the mathematician was grateful to have his job back and grateful to have another project on which to focus his considerable energy; in the imbroglio's aftermath

145

the Institute for World Government was eliminated, ostensibly because there were no funds available. More likely, the institute was a casualty of Cold War wariness. Who would place their trust in a federation of foreigners when there were hostile sovereign nations that possessed, or might soon possess, atomic weapons? Neither the U.S. nor the Soviet Union, which successfully tested its own atom bomb in 1949, was willing to take the risk. With McCarthyism and the Red Scare running rampant, internationalists often found their names on lists of communists and other fellow travelers. In any case, the college was in no position to agitate anyone.

"When I first started lecturing on the United Nations, atomic energy and international control of armaments for peace, it was popular," said Sauté in a 1969 oral history interview. "And then suddenly it got very unpopular. I would be lecturing or debating, and someone would say, 'You're from Belgium, aren't you? Well, then you're not an American.'" Further, although McKean was a Holt protégé, he was no crusader, and did not share his mentor's political fervor. He had a college to save, after which, it was then assumed, he would return to teaching, curating and painting.

The final adult education program — in the winter of 1951, during the Wagner regime — was not unlike Holt himself during his final years: game but bone weary. A six-lecture series, "Primitive Man: The Inventor," had been offered by Frederick W. Sleight, consultant in archaeology, who in 1955 would become the first director of the Central Florida Museum (now the Orlando Science Center). William H. Worrell, retired professor of semantics from the University of Michigan who then lived in Melbourne Beach, had delivered a half-dozen discourses on "Geography and Ethnology of the Near East," while the college's venerable Inter-American Council, founded in 1898 during the Spanish-American War, had screened a lineup of educational films, "many of them in color," concerning Central and South America. Noncredit courses had been offered in equitation (the care of horses), printmaking, public speaking, outdoor sketching, conversational Spanish and piano sonatas by Beethoven. Edwin Granberry's creative writing seminar, a mainstay since the early 1930s, had again been offered and, as always, had commanded the highest fee: $50 for 10 weeks. While undoubtedly interesting, such a limited lineup of locals could not compare to the robust rosters of eminent academicians from the heyday of "winter school" in the late 1930s and early 1940s.

On July 14, the first Committee for Community Courses, chaired by Sauté, met in Smith's office to decide how to move forward. Sauté and Smith were joined by Halsted W. Caldwell, secretary of the board of trustees; Royal W. France, professor of economics; Gladys Stanaland Henderson, chief reference librarian; Dorothy I. Koehler, registrar; Chloe M. Lyle, cashier;[12] and William R. Shelton, an English professor who

---

12 Lyle's mundane job title diminishes her importance to the college, which was her alma mater and her employer from 1929 to 1963. When she died in 1974, her service was held in Knowles Memorial Chapel and the college released this statement: "Chloe Lyle's service to Rollins College was an inspiration to those who knew her. She was the guardian of college funds in days when the financial situation was so critical that the continued existence of the college depended on a successful collection of its accounts and a minimum of expenditures. But what made her a great woman was her great heart. It was her responsibility to administer the scholarship program, and during her 35 years of service she worked out plans to help thousands of students who could not have gone to Rollins without help. With much too little funds available, she would spend unlimited time with each individual student working out plans for scholarships, loans and jobs so that somehow ends could meet, and they could attend Rollins. Probably her greatest memorial is the affection and loyalty which these students still feel for her. If there is a Rollins spirit, it is the spirit of those who have made Rollins, and Chloe Lyle was one of those wonderful people whose devotion to the college and its students made the Rollins spirit a reality."

was also the college's public relations director.[13] The group agreed to extend invitations to William Fort, a professor of philosophy and psychology; Audrey Packham, an associate professor of education; and James H. Russell, a professor of psychology; as well as to recent graduate Benjamin Aycrigg, an assistant in the admissions office and a broadcaster on WDBO-AM.[14] McKean, in a memorandum to Sauté, offered scant guidance. He wanted the adult education program's replacement — whatever that replacement turned out to be — to offer programs year-round, not just in the winter. He emphasized that current faculty, not adjuncts, should teach, and noted that "it has been presented to me forcefully that the plan is a college one and community teachers would complicate matters considerably." This opinion would be presented just as forcefully decades later.

Although McKean declared that Courses for the Community "should be sound financially," he offered no specific goals for enrollment or revenue. Succinct minutes from the organizational meeting indicate that ideas for topics and instruc-

---

13   Shelton, a 1948 Rollins graduate, had won an O. Henry Memorial Award for *The Snow Girl*, a story he wrote while still a student. (His professor, Edwin Granberry, had won the same award for *A Trip to Czardis* in 1932.) Shelton would go on to a distinguished career in journalism as space affairs correspondent for *Time* and *Life* magazines as well as contributing editor for *The Saturday Evening Post*. He was awarded the college's Decoration of Honor in 1962 for achievements in writing. After moving to Houston in the late 1960s, Shelton wrote several space-related books, including a science-fiction novel called *Stowaway to the Moon: The Camelot Odyssey* (Doubleday, 1973), which was filmed in 1975 as a TV movie starring Lloyd Bridges of *Sea Hunt* fame. Shelton also wrote, directed or produced more than three dozen documentary and educational films for the NASA, the U.S. Air Force and the U.S. State Department. He died in 1985.

14   Aycrigg would become known as "the Walter Cronkite of Orlando" during a 35-year career at the local CBS affiliate, now known as WKMG Channel 6, much of it as news director and anchor for the 6 p.m. newscast. Aycrigg had been one of the part-time employees fired by Wagner. He died in 2014.

tors were discussed, although none are specified. Sauté volunteered to ask the ever-feisty John Martin if he was interested in continuing the lecture series (apparently, Martin was not interested.) A suggestion was made that a survey be taken of local civic groups to see what sorts of courses might be popular, but there was no time for even the most rudimentary market research. A makeshift program including lectures, special-interest courses and for-credit courses was cobbled together and set to debut on September 28. The rollout was inauspicious, which is unsurprising considering the haste with which it was planned.

SAUTÉ REPORTED TO McKean that, after expenses, the improvised fall term of Courses for the Community netted a modest $2,171 for the college. Enrollment totaled 33 for a certification program in elementary education, which encompassed a series of for-credit college courses. Noncredit courses in Russian and Spanish drew a cumulative 25, while Granberry's creative writing workshop attracted 23. Other courses did not fare as well; play production and outdoor sketching drew seven registrants each, while a series of gerontology seminars averaged about 15 attendees per session. The most popular program was "Orchestral Music for Listeners," a series of 11 lectures offered in conjunction with the newly formed Symphony Orchestra of Central Florida. The talks, delivered by Edna Wallace Johnston, an associate professor of flute at the conservatory and minister of music at First Congregational Church of Winter Park, were moved off-campus to the nearby Woman's Club of Winter Park when crowds of 100-plus exceeded the capacity of the Dyer Memorial Building.

Children's activities, under the direction of Harvey L. Woodruff, director of the conservatory, and Mary Jarman Nelson, assistant professor of music, were also well-received, with about 160 youngsters from pre-school through junior high school taking lessons in voice and choral singing. "There is evidence to indicate that the increase in goodwill for Rollins College in the Central Florida community is considerable," wrote Sauté. "Furthermore, as long as we are able to present an imaginative, interesting and balanced program which can be done with our resources, the benefits will accrue in years to follow." McKean echoed Sauté's confidence in a subsequent report to the trustees, pointing out that the college could (and, in fact, did) boast that it educated more than 1,000 people: 600 day school undergraduates, 207 Bootstrappers and more than 200 adults who enrolled in one or more Courses for the Community.

As the 1950s progressed, the program adopted a relatively consistent format, with modestly priced ($5 to $20) lecture series and noncredit "special courses" held mostly during the winter term, as they had been during the Holt Era. A handful of for-credit courses, primarily the series leading to elementary-school teacher certification, were offered year-round, as were some language courses and a seemingly random smattering of such night-school standards as typing, shorthand and basic accounting. The children's program listed dozens of after-school sessions in art, dance, theater and the playing of musical instruments. Founders' Week activities, such as the Animated Magazine, and concurrent cultural events, such the Bach Festival of Winter Park, were promoted during the winter term. Faculty recitals and Sunday Organ Vespers in Knowles Memorial Chapel were often packaged with lectures and courses in promotional brochures.

Operation Bootstrap, in which civilians were always welcome to enroll, initially operated independently from Courses for the Community and seems to have been informally administered by Rhea Marsh Smith, in cooperation with base commanders. Why this changed is unclear but Operation Bootstrap, including its "College of Knowledge" at Patrick Air Force Base, was placed under Sauté's purview in 1954. Although the Brevard operation was initially unaffected by the consolidation, most courses previously offered at the Orlando Air Force Base and Pinecastle Air Force Base were moved on campus in 1956 and the military linkage was deemphasized. As a result, more civilians than service members enrolled. "Bootstrap courses are not crip courses," Sauté told the *Orlando Morning Sentinel*. "They're difficult." But by 1960, Courses for the Community had subsumed Operation Bootstrap, which was phased out despite having enrolled more than 4,000 civilians and service members from 1951 to 1959. Change would be seismic at the turn of the decade, but for most of the 1950s — apart from Operation Bootstrap, which was always about academics — Sauté's program generally retained an elite cultural tourism vibe.

In the winter of 1954, for example, McKean offered a series of six art-history lectures through Courses for the Community. William A. Constable, associate professor of English, delivered 10 lectures on modern English drama, augmented by dramatic readings from his wife, Wilna L. Constable, with whom he had co-pastored the First Unitarian Church of Orlando. Franklyn A. Johnson,[15] associate professor of polit-

---

15 Johnson had a harrowing experience during World War II. While an undergraduate at Rutgers University, he enlisted in the ROTC as a second lieutenant. After completing basic training, infantry school and the company commander's course, he was sent overseas and was among those who landed with the first wave of Allied troops on Omaha Beach in the invasion of Normandy. He was later wounded behind enemy lines and reported killed in action. However, he was a captive in a prisoner of war camp in northern France until he managed to escape in 1944. Upon his return to the U.S., he completed his master's and Ph.D. degrees in political science at Harvard University and embarked upon an academic career. He later became president of Jacksonville Junior College, which became Jacksonville University.

ical economics, held court with a six-lecture series on world politics, while Melvin L. Greenhut, associate professor of economics, offered a 10-lecture series on investment strategies. Edna Wallace Johnston's series on symphonic music, now held at the Woman's Club of Winter Park and the Sorosis Club of Orlando, returned with a series of presentations related to works to be played that season by the Symphony Orchestra of Central Florida. There were also courses on drawing and painting, motion-picture production, speech and acting techniques and conversational Spanish.

In 1956, British-born actor Peter Dearing,[16] director of the Department of Theater Arts, presented a dozen readings from popular Broadway shows, while S. Gale Lowrie, visiting professor of history and government and a past lecturer at Tsinghua College in Peking, held five sessions about East Asia. In 1957, Paul F. Douglass, professor of government and advisor to South Korean President Syngman Rhee from 1951 to 1953, offered five talks about circumstances leading up to the Korean War, while Theodore S. Darrah, dean of Knowles Memorial Chapel, led six discussions about the Old Testament prophets. Much to the amazement of instructors, students even began to form independent discussion groups.[17] "The

---

16 Dearing left the college the following year to become artistic director of London Little Theatre in London, Ontario. "I wasn't brought here ... to win a popularity contest," Dearing said when his demand for perfectionism ruffled feathers. "I somehow think that's what they wanted but they chose the wrong person ... Basically, what I have tried to do is create theatre. Good theatre, bad theatre, professional theatre, amateur theatre." Three years later, having revitalized the theater with splashy musicals, Dearing died at age of 57. At a memorial service held at the venue, there were no flowers; Dearing had requested that instead donations be made toward buying a curtain for the stage.

17 In his report to McKean on the first term of Courses for the Community, Sauté noted: "I should mention that during fall term an interesting form of adult education was initiated in the discussion club known as The Orlando-Rollins Forum. Twenty individuals subscribed

result [of Courses for the Community] is that for old as well as new students there is a wide variety of interesting things to hear, to see, to read, to think about and to do," Sauté told the *Orlando Morning Sentinel*, which wrote an editorial lauding the program.

Courses for the Community was inoffensive to liberal arts adherents on the faculty, who earned an additional stipend and enjoyed interactions with adult learners. In the wake of a public relations disaster, no one questioned the wisdom of offering courses and lectures to engender community goodwill. Operation Bootstrap raised no hackles because it was distinct from the college, and unlikely to dilute or disrupt its core mission. But the hybrid program taking shape lacked focus and would become further muddled in the 1960s and 1970s when social, economic and demographic factors converged to ignite a boom in continuing education. There was not, as far as can be determined, a long-range plan or even a serious discussion about what role — if any — continuing education should play within a small liberal arts college.

McKean ultimately decided that while the day school should remain true to its historic mission, the continuing education program should adopt a more expansive approach that would both meet a need in the community and generate revenue to bolster the day school's operating budget. Positioning the two programs as equivalent would later cause controversy, but by the early 1950s, Courses for the Community seemed to be achieving what McKean had promised. He

---

to a series of six evenings of discussion on topics of their choice. The discussions were led by members of the faculty selected by the group. The range of subjects covered can be judged from the list of speakers: [Nathan] Starr (English), [Paul] Vestal (biology), [George] Sauté (math), [Charles] Mendell (English), and [Arthur] Enyart (dean of the college). It is very likely that similar groups will be formed when the idea becomes better known."

reported to the trustees: "The college, we believe, is making fast friends by the logical means of brightening and enriching [their lives]."

ANARCHY ON OLLIE AVENUE? An overstatement, perhaps, but it can certainly be said that Courses for the Community brought children to the campus in droves: singing children, dancing children, painting children, acting children, swimming children, weaving children and musical-instrument-playing children. Thousands of present-day baby boomers fondly recall attending after-school classes, which were sometimes taught by highly credentialed day school faculty, or the program's popular summer day camp, which began in 1967 and ran through the summer of 2015. Community Courses for Young People, as the ancillary program was then known, offered piano lessons as well as rhythmics (dance), choral singing, junior theater, and arts and crafts in a barracks-like studio behind the infirmary near Dinky Dock (where the parking garage now stands).

Lessons in other musical instruments were added, along with instruction in swimming and canoeing. By the late 1950s, each eight-week quarter attracted more than 500 youngsters from pre-school to high school. From 1953 to 1958, participants showcased their skills in *The Spring Thing*, a collection of short plays, some of them original, as well as scripted and improvised skits. Art students displayed their works in the lobby, while crafts students helped created sets, props and costumes. Music students provided accompaniment and beaming parents packed the beautiful Annie Russell Theatre.

Peter Dearing offered his young charges opportunities to perform with the Rollins Players onstage at the campus's storied 400-seat venue. A former professor at the Royal Academy of Dramatic Arts in London, Dearing began his career as a child actor in films before touring the U.S. and Europe with the Ben Greet Players, a stock company that specialized in open-air Shakespeare.[18] In 1955, Dearing cast 9-year-old Annette Moore and 12-year-old Danny Carr in an Annie Russell Theatre production of *Mrs. McThing*, a fantasy about children and witches written by Mary Chase of *Harvey* fame. Although a critic from *The Sandspur* savaged the play, opining that "the progression of innumerable ideas is exceedingly awkward," he managed to coherently praise young Annette for "stealing the show" with her poise and stage presence.[19] Dearing later drafted youngsters for campus productions of *The Crucible* and *A Midsummer Night's Dream.* And in 1957, when he directed Maxwell Anderson's *The Bad Seed* for the Orlando Players, Dearing plucked a junior-high schooler for a plumb role. Precocious Anne Hathaway, 11, chewed up the scenery as pigtailed psychopath Rhoda Penmark in a performance the *Orlando Morning Sentinel* described as "brilliant ... [Anne] was able to project a chilling ruthlessness, which told her audience that under the smile a twisted brain was plotting murder."

Marion Marwick, a pianist who had tickled the ivories

---

18   Ben Greet was the stage name for Sir Philip Barling Greet, who may have inspired Dearing's interest in children's theater. When Greet managed London's Old Vic Theater from 1914 to 1918, he persuaded the U.K. Department of Education to sponsor school visits to the historic 1,000-seat venue. Over the course of four years, Greet presented Shakespeare plays to more than 20,000 elementary school students. Dearing joined the Ben Greet Players at age 14 and remained until Greet's death nine years later.

19   Also appearing in *Mrs. McThing* was Rollins drama student Ann Derflinger, who would become a legendary drama teacher at Winter Park High School. The auditorium at the school is named for Derflinger, who died of cancer in 1983. She often cited Dearing as a major influence on her decision to teach. Derflinger, in turn, inspired actors such as Tom Nowicki (*The Blind Side*) and Amanda Bearse (*Married With Children*).

with the Toronto Symphony and the Orlando Symphony Orchestra, enjoyed playing jazz and was good at it. She also enjoyed teaching others to play the piano and was among several adjunct instructors in 1957, when Community Courses for Young People was inexplicably renamed Community Courses for Children. She later became director of the program's music division and finally director of all activities under the auspices of the Rollins College School of Creative Arts, which subsumed the children's program in 1962. Under Marwick, a graduate of the Royal Conservatory of Music in Toronto, piano instruction dominated after-school offerings. By Marwick's account, she taught more than 1,000 people of all ages to play. "Everyone who took piano lessons from my mother loved her," recalled Robert Marwick, her son. "She was dedicated. She built that program into a major force in the community and something that meant a lot in the lives of young people." Indeed, a social media post from Robert Marwick seeking memories of his mother drew dozens of nostalgic responses recounting how Mrs. Marwick had made a difference — as good piano teachers often do — by becoming a friend and confidant.

Marwick's jaw-dropping numbers, however, were possible because in addition to individual instruction she was an exponent of the Pace Method — created by pianist and educator Robert Pace — which advocated teaching piano in large groups.[20] The School of Creative Arts was one of the first in the

---

20 Pace, who graduated from of the Julliard School of Music and held a doctorate from Teachers College, Columbia University, became Director of the National Piano Foundation, a position he held from 1963 to 1977. He later formed the International Piano Teaching Foundation to more specifically promote the learning theories he espoused, which included group instruction and discussion of musical concepts. Visitors to the School of Creative Arts when it moved to R.D. Keene Hall in 1974 remember the second floor containing dozens of pianos of every sort, many side by side, and youngsters playing them while wearing headphones.

U.S. to adopt the method. Pace, director of the piano department at Columbia University Teachers College and director of the National Piano Foundation, consulted with Marwick and visited Winter Park each year to check the program's progress. By the mid-1960s, the school offered nearly 30 courses per term and attracted some 1,200 students who could choose from sessions in piano, voice, brass and woodwinds, violin and viola, and guitar and banjo.

There was also instruction in painting and sculpture, ceramics and weaving and, somewhat incongruously, conversational Spanish and French. An annual Rollins Piano Festival of the School of Creative Arts was launched and attracted music students and educators from around the U.S. Pace, among others, attended as an adjudicator for student competitions. By now most classes were taught by adjunct faculty, often teachers from Orange County Public Schools. One prominent conservatory musician, however, found a mission at the School of Creative Arts and in so doing created a lasting but underappreciated legacy by establishing the Florida Symphony Youth Symphony.

Vioinist Alphonse "Phonsie" Carlo, during an interview for a job at the conservatory, was asked by Hamilton Holt — a lover of music who had sung first tenor in the Yale Glee Club — if he knew an obscure Irish folk tune, "Londonderry Air."[21] Carlo did indeed know the song, and played it as Holt accompanied him on an old stand-up piano. Delighted, Holt offered Carlo a job as an assistant professor of music in 1943. Carlo, who studied violin at Yale University and the Julliard School of Music, later helped organize the Bach Festival

---

21 "Londonderry Air," which originated in County Londonderry in Ireland, is familiar throughout the world. The tune is played as the victory anthem of Northern Ireland at the Commonwealth Games, an international multisport competition. The popular song "Danny Boy" uses the tune.

Orchestra and the Florida Symphony Orchestra, serving as concertmaster for both. Then in 1953, he was recruited to teach violin through Community Courses for Young People. By all accounts a kind and patient man who enjoyed instructing students of all ages, Carlo agreed and offered after-school lessons, as did his accomplished wife, Katherine, a concert pianist with whom he frequently performed.[22]

Shortly thereafter, Carlo convinced the Orange County School Board and the Florida Symphony Orchestra that a youth orchestra would benefit everyone involved. Through such a program, schools could offer orchestral training without the expense of starting orchestral programs.[23] And the symphony could have players-in-waiting as well as an expanded base of support through the proud parents of school-age musicians. Announcements were made, an article was published in the newspaper and on the first Saturday in November more than 100 students from middle school through high school, their instruments in tow, assembled at Howard Junior High School. On subsequent Saturdays, there were free classes for beginning and intermediate players followed by a rehearsal for students who were sufficiently advanced to become the first members of the Florida Symphony Youth Orchestra. Assisting the busy Carlo, who also played in a baroque ensemble, were several other symphony players and public-school music teachers.

---

22   Katherine Carlo, like her husband a Julliard graduate, was the pianist for the Florida Symphony Orchestra and the Bach Festival Choir. The Alphonse and Katherine Carlo Music Scholarship, which was established in 1993 thanks to a gift from the Alphonse Carlo Trust, provides scholarships for students to study piano or stringed instruments. There is also a Carlo Room in the R.D. Keene Music Building. Katherine Carlo died in 1990; her husband died in 1992.

23   Glenridge Junior High School was the first local public school to form an orchestra, in 1957. Winter Park High School did not have an orchestra until 1962.

Forming a competent, much less a good, youth orchestra was no small feat in 1953, when the music programs in most public schools were centered upon brass-heavy marching bands. Still, Carlo had a gift for recognizing and cultivating talent. In 1954, the 30-member youth orchestra — perhaps seeded with some collegiate ringers — played alongside the professionals at the Florida Symphony Orchestra's annual Spring Pops Concert at Orlando Municipal Auditorium (now the Bob Carr Theater). "I've never seen a group of students with more self-discipline and more earnestness in their work," said Edward Preodor, head of the violin department at the University of Florida in an interview with the *Orlando Morning Sentinel*. "Students who will give up their Saturday mornings to study are the best type of students. But more important still is the leadership of your conductor, Alphonse Carlo. He is obviously a leading musician who understands young people and who loves to work with them." The fledgling youth orchestra also performed solo concerts, including at least two that were televised locally.

Carlo stepped down as conductor in 1960 but remained a steady and supportive presence. The college covered some operating expenses and was listed for several years in the 1970s as the youth orchestra's sponsoring organization — although the nature of the partnership appears to have been informal. The Florida Symphony Orchestra's Women's Committee, meanwhile, provided scholarships for young players to study with Carlo and others at the School of Creative Arts. The youth orchestra, despite its popularity, received scant attention from the professional orchestra's management team until 1978, when it was granted "full arm" status. Ironically, the junior partner emerged unscathed even after the senior partner collapsed under financial pressure in 1993.

"Because we remained attached at the hip for so long, our

historical narrative has been told from the Florida Symphony Orchestra's perspective," said Don Lake, president of the youth orchestra's board of directors. "But Rollins College, through its former School of Creative Arts, was a profound co-sponsor and financial supporter. Our organization would not even exist without the help the college gave us." Today, Phonsie's pet project is a thriving 501(c)(3) organization with three full orchestras, a string training orchestra, a chamber music ensemble and a 24-piece jazz orchestra. Although the college is rarely given credit, the Youth Orchestra is an enduring (and sonorous) legacy of Courses for the Community and the School of Creative Arts.

Chapter 6

WORTHY OF THE STARS

IN 1957, THE Martin Company (previously Martin Marietta and currently Lockheed Martin) bought 6,700 swampy acres in Southwest Orange County and began building a complex for production of Pershing, Bullpup, Lacrosse, Sprint, Patriot and Hellfire missiles. In short order, the aircraft and aerospace manufacturer — buoyed by the high-tech boom that followed the Soviet Union's launch of Sputnik, the first artificial Earth satellite — grew to more than 8,000 local employees. Orlando's motto was changed, albeit temporarily, from the City Beautiful to the Action Center of Florida. Concurrently, junior colleges were sprouting up throughout the state, offering associate degrees and preparing students for careers in technology-oriented fields. Because of Martin's burgeoning presence, few regions needed such an institution more than Central Florida, where Rollins — with its four-year, liberal arts curriculum — held a monopoly on higher education.

Orlando did have a vocationally oriented junior college, but it was an odd hybrid that carried significant baggage.

Orlando Junior College, founded in 1941, was meant to "carry on the work started in high school with specialization in work which will help the student to find a job when he gets through his course," according to Judson Walker, the longtime super-intendent of education in Orange County who championed its founding during World War II. OJC, although it operated under the auspices of the Orange County School Board, was independent and privately funded. The president, Morris Smith Hale Jr., was a religious zealot who refused to admit blacks and was not bound by the U.S. Supreme Court's 1954 *Brown v. Board of Education* decision outlawing segregation in public schools. OJC's homogeneous 600-plus students attended classes on a 20-acre campus at Marks Street and Highland Avenue, home today of Lake Highland Prep.

In 1961, the Florida Legislature, at the recommendation of the state's Community College Council, authorized funds for a state-supported junior college in Orlando. But Gover-nor Farris Bryant vetoed the appropriation at the behest of powerful *Orlando Morning Sentinel* publisher Martin Andersen,[1] who believed that OJC could become the four-year "space university" for which he had long advocated. The Mississippi-born Andersen, by no means a racial progres-sive, was unfazed by Hale's discriminatory practices. But it was boosterism, not bigotry, that guided his thinking. Anoth-er junior college, he surmised, would compete for tax dollars and students, and might preclude a new university altogeth-

---

1   Here, in part, is how Andersen was described in his 1986 obituary: "Tough, savvy, blunt, down-to-earth, controversial, at times strident and hot-tempered, at times generous and compassionate, he was one of the last two-fisted publishers of the old roughhouse school of one-man newspapering." Andersen had said: "[Orlando] was a small town, unac-customed to strong and independent newspapers, and some of my poli-cies were unpopular. It was new journalism for the little town ... I made them get up at dawn, go out into their yards in their shirttails, walking barefoot in the dew, to get the paper."

er. So his newspaper crusaded against a state-funded junior college as an egregious waste of taxpayer dollars. "OJC has accomplished the remarkable achievement of living within its income from student fees and tuitions," read a 1957 editorial likely written by Andersen. "And it has been able to start a building program that, when completed, will make its campus one of the most beautiful anywhere."

In 1958, OJC rather presumptuously changed its name to the University of Orlando, although it continued to operate as a junior college. Hale hoped that OJC could one day become a private university — much as Jacksonville Junior College had become Jacksonville University in 1956 — and retain its ostensibly Christian values and exclusionary admissions policies. The more pragmatic Andersen just wanted a university, period, and would later use his clout to steer Florida Technological University, now the University of Central Florida, to Orlando.[2] UCF, which opened in 1968, is today the second-largest university in the U.S. An official history of Valencia College, which opened in 1967[3] — notably after Andersen's retirement — claims that Edward G. Uhl, vice president of Martin, offered Hale and the OJC trustees $1 million if they would overturn their policy against admitting racial and religious minorities and initiate technical

---

2 In addition to pressing his friend Governor Farris Bryant to move FTU ahead on the state's capital outlay priority list, Andersen and the Central Florida Development Committee raised more than $1 million to buy land for the university along Alafaya Trail.

3 In an ironic Rollins connection, attorney Raymer F. Maguire Jr. of Maguire, Voorhis & Wells was appointed by Jack Jennings, then chairman of the Orange County School Board, as his representative to the initial Valencia Community College Advisory Committee. Valencia historians credit the respected Maguire's support as crucial in helping overcome opposition to the state-supported school. Maguire had been the Rollins attorney during the Wagner fiasco, and resigned in protest when Wagner was dismissed at a meeting that he had deemed illegal.

training programs for employees (and potential employees) of the fast-growing company. Hale refused, according to the account, thus sealing the eventual doom of the intransigent institution. Rollins, which is scarcely mentioned, supposedly "remained steadfast in its commitment to the liberal arts and was uninterested in expansion" despite the opportunity that presented itself when OJC fell out of favor with Martin.

The company may well have made the infamous $1 million offer — the story is generally accepted as true — but would have done so without fanfare. In any case, Martin sent students to OJC, which in 1957 offered upper-level evening courses in electrical engineering and business administration through an extension program of the University of Miami. Between the two institutions, it was possible — in theory, at least — to earn a Bachelor of Science degree. Completing the program, however, was almost impossible in practice, especially for anyone who was gainfully employed. To graduate, a student was required to spend his or her final year in residence at the university's campus in Coral Gables — a pertinent provision that numerous stories in the *Orlando Morning Sentinel* somehow failed to mention.

Still, Andersen's newspaper praised the "unique agreement" that was "designed to meet the growing demands of local industry to provide better educational opportunities for their employees." Hale told the newspaper that more than 140 Martin employees had enrolled on the first day of registration, and that he was fielding at least 25 phone calls per day from other interested companies and individuals. After the OJC-University of Miami partnership was announced, Sauté wrote a letter to the editor that praised, albeit faintly, the ballyhooed joint venture. "Nevertheless," he added, "in fairness to the many newcomers here, it should be pointed out that for many years Rollins College has been providing extensive educational services for the people of Central Florida" through Holt's winter program and, more recently, through Operation Bootstrap and Courses for the Community, both of which the letter described in some detail.

Andersen, who rarely allowed readers to have the final word, tacked a response on to the end of Sauté's missive: "Rollins College has certainly always been in the forefront in offering educational opportunities for the people of Central Florida, and the Courses for the Community program is to be highly commended. The Orlando Junior College-University of Miami program, however, is designed to supplement the liberal arts curriculum with technical and engineering courses needed in industrial expansion. Both programs are a vital part of the educational process." Sauté's letter sounded more than a little petulant, and Andersen's reply sounded more than a little preachy. But the college, having been put in its place, would not quietly stay there.

The OJC program, perhaps inevitably, floundered. In 1959, E.J. Fallon, Martin's education and management development director, wrote McKean and implied, rather sternly, that it was his civic duty to help keep the OJC-University of Miami partnership afloat. McKean, in his capacity as education subcommittee chair of the newly formed Central Florida Development Committee,[4] ought to encourage enrollment and find ways to assist overworked OJC staffers with administrative matters, Fallon wrote, adding that "we at Martin believe there should be greater participation [by members of the business community] to assist Orlando Junior College as

---

4 The Central Florida Development Committee was started by the Orlando Chamber of Commerce as the Committee of 100 with the goal of "bringing about the sound growth, beautification and healthy development of Central Florida." Most major movers and shakers were members, including the Martin Company's Edward G. Uhl, one of the organizers who served as chairman in its first year.

evidence of support." The crux of the problem, not surprising-ly, was that students now within a year of graduation — about 50 in all, mostly Martin employees — did not plan to reenroll because they could not take sabbaticals and move to Coral Gables. Clearly, Martin officials had entered the agreement anticipating that strong enrollment would encourage a newly enlightened OJC to offer four-year degrees or, failing that, persuade the University of Miami to establish a degree-grant-ing branch. When the grand partnership fizzled, not a word about it was written in the *Orlando Morning Sentinel.* Surely Andersen, who had championed Hale, now realized that OJC would never become a great space university — or any other kind of university, for that matter.[5]

McKean's reply to Fallon's entreaty is unknown, but it is not true that Rollins was "uninterested in expansion." The day school, of course, was not going to become an incubator for missile engineers. But in 1957, at the specific behest of Martin, the college launched an evening program leading to a Master of Business Administration (MBA) degree — its first master's degree. Two years later, the college added an evening program leading to a Master of Science in Physics degree with an optional concentration in physics engineering. Most students in both programs were employees of Martin. The evening program, it seemed, could be anything and every-thing. For a time, it tried to be.

IN 1960, DWIGHT D. Eisenhower was still president of the Unit-ed States, but John F. Kennedy and Richard M. Nixon were headed for the Democratic and Republican nominations,

---

5   Orlando Junior College, which began calling itself the College of Orlan-do in 1969, started Lake Highland Preparatory School in 1970 to com-pensate for plummeting enrollment due to competition from public junior colleges. The college ceased operation in 1971.

setting up an epic battle that would culminate with a narrow win for the young senator from Massachusetts. The tumult associated with the decade — Vietnam, assassinations, mass protests, racial unrest, the sexual revolution and more — was largely yet to come. Beatniks weren't yet hippies, and Elvis — back home from serving in the U.S. Army in Germany — notched two of the year's Top 10 records: "It's Now or Never" and "Stuck on You." The 1960s are remembered, at least by those who were cognizant, as a time of change. Certainly that is true with the college's continuing education program, which adopted new names and new structures during the decade but, most significantly, became the most direct precursor to the present-day Hamilton Holt School when it began granting a Bachelor of General Studies degree through the Rollins College Institute for General Studies, which was announced in October 1960.

There were, as yet, no specific majors — only areas of concentration. Still, the college at least offered a four-year degree that was accessible for working adults and other nontraditional students. "The general studies degree will differ in many ways from that offered in the resident liberal arts college," McKean told the *Orlando Morning Sentinel*. "The requirements for candidacy will be different, but the standards of the courses taught will be those of Rollins." Indeed, the primary admission requirement to the lower-cost continuing education undergraduate program was a high school diploma or a GED. Transfer college credits were accepted, and additional credits could be earned from military service and college-level proficiency tests. Required courses were in the general categories of English composition, humanities, social studies and mathematics or science, but 30 of the 128 semester hours needed for a graduation could be in areas of concentration that included those disciplines as well as business and preparation for teaching. Generally, those under age 20 would not be admitted unless they were employed full-time or could present other valid reasons why attendance at a day school was impossible. And the program was a bargain. At $12.50 per semester hour with 128 hours required, a night school degree could be earned for $1,600, not including books and fees, while a day school degree cost at least $8,940 for the four-year residential program.

The institute, said McKean, was modeled on the evening divisions found in most larger universities but particularly that of the School of General Studies at Columbia University, which was founded in 1947 to serve returning veterans of World War II. That program's stated purpose was to offer a bachelor's degree program for "qualified students who, because of employment or for other reasons, are unable to attend other schools of the university." Columbia, in fact, pioneered the use of the term "general studies" when naming the college, adapting the medieval term for universities, "studium generale."

At Rollins, the fledgling institute — which held classes year-round — was divided into three divisions: Courses for the Community, with noncredit lectures, forums and the School of Creative Arts; the School of General Studies, with for-credit college courses leading to a Bachelor of General Studies degree; and the Graduate Programs, with master's degrees including an MBA, a Master of Science in Physics and a Master of Arts in Teaching. The Patrick Air Force Base extension, now under the jurisdiction of the School of General Studies, concurrently became a degree-granting branch of the college. Who, though, oversaw this profusion of programs? No one, specifically, and everyone, generally. Dean of the College Schiller Scroggs chaired a 10-member Committee on the Institute for General Studies on which each member had responsibility for some aspect of the institute's operation.

The panel included McKean as well as Tiedtke, who was both second vice president of the college and dean of the Graduate Programs. George Sauté was director of Courses for the Community and the School of General Studies; while Charles Welsh and Dan Thomas were directors of the Graduate Program in Business Administration and the Graduate Program in Physics, respectively. Other members included Richard Wolfe, college registrar; Murray J. Landsman, assistant professor of psychology; George Schlatter, resident director of the institute's Patrick Air Force Base Branch; and Harry J. Carman, a trustee who was formerly dean of Columbia College, where the concept of a general studies degree was born. Marion Marwick, director of the School of Creative Arts, was not in the loop, perhaps because she was a part-time independent contractor.

An executive committee consisting of Carman, Sauté and Wolfe conducted the day-to-day work of establishing curriculum, issuing publicity and administering the institute's operation. Although an early organizational chart indicated a placeholder for an institute dean, such a position was not filled. In fact, no iteration of the college's continuing education program had a dean until Daniel F. Riva's arrival in 1970. "There is no immediate need for a dean," according to an internal memo describing the program. "His duties are distributed among the other offices; but providing for future growth of the administrative scheme makes the division function clearer." Growth came, but neither a dean nor enhanced clarity immediately followed. Indeed, between contradictory documents, no organizational charts and confused press releases, it is frankly difficult to determine who had ultimate responsibility for the institute's success or failure. Or, for that matter, how success or failure would be determined.

As of winter 1961, the School of General Studies, formerly Operation Bootstrap, had 605 students and 51 part-time
instructors plus Sauté (most students and instructors were at
Patrick Air Force Base); the Master of Business Administration program had 123 students and seven part-time instructors
plus Welsh; and the Master of Science in Physics program had
55 students and four part-time instructors plus Thomas. The
new Master of Arts in Teaching program, directed by William
T. Edwards, expected to enroll its first students in the fall of
that year. The School of Creative Arts made the biggest foot-
print locally, with 928 children, 163 adults and seven part-time
instructors plus Marwick. Courses for the Community — the
non-credit offerings — dwindled although a handful were still
offered, including one on coaching football, basketball and
baseball offered by Joe Justice, the college's athletic director.[6]
Tiedtke would later call the continuing education program
"the tail wagging the dog," but for now, it was too amorphous
to define, except perhaps as a community service or a means
through which programs could be introduced that the venerable day school might otherwise resist.

Meanwhile, McKean looked skyward. Rollins, with its prox-
imity to Cape Canaveral and the Space Coast, seemed ideally
situated for what McKean dubbed the Rollins College Space
Science Institute, which would be the crown jewel of the Institute of General Studies. He even had a facility in mind: Andersen Hall, a Mediterranean-style mansion overlooking Lake
Ivanhoe that had been given to the college by *Orlando Morn-*

---

6   Justice was certainly a qualified teacher. While a student at Rollins he
    had played baseball, basketball and football. He would go on to coach
    those sports, plus soccer and golf. In 1954, his eighth year as baseball
    coach, he took the college all the way to the championship game at the
    College World Series in Omaha, Nebraska. Rollins became the smallest
    school ever to reach the College World Series, a distinction the school
    still holds today.

ing Sentinel publisher Martin Andersen, with whom McKean enjoyed a friendly relationship. "Central Florida is uniquely situated for such a project because of the nearness of Cape Canaveral, the numerous strong Air Force and Navy installations and the rapidly multiplying industries pioneered by the Martin Company, especially in the field of missiles, electronics and kindred auxiliary enterprises involving advanced mathematical and scientific knowhow," wrote McKean in an undated report, possibly prepared for the trustees. In the same document, he estimated that $500,000 would be enough to outfit and operate the space institute for three to four years, after which research grants would provide income.

In 1961, McKean touted the project as integral to national security before an audience of businesspeople at the Orlando Country Club. "We may not yet be at war, but we certainly are at something," he noted. "Whatever it is, we must win it decisively. Coexistence means tension, billions spent on hellish devices while we wait for some low-grade mentality to decide when to bomb us. We should leave our coexistence philosophy behind us and take a vigorous offensive in the ideological struggle." The speech was hardly the clarion call for world unity that Holt would have delivered. However, the offensive to which McKean referred was an intellectual one. "Russia's rulers see the importance of the race for knowledge," he continued. "Knowledge is a powerful weapon any time. It may be the deciding factor in this present conflict. The ability to defend ourselves, dedication to our ideals, determination to acquire knowledge faster than our enemies and a determination to see freedom triumph will give us eventual victory."

Perhaps McKean saw some irony in retrofitting Andersen Hall as a mini-NASA, since the home's erstwhile owner had suggested that the college remain in its liberal arts lane during the abortive OJC-University of Miami partnership.

Andersen, though, was all in, and viewed the college's plan as complementary to, not competitive with, his hoped-for space university. "As envisioned, [the space institute] would deal in pure science, while an institute of technology would deal with applied science such as engineering," noted the *Orlando Morning Sentinel* in an editorial that encouraged community support. "Business and industrial leaders of the area should be interested in seeing an early inauguration of the Space Science Institute, for it will make the establishment of an institute of technology easier."

The *Orlando Morning Sentinel* followed up with several front-page stories about the space institute and had a reporter and a photographer at the ready when officials from the Air Force Office of Scientific Research in Washington, D.C., visited the campus to offer advice and to tour and evaluate Andersen Hall.[7] McKean, obviously, had received Andersen's blessing well in advance of announcing his ambitious plan. No one in Central Florida dared embark upon a major initiative without first being assured of the pugnacious publisher's support, or at least of his relative disinterest.[8] And, as Andersen's unyielding opposition to a state-supported junior college demonstrated, educational issues could become particularly dicey.

---

7   The visit appears to have been purely a publicity ploy. The Air Force officials agreed that Andersen Hall was a lovely facility and could potentially be retrofitted as a research facility. McKean told the *Orlando Morning Sentinel* that the scientists had offered "endless good ideas" and that their input was "an unbelievably rare opportunity to get advice from all these men before we even start on this."

8   In 1958, *Florida Trend* named Andersen one of Florida's six most powerful men, writing: "[Andersen is] the first to be consulted by a public official on some project that is controversial, because the official knows that to propose something that does not meet with the approval of Andersen might well be to kiss the project goodbye." Rollins, of course, was a private institution and McKean was not an elected official. But Andersen's newspapers were effective at marshalling support — or opposition — to projects (and people) of all kinds.

At a Founders' Week dinner in 1962, McKean touted the space institute as though it were a fait accompli, announcing that the facility would be staffed by four leading scientists who would devote their time to basic research, assisted by elite graduate students seeking master's or doctoral degrees in space science. Wernher von Braun, aerospace engineer and first director of NASA; Edward Teller, theoretical physicist known colloquially as the Father of the Hydrogen Bomb; and Lieutenant General Bernard Schriever, chief of the Air Force's ballistics division, had all been briefed and expressed enthusiasm for the effort, McKean said.[9] Each, in fact, had sent telegrams of congratulations. "The new Space Science Institute will have only one limitation — the extent to which Orlando and Central Florida will support it," he added. "With sufficient funds it will be one of the leading research centers of the world." Curiously, according to the *Rollins Alumni Record*, McKean reported that enough money had been pledged to begin the project, although he did not specify how much or from what source.

The Final Frontier was clearly on McKean's mind in the winter of 1962, when he presented an Animated Magazine themed around the question, "What Lies Ahead?"[10] Contributors, including U.S. Senator George Smathers, Governor

---

9 Teller and Schriever were both honored during Founders' Week in 1961. Teller had been presented an L.H.D. by McKean, who described the scientist as "a superb example of the good that comes when intelligence and training are combined with freedom." Schriever, who gave a speech on advances in technology and the challenge posed by communism, was presented an Sc.D. Von Braun spoke at the final Animated Magazine in 1969.

10 Members of the faculty also spoke regarding the future of Rollins. Bruce B. Wavell, associate professor of philosophy, predicted that the college would have larger classes and multiple campuses, and might become a university. McKean, too, foresaw a future in which the college would have multiple locations, each with a different purpose, such as the space institute and possibly a fine-arts school.

Farris Bryant and NASA Administrator Robert C. Seamans, lauded the space institute as though the drapes were already being hung at Andersen Hall. "What Rollins College has done today will not only affect the future of Florida, but the nation and the world as well," said Smathers, who warned that the U.S. had fallen behind the Soviet Union in science education and must quickly make up ground. Shortly thereafter McKean announced that the college had offered to host and provide administrative services for a graduate branch of the University of Florida School of Engineering in the former Park Avenue Elementary School (now SunTrust Center), recently bought by the college for use as office space and classrooms for the Institute for General Studies.

The Rollins College Space Science Institute, of course, never took flight. The project was not mentioned in print after 1963 and Andersen Hall was sold in 1969. But the episode demonstrates the fickle fervor with which McKean pursued ancillary programs that bypassed the day school, and how easily distracted he could become when intrigued by an alluring program or project.

During the space institute campaign, the mercurial president may have sensed some discomfort among students and faculty who feared that he had lost interest in the intimate liberal arts institution. McKean addressed the issue in a 1962 edition of the *Rollins Alumni Record* that also contained reams of space-related hoopla. In a brief letter headlined "Liberal Arts Basic," he assured readers that the college's foundational principles were not at risk: "The humanities — philosophy, history, literature, art and music are related to research in space and science since they lead to the development of man. I see the humanities as the most effective way of bringing man to higher levels. We must not only advance in technology, we must advance in goodness if we are worthy of the stars."

By May 1964, when the Institute for General Studies conducted its first commencement exercise for 148 graduates, the college could boast that 778 adults in Winter Park and 475 in Brevard County were working toward Bachelor of General Studies degrees, with 312 in the Master of Arts in Teaching program, 306 in the MBA program and 65 in the Master of Science in Physics program. About 40 students were enrolled in a televised course, Mathematics and Western Culture, offered in conjunction with WDBO-TV (now WKMG-TV, the region's CBS affiliate) and Sunrise Semester, a syndicated educational television series produced by New York University. Total day school enrollment, by contrast, stood at about 900.

And yet, according to the *Rollins Alumni Record*, "every now and then President McKean still gets the suggestion that Rollins should consider offering programs at night for people in the community." Editor Marcus T. Young, the college's director of alumni affairs, went on to praise the institute as "much more than a fine community-service gesture" and to describe Sauté as "not interested in press clippings and service awards; he is interested in education. And his long hours of work have resulted in just that — educational opportunities for many hundreds of Central Floridians."

But it was true that the institute — without a dean to advocate for it, without a building to distinguish it and without a student body that could participate in campus activities — was all but invisible to the college community. Other than the division directors, there were no full-time faculty members in Winter Park and only six in Brevard County. The Martin Company — whose employees comprised virtually all the master's degree students in physics and more than half the master's degree students in business administration — supplied most of the science and business instructors. Day school faculty taught some night courses to supplement their incomes, but about two-thirds of the 60-plus instructors in the College of General Studies were part-timers from the community. Adjuncts were hired with the approval of the corresponding department in the day school, but their number — and in some cases their performance — would become an issue of contention. Sauté told the *Rollins Alumni Record* that he dreamed of one day operating a major "continuing education center" with dedicated facilities. Now he was scrambling to find rooms for evening classes, some of which were taught at Winter Park High School (now the Winter Park Ninth Grade Center).

There were, however, challenges. The Committee on the Institute for General Studies, now chaired by Dean of the College Edwin S. Burdell[11] — Scroggs had retired the year before — met just prior to the first commencement to discuss a Southern Association of Colleges and Schools report that had expressed concerns regarding the program. Present were, among a handful of others, McKean, Teidtke, Edwards, Sauté and Schlatter from Patrick Air Force Base. The report read, in part: "[The SACS] suggests that every effort be made to prevent a further splitting off activities of the institute from the regular activities of the college. Under no circumstances should faculty members of the resident liberal arts college be given to regard the programs of the institute as inferior to those for regular students and of no concern to the regular faculty." Perhaps, the report added, the director of the insti-

---

11   Edwin Sharp Burdell was former director of the Cooper Union for Advancement of Science and Art in New York City. In 1934, Burdell had been appointed by M.I.T. President Karl Compton to develop a liberal arts program for engineering majors. The program was so successful that Burdell was awarded a $40,000 grant by the Carnegie Foundation to head a committee that would make recommendations on how other technically oriented institutions could incorporate liberal arts programs.

tute — currently Sauté — should report directly to the dean of the college instead of to a 10-person committee.

Although no one addressed organizational restructuring, other problems were acknowledged according to minutes of the meeting. For example, it was reported that some adjuncts routinely dismissed their classes an hour or more early. This was unacceptable, of course, and it was agreed that program directors must hold adjuncts accountable. Full-time day school faculty members who also taught in the evening program should likewise monitor adjuncts, it was determined, although how this could be accomplished — and why full-timers should be expected to assume uncompensated supervisory responsibility — was unclear. A faculty meeting for those doing double duty would be scheduled to discuss the matter further.

The most pressing issues regarded Patrick Air Force Base Branch. According to SACS guidelines, if the base operation was truly a branch of the college then it needed an on-site library, and more than half the faculty should be full-time. McKean insisted that he would shut down the branch if it could not meet SACS standards, and Burdell replied that a "crash course" for hiring full-time instructors was underway. Problems in Brevard County were, for the time being, resolved when five more full-time hires were made and a rudimentary library was established. Securing instructors who held doctoral degrees had been no easy task, Burdell later told McKean, since the college's $6,000 to $7,000 salaries were comparable to what elementary school teachers without master's degrees earned.

In 1964, one of the institute's master's degree programs was spun off, thanks to a $1 million gift the college received from Roy E. Crummer, a businessman who helped Florida refinance its bond indebtedness after the economic collapse of 1929. The money was used to build and endow the Roy E. Crummer School of Finance and Business Administration (now the Roy E. Crummer Graduate School of Business), which originally offered both MBA and Master of Commercial Science degrees.

At the announcement dinner, Crummer — who had lived in Winter Park until 1942, when he moved to Reno, Nevada — explained the rationale behind his gift: "In a free economic system such as we enjoy, difficulties must be met by independent leaders. We must not leave the solution of our economic problems up to government officials. I look to this school to train business leaders with a sense of rightness, a sense of responsibility, and with the preparation necessary to meet and solve the problems and difficulties which confront them." Added McKean: "[The Crummer School] will help to strengthen the human element in business. It will strive to make men of its students, not machines. The business world needs leaders prepared to think responsibly, not rely on pushing buttons and pulling levers."

Rollins, which began offering an undergraduate business degree in the 1920s, had since 1954 provided a pathway to an MBA via a partnership with John Tiedtke's alma mater, the Amos Tuck School of Business at Dartmouth University in Hanover, New Hampshire. Through the program, business administration and economics majors — males only, it was specified — could complete three years at Rollins and two years at the Tuck School, thereby earning both a bachelor's degree (from Rollins) and an MBA (from Tuck) in five years.[12] With the opening of the Crummer School, a student

---

12   The Crummer School, as of 2019, offers a similar program. Through the 3/2 Accelerated Management Program, students spend their first three years in the day school while their final two years are spent in the Crummer School's Early Advantage MBA Program (EAMBA).

— regardless of gender — could accomplish the same goal without relocating to the Granite State. Although the Crummer School would not have a full-time faculty until 1980, it did have a $700,000 building under construction, an endowment totaling $800,000 ($300,000 from Crummer and $500,000 from the college trustees), a relatively autonomous dean (Charles A. Welsh) to steer the ship and the unqualified support of McKean. The Institute for General Studies had none of these things.

Then, in April 1965, the institute was dissolved and replaced by the Central Florida School for Continuing Studies. Sauté, who remained director of both the school and the Patrick Air Force Base Branch, now reported to the Faculty-Administration Committee chaired by Burdell. The remaining graduate program directors, who had previously reported to Tiedtke, now reported to the newly formed Graduate Council, also chaired by Burdell, who had for all intents and purposes become the dean of continuing education, although this designation was never explicitly stated. Burdell told the *Orlando Morning Sentinel* that "operating efficiencies" prompted the reorganization — but surely there was symbolic significance to discarding the ambitious-sounding "institute," particularly considering that word's expansive implications.

Further — and perhaps of even greater significance — the college had jettisoned its prestigious brand and adopted instead a generic descriptor of the region, thereby obscuring any obvious connection between the day school and the night school. Many inferences, none of them good for the continuing education program, can be drawn from such purposeful distancing. Also telling: Burdell initially overlooked the School of Creative Arts, which had for years occupied an administrative twilight zone, and retroactively placed Marion Marwick and her team under the School for Continuing Studies umbrella only after McKean noted that the children's program was missing from his organizational chart. The components of the continuing education program, and how they related to one another, were obscure even to some administrators.

Indeed, no one appeared to pay much attention to the School of Creative Arts except McKean, who seemed perpetually annoyed by Marwick's casual management style. Several times, in fact, he threatened to shutter the program over administrative snafus. "I have appointed no one to teach in the [School of Creative Arts] for this fall term," McKean wrote in a 1962 memorandum to Marwick. "If anyone is actually teaching, by this memorandum I will direct the treasurer to discontinue their salaries. No department of this college can or should make laws for itself. Unless the [School of Creative Arts] can conform to the principles and practices of the college, I will recommend to the trustees that it either be discontinued or reorganized." While McKean was justified in insisting that Marwick follow established protocols, such as securing proper approvals for instructor appointments, his tone seemed unduly harsh. The School of Creative Arts was, after all, a nonacademic, noncredit program that primarily taught arts, crafts and music to children. It is also not quite clear why McKean did not first take the matter up with Sauté, who was nominally Marwick's supervisor.

But Sauté, too, at times incurred the patrician president's icy ire. In 1963, McKean expressed concerns to Sauté about the caliber of the adjunct faculty: "No one who would not qualify as a member of the College of Liberal Arts is to teach in the Institute for General Studies," McKean wrote. "Unless it is possible for us to maintain identical standards in the institute and the liberal arts college, I will recommend that the trustees discontinue the institute at the end of the year." Of course, Sauté by necessity used primarily adjuncts who were subject-matter experts but not necessarily academicians. McKean was also angered when night school students who had been denied admission to the day school nonetheless finagled their way into day school courses. In 1964, one such breech was reported by Burdell. This alone was egregious enough, but the young woman, according to Burdell, "is also to be found continually on campus, in residence halls and generally conducting herself as a regularly enrolled boarding student." At the bottom of Burdell's memorandum, McKean scrawled: "This must not continue."

McKean demanded excellence but never defined what, exactly, excellence meant within the context of the continuing education program. Nor did he supply the tools — physical, intellectual, human, financial — that could have elevated the erratic effort beyond mediocrity. Sauté must have been frustrated that McKean was displeased — few people purposely fail to meet expectations, assuming those expectations have been communicated and understood — but the mathematician shared some responsibility. Sauté, under the circumstances, might have seized the opportunity to present his own way forward and to become continuing education's strongest internal advocate. His affability and deference to higher-ups — Holt, Wagner (initially, at least) and now McKean — may explain why he apparently failed to assert himself. The *Corner Cupboard* reporter who had profiled Sauté had described him as one who "lives life as it comes" with "the patience and the self-control to await the outcome of events." In retrospect, that description appears to have been quite insightful.

McKean, meanwhile, was still churning out big ideas. In 1967, he made headlines with a proposal to create a national university through which a student of any age and in any loca-

181

tion could earn a low-cost bachelor's degree through courses on television and radio, videotape recordings and correspondence instruction without setting foot on a physical college campus. "We cannot send everyone to college," he said. "But we can send college to everyone." Subject-matter mastery would be demonstrated through examinations administered by the National Education Testing Service. "We could tailor the instruction from the most remedial level all the way through honors candidates who would have to stand before a comprehensive board of oral examiners before graduation," he told an *Orlando Morning Sentinel* reporter. While McKean's plan would not replace traditional colleges and universities, it would make a college education accessible to those unable to attend. "Maybe the whole idea of a degree for everyone is absurd," he said. "But knowledge for everyone isn't."

McKean's idea presaged later notions of virtual universities and the "colleges without walls" concept. He was, to be sure, an adherent of the specialized liberal arts model with individualized personal instruction. But, as evidenced by his "Everyone's College" proposal, he also sought to bring higher education to a wide spectrum of lifelong learners. His reluctance to abandon the continuing education program as president likewise demonstrates that McKean was not an educational elitist. Courses for the Community, the Institute for General Studies and the Central Florida School for Continuing Studies — haphazard as they may have appeared (and, in fact, were) — opened educational doors for many thousands of people when there were no other higher-education options available in greater Orlando.

McKean, who had become an iconic figure in the region through his high-profile presidency, announced that he would retire and assume the newly created role of chancellor by the beginning of the school year in September 1969. An affable intellectual, he had calmed the campus and connected with the community. "I'm just an old art teacher," he would later tell the *Orlando Morning Sentinel*. And perhaps he would have preferred to paint, ensconced in his scriptorium turning out haunting, impressionistic images dominated by blues, greens and blacks — some containing the sort of supernatural elements, such as ghosts and angels, often found in folk art. Steeped in nostalgia for the Holt Era, McKean could never quite come to grips with the decade's sweeping social changes — some of which were reflected at the college through non-conformist students and noncompliant faculty members. Indeed, the issue of the *Rollins Alumni Record* announcing McKean's departure from the presidency also included a story from a 1967 graduate now serving in Vietnam headlined "Find Charlie and Kill Him" as well as an essay from a 1965 graduate now studying for a Ph.D. at Columbia University headlined "Chaos on Campus."

McKean stepped away from the college but not away from the spotlight; he would spend the rest of his long life engaging the community through the artistic treasures that he and Jeannette had gathered. In 1995, he would be posthumously named Floridian of the Year by the *Orlando Sentinel*. "[McKean's] ability to restore the Holt patrimony and to bring harmony and hope back to a dispirited college was his greatest achievement," wrote college historian Jack C. Lane. "But restoration of that patrimony may also have been the source of his most salient weakness. In a period of dramatic educational change, McKean seemed stuck in the past, unable to move beyond the world of his most cherished memories. ... At the beginning, he had told the trustees that he was an artist who should be teaching instead of undertaking the role of president. ... However, McKean relished serving as president of Rollins College; that early self-assessment of his own abilities was as much an insightful self-perception as it was an act of modesty."

IN FEBRUARY 1969, Dean of the College Donald W. Hill sent a brief memo to McKean: "Mr. Sauté, age 65, may be retired, if desired." Obviously, McKean desired precisely that. In March, he notified Sauté by letter that it was his "unpleasant assignment ... to tell you that the board of trustees have agreed, in view of the fact that you are 65 years of age, not to reappoint you to the position of director of the Central Florida School for Continuing Studies. This comes in conjunction with the board's decision to make some changes in the organization and administration of the school." Sauté was thanked for his years of service and offered an opportunity to teach — likely at an adjunct's stipend — if he wished.

Sauté, however, resisted. He was healthy and, in his estimation, had done a good job given the limited resources at his disposal. True, enrollment in his program had dropped from a peak of 1,155 in 1966 to 828 in 1969, but Sauté had planned to introduce new courses for law enforcement officers as well as programs for public servants in recreation, finance and fire safety.[13] The School of Creative Arts, which he allowed Marion Marwick to run as she saw fit, had launched a successful summer day camp and had continued to foster goodwill in the community. But McKean would not back down — he had, in fact, already extended an offer to someone else — and Sauté's plea to incoming president Jack B. Critchfield, the 36-year-old chancellor of student affairs of the University of Pittsburgh, was politely rebuffed. "In attempting to learn as much as I can about your retirement, it appears that the exec-

---

13   Criminal justice and fire safety degree programs would cause significant controversy when they were introduced under Sauté's successor, Daniel F. Riva.

utive committee of the board of trustees, along with President McKean, decided that this action was necessary and that it should be a firm decision," wrote Critchfield to Sauté. However, the incoming president continued, he hoped that he could count on Sauté's wisdom and guidance in the coming months.

In academia, it seems, pink slips are often accompanied by plaudits. Sauté, for his part, was dismissed with decorum at the May 1969 commencement. McKean read a citation, which surely sounded more like an elegy to the honoree: "George Sauté, dedicated professor, concerned citizen, leader in common ventures; as one who has helped lift our vision of world peace, given new directions and dimensions to the education of adults, and helped so many to carry on past their discouragements and even their small hopes; for what you have done and the tradition in which you stand, it is my privilege to bestow upon you as a faithful servant of Rollins, the Rollins Decoration of Honor."

And so ended a 26-year career at the college. Sauté pioneered the program that would become the Hamilton Holt School, yet his name is little remembered today. His legacy, however, can be seen most nights on campus when classrooms fill with men and women of all ages and backgrounds — most of whom have already put in an eight-hour day. Although he was also named professor emeritus, there is no record that George Sauté, dedicated professor, concerned citizen and faithful servant, ever again taught at Rollins.

Chapter 7

LIBERAL ARTS AND LAW ENFORCEMENT

JACK CRITCHFIELD, the 11th president of Rollins College (1969-78), told the *Orlando Morning Sentinel* that he was looking forward to running a small institution. "Comparing the University of Pittsburgh to Rollins College is like comparing the fruit of a coconut to that of a radish. Sheer numbers make the multiversity many colleges under one roof. The role of a small college is to maximize its service without maximizing enrollment — I would hope to see this be the goal of Rollins." His philosophy of education? "Essentially, it's this: I think colleges must create exciting teaching-learning situations. A campus should be one of our most democratic institutions, a place where the right to criticize and dissent responsibly is protected." Critchfield, though, quickly found himself confronted with less lofty financial issues: To balance the budget he began selling off properties, including the Pelican Beach House[1] on New Smyrna Beach and Martin Hall

---

1 Located on New Smyrna Beach, the Pelican House was a two-story,

on Genius Drive, which had been bequeathed to the college by lecturer John Martin and used as headquarters for the conservatory until the construction of R.D. Keene Hall on campus in 1974.

After a decade at the college, Critchfield would enter private business and become president of Winter Park Telephone, then group vice president and ultimately CEO of the $3.5 billion Florida Progress Corporation (its subsidiaries included Florida Power).[2] Clearly, Critchfield had the pragmatic persona required to establish strong ties between the college and the business community in ways that neither the idealistic Holt nor the artistic McKean ever could.[3]

---

white-frame building that had been built as a conference center by Presbyterian Church USA in the 1920s. It was later sold to Fred Lewis Pattee, professor of English literature, and his wife Anna Lura Plumer, who operated it as a casino. When the casino closed in 1927, the couple donated it to the college, where it was used to hold classes and then as a shelter station for the U.S. Coast Guard during World War II. Later, the house, occupied by a housemother to prevent untoward behavior, was used as a recreational destination for students and faculty. The college sold the property in 1978 for $150,000.

2   Upon his retirement from Tampa-based Progress Energy in 1998, Critchfield told the *Tampa Bay Times* that he was hired at Rollins "because there was a movement all of a sudden that said if we can get younger college presidents, they'll relate better to the students than the old guys." However, he said, he did not have much time to cultivate student relationships: "All I did for nine years there was to raise enough money to pay off [the college's] debt and get it on firm financial footing." Although the *Times* reported that his record at Progress Energy was mixed, he had become a civic titan in Pinellas County, serving on the boards of 15 major organizations and helping to assemble an ownership group that brought Major League Baseball's Tampa Bay Rays to the region.

3   Most importantly, Critchfield developed what would become a historically important relationship with Harold Alfond, founder of the Dexter Shoe Company, and his wife, Dorothy "Bibby" Levine Alfond. The Alfonds' son, Ted, and daughter-in-law, Barbara Lawrence, met at the college and were 1968 graduates. The Alfond name is a familiar one on campus. The Alfond Swimming Pool (1973) was followed by the Alfond Baseball Stadium at Harper-Shepherd Field (1984), the Alfond

Due to a new governance structure that shifted responsibility for academics to the faculty, Critchfield was able to focus on financial and operational issues while the day school embarked upon another curriculum revision.

The Central Florida School for Continuing Studies, now unfettered by a reticent director and a reluctant president, was also remade under new director Daniel F. Riva, a gung-ho retired Air Force colonel who had been commandant of the Academic Instructor and Allied Officer School at the Air University Teachers College in Montgomery, Alabama. With a Ph.D. in general education from the University of Missouri at Kansas City, Riva had earned 32 military decorations, including the Distinguished Flying Cross (twice). "Adult education is being altered just as is the education of young people," he told *The Sandspur* when he arrived on campus in 1970. "We plan to introduce new courses and programs responsive to the urgent needs of our changing society."

In 1972, Riva's position was upgraded from director to dean of the rebranded School of Continuing Education. By the fall of 1973, the program had more than 2,600 students enrolled, about 600 of whom were at the Patrick Air Force Base Branch (now sometimes referred to as "Rollins-by-the-Sea.") There were nearly 100 for-credit courses from which to choose — the number would quadruple by the decade's end — as well as preparatory courses for certification in real estate sales and mortgage finance. Mini-courses covered such topics as estate planning, income tax preparation and the problems of aging. A

Boathouse (1990) and the Harold & Ted Alfond Sports Center (2001), a joint gift with son, Ted. In December 2010, the Harold Alfond Foundation awarded a grant of $12.5 million — the largest single gift in the college's history — for construction of the Alfond Inn. Revenue from the boutique hotel will flow to the Alfond Scholars Fund, where it will accumulate for 25 years or until the endowment reaches $50 million, whichever is later.

course in speed-reading, while it did not offer credit, did offer a money-back guarantee. Undergraduate degree options included not only the original Bachelor of General Studies, but also a Bachelor of Arts, a Bachelor of Science and even an Associate of Arts comparable to two-year degrees typically offered by junior colleges. Areas of concentration were available in business and economics, education, English, humanities, mathematics, and science and social sciences.

Although the Master of Science in Physics degree was dropped in 1973, the Master of Arts in Teaching degree was augmented by a Master of Education degree and a post-master's program leading to a Specialist in Education degree, which attracted primarily school administrators.[4] To the chagrin of some, in 1971 the continuing education program initiated a bachelor's degree program in criminal justice. Enrollment by police officers was bolstered by tuition reimbursement through the Law Enforcement Assistance Administration, an agency of the U.S. Justice Department. Any of the three undergraduate degrees — even the Bachelor of Arts — could become a criminal justice degree through such courses as capital punishment, correctional management, civil liberties, constitutional law, criminology, crisis intervention, forensic chemistry, legal research, police intelligence, private security, trial techniques, and traffic control and accident investigation.

In 1974, a Master of Science in Criminal Justice degree was introduced. The 36-hour graduate program included courses in advanced criminology, comparative legal systems, economics of criminal justice, emerging correctional systems, philosophy of justice, and legal research and reasoning. "Central

---

4   A Master of Arts in Guidance and Counseling degree was introduced in 1977.

Florida's police, courts and probation officers are finding that they have a lot more in common than just criminals," wrote the *Orlando Sentinel* in a story about the master's program, said to be the only one of its kind in the country. "Also Aristotle, Thomas Hobbes and John Stuart Mill."

These degree offerings — and subsequent specializations in arson investigation and fire safety administration — caused consternation among day school faculty members, some of whom had previously been content to ignore the continuing education program even as it veered further afield from the generally accepted definition of the liberal arts. Riva, though, forged ahead. "Society is expecting law enforcement officials to be solving more and more highly complex crimes than ever before," he explained to the *Orlando Morning Sentinel* in the summer of 1970. "Our goal is to assist law enforcement personnel toward sophistication as well as competency. We don't make it overly theoretical and we try to keep the benefits obvious, thus avoiding the motivational problems of students who say their courses lack relevancy."

Perhaps responding to day school pushback regarding the criminal justice curriculum, Riva composed an antagonistic article for the *Rollins Alumni Record* that excoriated college officials who had preceded him for their short-sightedness. "What caused the [continuing education] program to falter and almost fail in the latter 1960s?" he asked. "The answer is easy. A continuing education program must be tuned in to the needs of the local community from whence it draws its constituents. It must not only be immediately responsive to perceived needs, but it must search for better ways to serve the community by anticipating, initiating and formulating courses before the needs become generally apparent. Course proliferation is not a no-no in continuing education. Rather, it is a must."

The continuing education program under the prior administration had failed to respond to the needs of the community, Riva added, because "Rollins authorities seemed to think in terms of day program values rather than in continuing education principles, and in such context new courses and programs proposed were neither desirable nor warranted." This hidebound approach had been officially discarded, continued Riva. Now, in fact, day school students — with the permission of their advisors — could take one night school course per semester and receive full credit. Riva, who conceded that while the day program offered more cohesion, opined that the night program "seems to me to have more interesting and exciting courses and more courses that can be immediately applied to real life situations."

Perhaps a little too real, for some tastes. Criminal justice classes began staging mock crimes, such as fatal shootings in the college infirmary and at the campus tennis courts, after which student sleuths sought to apprehend the perpetrators and bring them to justice in the city's municipal court using community volunteers as jurors. The *Orlando Morning Sentinel* covered these exercises extensively, running photographs of "victims" splayed on the ground as investigators interviewed bystanders and gathered evidence. "There can be no clearer method of teaching the process than by complete dramatization of its mechanics," said Paul Lee, a local attorney and an adjunct instructor.

By 1976, the criminal justice programs had 450 students enrolled. By 1979, the number had swelled to 650 students, most of whom already worked in law enforcement but sought advance in their departments. A college degree was now required in many larger police agencies for promotion beyond the rank of sergeant — and some local police chiefs set an example by enrolling in the program themselves. Titusville

Chief of Police Clarence Kirkland was among the first graduates, followed by Maitland Chief of Police Ralph Jones and Kissimmee Chief of Police Don Adams. Orlando Police Chief Bob Chewning also signed up, as did Orange County Sheriff Mel Colman.

"If this thing continues, the day of the dumb cop is gone," said Riva, who had been elected president of the Florida Criminal Justice Educators' Association. "The School of Continuing Education, in accordance with the new thinking in police management, has become one of the educational leaders in this field. We have succeeded in making the program academically sound while at the same time providing a balance between short- and long-term tactical gains for the men." The criminal justice programs were also offered at Patrick Air Force Base Branch and at more far-flung locations in Ocala and Bartow. Instructors included Orange County Jail Chaplain James Bryan, Orange-Osceola County State Attorney Rom Powell, Orange County Corrections Director James Schoultz and Orlando Police Chief James York. Others included former Juvenile Court Judge J. Chester Kerr and Sanford Crime Lab Chief Sam Ragsdale.

While no one doubted that improved professionalism among law enforcement personnel was a desirable goal, and that continuing education for employees of police departments was worthwhile, some questioned whether the college — even through its separate continuing education program — was a suitable venue for such offerings. Riva, however, was convinced that criminal justice and the liberal arts melded perfectly. In an article he wrote for a 1979 issue *The Forum for Continuing Education*, he sniped that "liberal arts purists" had grudgingly accepted the criminal justice programs only after being assured that they would not impinge upon the day school. "After all," he noted with more than a hint of sarcasm, "the School of Continuing Education was only an evening addendum to the main college, populated mostly with adults from the local community. It seemed to be strangely flexible and to have a different set of admissions standards, so perhaps a criminal justice program could be tolerated there."

Most criminal justice programs were purely vocational, Riva noted, adding that the Rollins program was superior precisely because of its liberal arts emphasis: "Rollins College took the whole-person concept as its guide, believing that criminal justice personnel should be men and women capable of dignifying the human mind, who would rank integrity above personal gain and who could comprehend diversity within order. They should possess innovative competence and have a deep and continuing concern for the quality of life in our towns and cities. They should respect and understand human values, rights and traditions, and be able to operate sensibly inside a framework of responsibility and accountability." Subjects such as philosophy, history, humanities, ethics, religion, sociology and behavioral science, he added, helped shape not only better police officers but better human beings who had the critical thinking skills "to seek answers to the questions about the drives and motivations of man, the human condition and the purpose of American society."

Riva had little patience with critics who complained that his all-embracing approach — his willingness to devise a degree for every need — somehow diminished the college's stature. In any case, throughout the 1970s the School of Continuing Education generated between $500,000 and $1 million per year in unrestricted income for the college, much to the delight of Critchfield, who had found fundraising to be much more burdensome than anticipated. Further, whatever the liberal arts faculty may have thought, students were generally satisfied. An early 1980 survey conducted by the College Planning

Committee, which had spent nearly 18 months assessing every aspect of the institution's operation at the behest of incoming President Thaddeus Seymour, found that 49.8 percent of night students rated their courses as "good," while about 40.5 percent rated their courses as "excellent."

When rating instructors, however, a disparity emerged between knowledge and teaching skills. While 62.6 percent said that their instructors had "excellent" knowledge, only 29.9 percent said that their instructors had "excellent" teaching skills. (A plurality, 40.7 percent, described the teaching skills of their instructors as "good.") In a program that depended heavily upon adjuncts, this could not have come as a surprise. "Some professors are truly outstanding," responded one student. "Others know the subject matter but not how to present it." In separate meetings, adjuncts told committee members that while they were proud of their affiliations with the college, they were also "made to feel that they were imposing" by day school faculty and were generally uninformed about standard college policies and procedures. The feedback from students and instructors, positive and negative, was duly noted.

Night school students were, not surprisingly, more ethnically diverse than day school students, although 87.2 percent described themselves as "white, non-Hispanic." Ages ranged from 19 to 82, with 54 percent between ages 23 and 26. Business administration was the largest area of concentration (33.6 percent) followed by criminal justice (24 percent), social sciences (13.7 percent) and preparation for teaching (9.3 percent). Mathematics, science and humanities lagged, although 6.5 percent said they remained undecided. Other than the tepid rating given to instructors — no small issue at a college renowned for its emphasis on teaching — there was nothing in the report to indicate that a wholesale restructuring was in the offing. The entire document, however, had yet to be released.

Indeed, by most metrics, the Riva years were a soaring success. While the continuing education program had drifted aimlessly under McKean and Sauté, it had grown rapidly under Riva, who found creative ways to engage new constituencies. Continuing education, he often noted, was less encumbered by tradition, bureaucracy and campus politics and could therefore be nimble enough to seize opportunities as they presented themselves. Perhaps, some argued, a few of those opportunities would have been better left for others to seize.

For Riva, however, the mission was to identify — better yet, to anticipate — community demand and be ready with applicable courses of study. "Apparently unknown to many, modern continuing education has shown the way toward new educational horizons," he had written in 1972. "Now others are becoming interested, and there is no good reason for dashing cold water on brave educators who thrill as they rediscover this new territory." Whether Riva's entrepreneurial philosophy would be compatible with that of Seymour, the genial giant who succeeded Critchfield in 1978, remained to be seen.

Chapter 8

PURSUIT OF
EXCELLENCE

THADDEUS SEYMOUR, the 12th president of Rollins College (1978-90), attended Princeton University and the University of California at Berkeley as an undergraduate before earning a Ph.D. in 18th-century English literature from the University of North Carolina. He then became an English professor at Dartmouth College, where five years later he was elevated to dean of students. In the nine years prior to his post at Rollins, he was president of all-male Wabash College, a small (800-student) liberal arts college in Crawfordsville, Indiana. The 6-foot-6 Seymour, in his youth a member of Princeton's nationally ranked crew team, cut an impressive figure as he strode across campus. But he also possessed a larger-than-life personality, as did Holt, and more than a touch of whimsy, as did McKean. An accomplished amateur magician, he loved to perform tricks for children — for anyone, really — and wasted no time in reviving Fox Day.[1]

---

1   Seymour was a lover of distinctive if sometimes silly college traditions.

Seymour, born in New York City in 1928, was described in the *Orlando Morning Sentinel* as "about as different from his predecessor as a Hush Puppy is from a patent-leather loafer." If Holt was the ideal college president, at least for Rollins in the 1920s, then Seymour seemed to fit the bill in the late 1970s and beyond. He had raised nearly $32 million in two-and-a-half years at Wabash College — said by *The New York Times* to have been "the most successful small college campaign in the history of higher education" — but remained a liberal arts educator at heart. "If you're going to be a liberal arts college, you've got to be a liberal arts college," was Seymour's mantra as he sought to lift the somewhat threadbare institution out of the financial and intellectual doldrums. "When I saw [Rollins], I saw a physical plant in quite serious disrepair," recalled Seymour in 2005. "I saw a place that was embarrassed by its Jolly Rolly Colly[2] reputation. I saw a place that needed to feel

---

While at Wabash College, he started a holiday called Elmore Day to honor a notoriously bad Indiana poet named James Buchanan Elmore. As part of the festivities, Seymour would read Elmore's works aloud at an outdoor assembly. When Seymour left for Rollins, the Wabash faculty wasted little time in abolishing Elmore Day. An example of Elmore's work: "In the spring of the year, / when the blood is too thick, / there's nothing so rare as a sassafras stick. /It strengthens the liver and cleans up the heart, / and to the whole system new life doth impart. /Sassafras, oh sassafras, / thou art the stuff for me! / And in the spring, I love to sing, / sweet sassafras, of thee."

2   "Jolly Rolly Colly" was the college's hard-to-shake nickname, which is of unknown origin but dates at least to the 1950s. Holt acknowledged what he believed to be the college's undeserved reputation for frivolity as early as 1936. "We are proud of the fact that we give our students extreme liberty at Rollins," he said during a lecture at Knowles Memorial Chapel. "We have reduced rules to the minimum and those few we do have are made by the students or by the deans in cooperation with the students. ... I suppose it is because our students are so contented and happy that some people have accused Rollins of being a country club. Now, if we only made them unhappy, if we assigned them more work to do than we knew they could accomplish, thus appropriating their leisure, if we hedged them about rules although we knew that few of those rules would be respected, if we allowed no questioning of authority, then I suppose

loved. It needed to feel good about itself."

Seymour, looking ahead to the college's centennial, appointed the blandly labeled College Planning Committee in 1978. The group, assisted by the New York-based College Board's Office of Adult Learning Services, would spend the next year and a half evaluating programs and setting a five-year institutional agenda. By 1985, its centennial year, Seymour wanted Jolly Rolly Colly to be nothing less than "the finest small college in the Southeast, standing among the finest small colleges in the country." Daniel R. DeNicola, dean of education and an associate professor of philosophy, was named chairperson. "In my 51 years in higher education, the person I have valued the most is Dan," said Seymour in 2005. "Knowing how important planning was — and knowing that Dan was the brightest, most enlightened, most engaging person I have known in my professional years — I asked him to head the committee. I depended on him, I turned to him, I was guided by him, I was educated by him. I count him as the major figure in my administration."

Other committee members included Betsy Benson, a student majoring in English literature;[3] Persis Coleman, assistant professor of biology; Frank Dasse, assistant professor of economics; Charles M. Edmondson, associate professor of history; T. William Miller Jr., a trustee; Frank O'Donnell, a student majoring in English and mathematics;[4] Maurice "Socky" O'Sullivan, associate professor of English; J. Walter Tucker Jr., a trustee; and A. Arnold Wettstein, professor of

---

there are people who would then say Rollins was a great educational institution and not a country club."

3   Benson was, as of 2019, a judge in the 17th Judicial Circuit in Broward County.

4   O'Donnell was, as of 2019, CEO of Biltmore Consultants, a financial services company based in Asheville, North Carolina.

religion. Roger G. Baldwin, a freshly minted Ph.D. in higher education from the University of Michigan, was hired as research director,[5] while Marsha L. Clore, a secretary in the department of education, was brought aboard as administrative specialist.[6] Notably not on the committee was Daniel F. Riva, whose School of Continuing Education — including the Patrick Air Force Base Branch, which was technically a branch of the liberal arts college but operated under Riva's supervision — was already in Seymour's cross hairs.

"We felt very strongly that in the planning process we needed to be clear about what liberal arts education was," said Seymour in 2005. "Liberal arts education was not the majority of your students studying business and the second-largest group studying communication, which is what was going on. Liberal arts education goes back to the founding of Harvard College or to Oxford [University] in the Middle Ages." One can easily anticipate — as Riva likely did — Seymour's view of such courses of study as criminal justice and fire safety administration.

"The concern was that the college, both in responding to community need and in opportunistically seeking additional revenue, had blurred its identity, scattered its energies and strayed from its mission and eroded its quality," said DeNicola. "[Seymour's] experience included both a hybrid Ivy League institution, Dartmouth, as well a traditional liberal

---

5   Baldwin was, as of 2019, Professor of Educational Administration at Michigan State University.

6   Said DeNicola: "I hired [Marsha Clore] and worked with her for nearly two years. *The Sandspur* published a picture of her in the president's office standing next to the pile of research documents the committee had assembled. When the committee ceased its work, she left to follow her husband, who worked for an oil company in Saudi Arabia, and she died there under mysterious circumstances — her death haunts me to this day." The photograph DeNicola reverenced is reproduced in this book.

arts college, Wabash. He and I shared the belief that we needed to re-center the college's mission, image and programs on a liberal arts ethos. Neither of us wanted to abandon programs to serve the local community, however, so long as they could be offered with high quality. I did not sense any divergence of goals between Thad and me."

When the 500-page *Report of the College Planning Committee* was released in October 1980, its introduction noted that Rollins, which professed itself to be a small liberal arts institution for residential students, had over the years added appendages, such as the Patrick Air Force Base Branch, "almost casually, and without a commitment of resources." For this and other reasons, the college had metamorphized into "a complex institution of diverse programs, each of which developed because of the initiative of one or two people, not because of any comprehensive design or community consensus." The continuing education program, for example, had been valuable in many respects — it had offered a community service, enhanced thousands of lives and exceeded the liberal arts college in attracting minority students and faculty — yet it did not "enjoy the full respect and moral support of a significant proportion of the Rollins community." Why should this be?

For one reason, the report surmised, the vast majority of night school students were seeking bachelor's degrees similar to those offered by the day school. It could, therefore, be assumed that the educational objectives of the night school were the same as those of the day school: "It is then a small step to conclude that the former offers a cheap imitation of the latter." Cheap is a relative — and, in this context, derogatory — term. But at $30 per semester hour with 128 hours required, a night school degree could be earned for $3,850, not including books and fees, while a day school degree cost at least $22,380 for four-year residential students. The idea that night school and day school degrees should be considered essentially interchangeable — as they are today — had not yet taken hold because of both quality and cost differentials.

The problem was exacerbated, the report theorized, because the $1 million in gross annual income generated by the continuing education program was used to subsidize the day school's operating budget — not to reinvest in facilities, equipment or personnel that would enhance the night school. This caused a "common perception ... that Rollins looked at [continuing education] primarily as a source of funds, secondarily as a community service operation and only thirdly as a program of academic integrity requiring support services and funding." In addition, faculty members — even day school instructors who taught at night school to earn extra income — rarely held meetings and evidenced scant interest in governance and policy-making. That situation, the report pointed out, was just one indicator of apathy caused by broader institutional neglect: "It is grossly unfair to our dedicated colleagues [in continuing education] to complain of academic quality yet to deny them needed resources and services; to always give their claims a low priority yet to rely on them as a source of personal or institutional funds."

The areas of concentration — offered in lieu of majors for continuing education students — were erratically organized with virtually no course sequencing and, compared to the day school, skimpy general education requirements: "Students come to feel as though they are simply accumulating credits instead of developing knowledge, skills and talents." Further, the report concluded, several areas of concentration simply did not belong in a liberal arts college — not even in a separate program that catered to adults. The criminal justice and fire safety administration programs, for example, should be dropped, as well as the courses in real estate. "College-level courses in such areas as secretarial training, welding and cosmetology would not normally be offered as electives or accepted for credit from a transfer student," the report read. "Yet, the School of Continuing Education and the Patrick Air Force Base Branch curriculum includes courses in real estate and fire safety administration as liberal arts electives. ... the intuition of the committee is that such courses are inappropriate even as electives in a liberal arts degree."

The report's most daring recommendation, however, was to do away entirely with the business administration concentration (and, in the case of the day school, the major): "Even in the liberal arts college, we find ourselves today with nearly one-third of our undergraduates enrolled in the business administration major — a remarkable shift from previous years and an odd balance for a liberal arts institution." Business administration, the report concluded, was rightly a graduate-level subject. If the undergraduate program were eliminated, the Crummer School could then staff up, focus exclusively on the MBA program and position itself for accreditation by the prestigious Association to Advance Collegiate Schools of Business.[7] A business administration minor, however, could be retained and would "offer an interested student a solid foundation for admission to graduate business schools and sufficient technical courses ... to enhance a transcript."

Whatever areas of concentration ultimately made the cut,

---

7   AACSB accreditation was awarded to the Crummer School in 1985. It was at the time just the 15th graduate school of business to be so designated, and by far the smallest, standing alongside Columbia University's Graduate School of Business, Cornell University's Graduate School of Management, Dartmouth College's Amos Tuck School of Business, Duke University's Fuqua School of Business and Harvard University's Graduate School of Business among others. Only 5 percent of business colleges around the world hold AACSB accreditation.

the report stated, each should have a full-time faculty coordinator. The coordinators, with joint appointments in the day school, should form a curriculum committee responsible for such matters as course development and adjunct evaluation. In addition, long-overdue professional development training should be available so that neglected community instructors could improve their classroom skills, while team-teaching using full-time and adjunct instructors should be explored for some courses. "Obviously, part-time faculty cannot expect the professional development resources made available to full-time faculty," the report continued. "On the other hand, it is appalling for the college to have supplied no professional development funds whatsoever to an adjunct who is now teaching in his 14th year for us."

Grading, too, came under scrutiny. Night students averaged a 3.27 GPA versus an average 2.75 GPA for day students, which appeared to indicate laxness unbecoming a college.[8] Finally, the report stated, the murky status of the Patrick Air Force Base Branch should be clarified. Instead of a branch of the liberal arts college, it should be a thoroughly integrated off-campus center of the School of Continuing Education. The base's resident director already reported to the dean of continuing education, and the two programs shared a virtually identical curriculum. Most students in Brevard County were now civilians, the report added, and would likely prefer to display a degree that did not reference a military base.

Riva, not surprisingly, was incensed by the report. It was true that the continuing education program had operated as something of a fiefdom. But Riva had done nothing more than his bosses had allowed — or expected — him to do. Now

---

8   Riva was known not to favor work-intensive courses for adult learners who juggled career and family responsibilities. He was not the first nor the only night school educator to have held this view.

it appeared that his program, and its seven-figure contribution to the college's operating budget, was under assault. He began to strongly push back. In a December 1980 memorandum to newly named Provost Robert Marcus, he warned of blowback from the Patrick Air Force Base Branch, saying that the college could expect "numerous lawsuits if the contents of this report became general knowledge among military personnel." Commanders, he said, would not "take the rap" if a perception took hold that the college had offered service members anything less than a quality education.

But the proverbial writing was on the wall. In January 1981, a dispirited Riva announced that he would retire in June, telling the *Orlando Morning Sentinel* that "knowing when to exit is as important as knowing when to enter ... a different kind of person is needed here now." Marcus, instead of expressing even cursory regret, told the newspaper that "Dean Riva's announcement that he will leave the school in June has encouraged us to take advantage of his time between now and summer to work with a series of consultants to re-evaluate the school and its programs." Seymour had little to add, noting only that further recognition of Riva's service would come in due course. Even the most obtuse readers would have sensed tension simmering between the lines of this otherwise unremarkable news brief.

At May commencement exercises, in typical college fashion, Riva was awarded an LL.D and elevated to the rank of dean emeritus. "You have brought energy, imagination and notable administrative skills to your work at Rollins," said Seymour, speaking truths that no one could have disputed. Riva — who died in 2009 — had indeed been a dynamo, reviving a moribund (and arguably failing) program and expanding it to reflect his wide-ranging vision for continuing education. But, in the final analysis, his statement to the *Orlando*

Sentinel was correct: With Seymour as president — a liberal arts Hush Puppy instead of a business-oriented patent leather loafer — a different kind of person was needed now.

NOT EVERY RECOMMENDATION from the College Planning Committee was adopted. But change came rapidly following Riva's departure with the announcement of both a Division of Continuing Education and a Division of Non-Credit Courses. "This new structure reaffirms [the college's] institutional commitment to educational outreach," wrote DeNicola in a February 1982 memorandum distributed campuswide. "It promises new options and higher standards for our continuing education students. It promises a set of significant new initiatives in non-credit programs. It provides for a closer integration of all undergraduate programs and it extends responsibility of full-time faculty to include these programs."

Dramatic steps were taken: some degree programs were dropped — criminal justice and fire safety administration, for example — while others were added. Perhaps most significantly, however, the business administration concentration (or major) was eliminated in both the night school and the day school. The Division of Continuing Education would confer only Bachelor of Arts degrees with full-fledged majors in communication arts, economics, environmental studies, English, humanities, international affairs, psychology and public affairs. Optional minors would be offered in any of those subjects, as well as in accounting, business administration, French, Spanish, theater and women's studies. General education requirements were bolstered to more closely mirror those of the day school. The two-year Associate of Arts degree, despite its community college connotation, remained for the time being.[9]

---

9   Valencia Community College's Winter Park Branch would not open un-

The Division of Non-Credit Courses would offer a cornucopia of cultural enrichment and professional development
programs for adults and operate the ever-popular School of
Creative Arts for youngsters. DeNicola noted that coordina-
tion of all noncredit offerings in a separate division made
good administrative sense while bringing the college into
more strict compliance with the standards of the Southern
Association of Colleges and Schools. The Patrick Air Force
Base Branch, which typically had 700 or more students
enrolled, was not consolidated with the revamped continuing education program. In fact, the operation gained some
additional autonomy when its longtime resident director,
Robert Earl Lee, was elevated to dean and began reporting
directly to DeNicola.

"It is both matters — quality and liberal arts ethos —
that equally informed our decisions," said DeNicola, who was
named dean of the faculty in 1980 and vice president and
provost in 1983.[10] "Our report did, however, try to meet other
concerns: financial solvency, marketability and community
need. We also tried to identify special opportunities, previously untried, that could fit these criteria."

At the same time, Bettina K. Beer, college registrar and
assistant professor of history, was named assistant to the
dean of the faculty for continuing education — in effect dean
of the Division of Continuing Education — and undertook
much of the heavy lifting during an at-times painful transi-

---

til 1998, and VCC's main campuses — in far west and far east Orlando — were still daunting commutes for residents of Winter Park and
Maitland. Rollins participates in a statewide Articulation Agreement
that governs the transfer of students from the state's public community colleges to the member institutions of the Independent Colleges and
Universities of Florida (ICUF).

10　Robert Marcus, the previous provost, had left the college for SUNY
　　Brockport, where he because vice president for academic affairs.

tion. "The philosophy underlying the new curriculum is to provide community residents with the opportunity to receive a liberal arts education combined with specialized preprofessional sequences of courses ... which are directly applicable to their careers," Beer told the *Rollins Alumni Record*. "The general education requirements are designed to provide those concepts and skills that adults need to clarify their past experience, and which have consequences for the future management of their personal and professional lives, whatever their occupations may be."

While reshaping the continuing education curriculum was exciting, Beer recalled, one of her less pleasant responsibilities was informing numerous adjunct instructors, some of whom had taught at the college for years, that their services would no longer be required. Many were competent instructors who had tolerated low pay and snobbish disdain from their day school counterparts but were nonetheless loyal to the college and resentful at having been discarded. "I had grown men crying in my office," Beer recalled. "The idea was to replace them with day school faculty. It was a tough decision, but it was the right decision, because it enabled the college to create a more academically sound night program." But what about the business majors, who comprised about 40 percent of the night school's enrollees? Although they were offered the option of transferring to the new program or completing their original business degrees, Beer found that these students were generally unenthused about the abolishment of their major, and many did not re-enroll.

Also in 1982, Richard "Rick" Bommelje, assistant to the dean under Riva, was named assistant dean and director of the Division of Non-Credit Courses.[11] "It is our intent to provide

---

11 Bommelje had earned his undergraduate degree in business adminis-

a broad range of experiences for all age groups," Bommelje told the *Rollins Alumni Record.* "We are in the process of consolidating the various existing noncredit courses at Rollins and are concurrently developing new programs for the future." Bommelje's division, which was in 1990 renamed the Center for Lifelong Education, grew rapidly with workshops on such topics as acting techniques, computer usage, foreign languages, graphic design, investment strategies, listening skills, problem solving, public speaking, speed reading, time management and a travel-film series, as well as recreational courses that taught fencing, sailing, tennis, scuba diving and water-skiing. The division's first offering was a creative writing course from Sloan Wilson — best known for his 1955 novel *The Man in the Gray Flannel Suit* — who had accepted a two-year stint as the college's distinguished writer in residence while completing a new book set in Florida.[12] The School of Creative Arts, coordinated by administrator Angela Moeller and piano teacher Bertha Eutsler — Marion Marwick, citing health problems, had retired in 1972 — expanded into sports camps led by college coaches and even offered some academic courses such as reading and mathematics.

"Over the course of a decade we built the team up to 14 full-time staff members," said Bommelje, who later became assis-

---

tration from the College of Continuing Education under Riva. He also administered the college's U.S. Department of Justice Law Enforcement Assistance Administration grant, which funded the criminal justice programs.

12 Wilson's book, *The Greatest Crime*, was about drug smuggling in South Florida. It received only tepid reviews, and in 1982 the author declined the college's offer to extend his contract by only one year. "For both professional and personal reasons, I don't like working on such a short-term basis," he told the *Orlando Sentinel.* "It takes time to build a program for the teaching of writing and I like to establish a home for more than a year at a time." His wife, Betty, later described Winter Park as filled with "stuffy, dull people, and they're all rich."

tant dean and then associate dean of the retooled continuing education program. "It was pretty sizable for this school." As many as 60 instructors taught every topic imaginable, and by the early 1990s more than 8,000 students per year enrolled in noncredit offerings of one kind or another.[13] Beginning in 1996, on-site professional development programs were offered at various large companies under the division's Corporate Learning Institute, which was directed by human resources specialist Cynthia Hasenau.[14] The noncredit business programs were absorbed by the Crummer School's Executive Training & Management Center in 1999.

DeNicola had anticipated that enrollment would decline as a result of the revamped curriculum, particularly without a business major. But he had hoped that offering a quality, well-rounded and eclectic liberal arts program would somewhat cushion the blow. However, the early numbers were ugly; between the fall of 1981 and the fall of 1984, enrollment had fallen by 40 percent — from 1,163 to 688. The annual contribution from the continuing education program to the college's operating budget had plummeted from nearly $1 million to about $200,000. Surely the college's bottom-line oriented trustees must have questioned the wisdom of essentially gutting a highly profitable subsidiary. And yet, everyone stayed the course.

---

13   The Rollins Center for Lifelong Learning, which is unrelated to the Center for Lifelong Education, began its STARS (Senior Tars) program in 2013, offering noncredit mini-courses aimed at adults over age 50. The college's non-credit programs are now primarily offered through STARS. The Rollins Center for Lifelong Learning was shuttered in 2018 following a strategic planning initiative. The senior enrichment program STARS was retained and aligned with the HHS under the Office of the HHS dean.

14   Hasenau earned a Master of Science in Human Resources management and Organizational Development in 2000 from what was by then known as the Hamilton Holt School. She was, as of 2019, executive director of Mead Botanical Garden.

The program was solid, DeNicola believed, and would stabilize and even begin an upward trajectory once the dust had settled. By mid-decade, fully 65 percent of continuing education courses were taught by full-time faculty from the day school versus 28 percent in 1979. It was, as Seymour described it, "a real college." DeNicola had assigned ad hoc facility committees to work on new courses in such areas as international psychology, computer information systems and Inter-American studies. "New offerings such as these ... should ameliorate the negative reaction in the corporate and business community to the abolition of the business major ... and would be responsive to the feeling that [the continuing education program] is not offering programs which meet the needs of their employees," he wrote in a 1985 report to the faculty Continuing Education Committee.

Beer, though, left to open a college preparatory school and eventually to become dean of the liberal arts program at the Ringling College of Art & Design in Sarasota. Someone else would have to lead the School of Continuing Education into a new era of excellence during its second quarter century.

A MAJOR STEP FORWARD was taken in 1984, when Robert A. Miller was hired as dean of the Division of Continuing Education from Northern Kentucky University, where he had been dean for institutional research. In the run-up to the 25th anniversary of the degree-granting program, Miller took several decisive steps that would finally set continuing education on firm footing and allow it to stand alongside what is now called the College of Liberal Arts — the day school — and the Crummer School as one of three equally important components of Rollins College. He quickly expanded an existing 18-member community advisory board, luring aboard several high-level executives, and hired savvy marketing and development directors, the first such positions dedicated to the continuing education program. Other firsts: Miller offered student scholarships and assembled a core full-time faculty through joint appointments with the day school.

While an open admissions policy remained in place, performing well on four required courses was mandatory for matriculating students. Introduction to Humanities, one of the requirements, was a team-taught interdisciplinary course developed through a $40,922 grant from the National Endowment for the Humanities. Initially the teaching team included Barry Levis, associate professor of history who wrote the grant; Hoyt Edge, professor of philosophy; Laura Grayson, associate professor of politics; and John Heath, assistant professor of classics. "We're now placing the humanities more at the center of our curriculum," Miller told the *Orlando Sentinel*. "What educators are saying now is that there may be some courses all students should take so that part of the educational experience will be a common one." These core courses would weed out those who were unable — or unwilling — to do college-level work.

Naturally, the name of the program was changed again. Now it was, for the second time in its history, the School of Continuing Education — not to be confused with the Institute for General Studies, the School of General Studies, the School for Continuing Studies or the School of Continuing Education. There were more than semantics at play, however. As a school, not a division, Miller's program gained institutional parity with the Crummer School. Both Miller and Martin Schatz, dean of the increasingly prestigious graduate business program, reported directly to DeNicola. Two new majors were introduced: organizational behavior and organizational communication, both of which it was hoped would appeal to business-oriented students without straying too

211

far afield from the college's mission. "We wanted to create a serious program at an elite college with a strong liberal arts bent," Miller told the *Orlando Sentinel.* "We're looking for students who wanted that kind of program. In the short term, a high-quality, demanding program attracts less students, but in the long run that's what makes the name of a school. We're not looking to double our student size." Enrollment, however, began to rebound, from 741 students in 1985 to 803 students in 1986 — the first consecutive year-over-year increases since the reorganization.

Miller, who had stanched the bleeding, wondered why a liberal arts college had no liberal arts master's degree. So in 1987 he and DeNicola turned again to Levis, who had successfully landed an NEA grant for the core undergraduate humanities course. Levis, who also directed the night school humanities program, got to work and snared a $150,000 grant for development of a Master of Liberal Studies (MLS) program. He would later call the MLS "my most significant contribution to Rollins." The faculty committee that designed the program included Levis, Miller, Grayson and Edge as well as Patrick Polley, assistant director of physics; Joseph Nassif, professor of theater, dance and speech; and Maurice "Socky" O'Sullivan, professor of English.

The MLS, perhaps the college's intellectual crown jewel and certainly the offering that most thoroughly epitomizes its liberal arts principles, was directed by Levis until 1995. For lifelong learners interested in just about everything, the MLS is rigorous but rewarding. Enrollees — who come from all walks of life and may range in age from twentysomething to sixtysomething — seek intellectual stimulation, personal enrichment and the company of curious kindred spirits. Very few, other than aspiring college humanities teachers, pursue the degree with the primary goal of mastering a more marketable trade.

Most MLS students are well-established in their careers. Classes are taught by an elite cadre of faculty that consists exclusively of tenured or tenure-track professors who are academic all-stars in such fields as art, music, literature, philosophy, religion, science and more. Core courses include The Human Order, The Origins of Modernity, Religion and Western Culture, Milestones of Modern Science and Masterpieces of Modern Literature. Electives differ from semester to semester, and final thesis projects have included everything from research papers to art installations.

Rollins launched the first MLS program in the state, but it is no longer the only one. Today there are four, with the University of Central Florida, the University of Miami and Barry University in Miami Shores offering comparable degrees. Nationwide, there are about 90 institutional members of the Association of Graduate Liberal Studies Programs, headquartered at Duke University. MLS programs or their equivalent are offered at such prestigious universities as Dartmouth, DePaul, Johns Hopkins, Georgetown, Stanford and Vanderbilt. But only about a half-dozen small colleges, including Rollins, offer graduate degrees in liberal studies. Some institutions appear to have cobbled together MLS programs by bundling seemingly random assortments of existing graduate-level courses. Rollins, however, requires five sequential core courses designed specifically for MLS students.

The 48-hour program can sometimes be completed in three years, although many students — especially those immersed in demanding careers — may take longer. Fast-track or slow-track, a liberal arts college is the most logical place for advanced liberal arts studies, noted President Grant Cornwell, who has written and spoken widely on the value of a liberal arts education in a world where STEM (science, technology, engineering and mathematics) is increasingly emphasized. "The MLS program encapsulates the essence of the liberal arts ethos," said Cornwell. "While every student leaves Rollins with a broad liberal education, MLS students' thesis or capstone projects further exercise their analytical and critical thinking skills."

All aspiring MLS students are screened by the program director. That is because college transcripts, which sometimes date back decades for MLS applicants, may be of limited value. Applicants must write two brief essays: one about why they are interested in the program, and one about a book, other than the Bible, that has influenced their thinking. "I have a special soft spot in my heart for students who undertake courses without even a hint of a vocational focus: humanities and English majors for instance," said Levis in a 2013 commencement address to Holt School graduates. "They major in these disciplines for the sheer love of knowledge. And then there are the Master of Liberal Studies students. Now there's a worthless degree if I ever saw one, and the one in my humble opinion with the most intrinsic value. But of course, I'm prejudiced." Levis added that such courses of study teach students to read, write and think. "If you master those skills, then no matter how much technology changes you will be able to adapt," he said. "If you can read a text closely and critically, then you will be able to master new materials and be able to judge the useful from the worthless."

MEANWHILE, AS THE School of Continuing Education's position solidified, Miller thought that the name should be changed — hopefully for the final time. The phrase "continuing education" sounded too vocational, he believed. Initially, Miller suggested to Levis that the program be named for former President Hugh F. McKean, who had begun the first degree-granting night school. Levis spoke to McKean on Miller's behalf, and the offer was graciously declined. Miller then had another brainstorm. "[President Thaddeus Seymour] had such a feel for the story of the place, so I said, 'How about Hamilton Holt?' And he said, 'Be patient, we'll think about it,'" Miller recalled in a 2005 oral history interview. "So, I wasn't patient. I was young and I kept on pressing it. Eventually Thad, I think, was very pleased with what had happened at the school, because his idea of a financially viable, very high-quality academic adult program was realized. And he did in fact bring it to the board of trustees and it was approved. That's how it got the name Hamilton Holt School."

The change was formally adopted in November 1987 at a special convocation at Knowles Memorial Chapel, during which Seymour presented Miller with a bust of Hamilton Holt.[15] Robert Jay Lifton, a psychiatrist and historian who specialized in war atrocities, was the guest speaker. His most recent book was *The Nazi Doctors: Medical Killing and the Psychology of Genocide*, which had won that year's *Los Angeles Times* book prize. Lifton, whose area of expertise was decidedly grim, seemed to be an unconventional choice for a celebratory event. But then, nothing about the Hamilton Holt School and its antecedents had ever been conventional. Lifton's topic: "Our Nuclear-Age Future: Directions of Hope."

As the 1980s drew to a close, Seymour could look back over a decade of successes. A $32 million capital campaign was successfully completed, and the college's endowment doubled, to nearly $20 million. The Olin Library was built with a $4.7 million grant from the Olin Foundation. Other physical plant additions and improvements included Cornell Hall ($4.5 million), Alfond Stadium ($1.5 million) and a renovation of the Mills Memorial Center as a learning resource center and

---

15   The bust of Holt was damaged and is no longer on display.

student government offices ($1.8 million). Four endowed chairs were added: Classics — a favorite of Seymour's, who delighted in its popularity — Latin American and Caribbean Studies, English Literature, and Finance in the Crummer School. *Time, Newsweek* and *U.S. News & World Report* now covered the college not for its controversies or its gimmicks but for its academic prowess. Seymour, who retired from Rollins in 1990, went on to replace Irving Bacheller as Winter Park's de facto First Citizen. The title was made official when he and his wife, Polly, were named Citizens of the Year by the Winter Park Chamber of Commerce in 1997. A beloved community icon, Seymour died in October 2019 at age 91.

Daniel R. DeNicola left Rollins in 1996 to become provost and vice president for program development at Gettysburg College in Gettysburg, Pennsylvania. He became that college's professor emeritus of philosophy and, as of 2019, lives in Gettysburg and writes about educational issues. Robert A. Miller left Rollins in 1991, but not before receiving the Hamilton Holt Medal from President Rita Bornstein. "You have led the Hamilton Holt School to prominence in its role of offering quality education to nontraditional students," said Bornstein when presenting the medal. "The Hamilton Holt School was named for my illustrious predecessor because of his commitment to the importance of lifelong education. You, too, have embraced that commitment." Miller went on to hold leadership positions in several colleges, including a seven-year stint as president of Nazareth College of Rochester in Rochester, New York. He is, as of 2019, retired and living in Orlando. Richard Bommelje, a specialist in the art and science of listening, has continued as a professor of communication at Rollins.[16]

---

16 Bommelje's wife, Quin, made national news in 2018 when, at age 71, she and 35-year-old dance partner Misha Vlasov made the semifinals on NBC's *America's Got Talent*. Quin Bommelje, who became an audi-

All recall the early 1980s as a heady time during which they took a stand for liberal arts education and built a program that Hamilton Holt himself, the ultimate lifelong learner, would likely have embraced. Future deans, some of whom served on an interim basis, built upon their extraordinary work: Charles Edmondson (1991-93) Robert Smither (1993-98 and 2003-05), Patricia A. Lancaster (1998-2003), Sharon Carrier (2005-09), James C. Eck (2009-10), Laurie Joyner (2010-11), Debra K. Wellman (2011-12), David C.S. Richard (2012-17) and Patricia A. Brown (2017-19). "I thought the program was in really great shape by the time I took it over," said Smither, who would serve as dean twice and would for nine years direct the MLS program. "The enrollments were growing. There was a lot of enthusiasm in the faculty. There were new programs and new majors. It was a great time."

It did seem as though DeNicola and Miller had, to a large extent, rehabilitated the continuing education program's image among faculty members. In a 1989 survey, conducted as part of the Cooperative Institutional Research Program conducted jointly by the American Council on Education and the University of California, Los Angeles, it was found that 70 percent of faculty members able to render a judgment believed that night school students were superior or equal to those in the day school. About 90 percent "strongly disagreed" or "somewhat disagreed" with the statement, "the Holt School detracts from Rollins' main mission of serving traditional students." A similar 90 percent agreed that the Holt School improves the college's reputation in the community, while 77 percent agreed that the Holt School "properly represents Rollins as a liberal arts institution." Nearly the

---

ence favorite and a social media sensation, had only begun taking ballroom dance lessons 10 years before.

same percentage agreed with the statement, "the school helps me maintain my enthusiasm for teaching." While only about half of full-time faculty members responded to the study, the results nonetheless indicated no great groundswell of opposition and, indeed, considerable enthusiasm. The results would likely have been quite different a decade earlier.

In the years following the reorganization, several older programs came to an end. In 2003, for example, the Brevard County branch — which dated to the days of Operation Bootstrap — was closed after 53 years. The college had moved in 1988 from Patrick Air Force Base to an industrial park in Rockledge, where it was known as the Rollins College Brevard Campus. In 1994 it moved again, to West Melbourne, and was dubbed simply Rollins Brevard. But by whatever name, venerable Rollins-by-the-Sea — which had tallied more than 5,000 graduates — could not survive when the University of Central Florida began offering upper-level classes at various campuses of Brevard Community College. Patricia A. Lancaster, who was concurrently dean of the Brevard campus and the Holt School, supervised the branch's closure over a two-year period. Later, in 2015, the college caught the community — and much of the campus — by surprise when it closed its popular summer day camp after 48 years, saying that it would divert its resources to more academic programs.

In other ways the night and day programs became more closely intertwined. In 2003 and 2009, respectively, the departments of music and English began cross-listing their courses and integrating their majors with those of the night school. John V. Sinclair, the college's director of music, said his department is able to field larger choirs and orchestras by including Holt School students.[17] "Everyone is treated

---

17   Sinclair began the Community School of Music in 1993 to offer locals

exactly the same way," said Sinclair. "The classes and require-ments are exactly the same, and the degrees are identical. No one ever told us in the music department that these students were anything other than first-class citizens. So that's the way we've handled it from the day we started the program." Paul Reich, chair of the department of English, agreed and added that the presence of night students — who are usually older and more diverse — enriched discussions. "Both populations are able to learn from each other," Reich added. "It's very diffi-cult now for us to imagine a world in which those voices would be removed."

The numbers tell the story. Night school students are older and more diverse than day school students. Under-graduates are 58.8 percent white in the day school, versus 39 percent white in the night school. Otherwise, as of 2018, the most recent year for which figures are available, the ethnic-ity of the respective undergraduate student bodies was: Hispanic/Latino, 17.9 percent (day) and 28 percent (night); Black or African-American, 3.9 percent (day) and 8.9 percent (night); and Asian, 3.1 percent (day) and 3.9 percent (night). The Hispanic/Latino category has been particular-ly durable in recent years, experiencing the most growth in raw numbers since 2011 (from 160 to 173) and the most growth as a percentage of total enrollees (from 20 percent to 28 percent). The average day school undergraduate was 19.8 years old, while the average night school undergraduate was 27.1 years old. Plenty happens between the ages of 19.8 and 27.1, and Holt School students bring those life experiences to the classroom.

In the years since the name change, the Holt School

noncredit private music instruction for all ages and levels as part of the Rollins College Department of Music, filling the void left when the School of Creative Arts phased out musical instruction.

continued to evolve and to push boundaries. In 2011, President Lewis Duncan (2004-14) faced significant internal opposition when he reorganized the undergraduate faculty — all of whom had been under the Arts & Sciences umbrella — and created a new College of Professional Studies through which the business management major was revived.[18] Among those pleased with the restructuring was Holt School Dean David C. S. Richard, who believed that night school students, in particular, wanted business degrees. But Richard was even more intrigued by the potential of health-related studies, and with approval from the new college initiated an undergraduate degree program in healthcare management as well as three master's degree programs in public health, health services administration, and applied behavior analysis and clinical science. His long-term goal was for the college to establish a presence in Lake Nona — a 7,000-acre master-planned community in east Orlando where a burgeoning "Medical City" encompassed hospitals, life-sciences research facilities and the UCF College of Medicine.[19]

However, it was not to be. Duncan received a vote of no confidence and a censure from the Arts & Sciences faculty before resigning in 2014. Two years later, under the adminis-

---

18 Rollins was not entirely lacking an undergraduate business curriculum. A major in international business was launched in 1998, under President Rita Bornstein. The multidisciplinary program, which linked economics, political science, cultural studies and language together with an international internship, became the college's most popular major — and reinforced the idea that students very much wanted a degree with "business" in the title.

19 Ironically, Richard's contact at Lake Nona was Thaddeus Seymour Jr., son of the former Rollins president, who was then senior vice president at Tavistock Development Company, owner of Lake Nona, before he retired in 2015. Seymour Jr.'s retirement was short lived, however. He joined UCF in 2016 and was serving as interim president of the university as of late 2019.

tration of President Grant Cornwell, the academic programs were recombined under the College of Liberal Arts, which was generally viewed as a welcome affirmation of purpose. Although the College of Professional Studies was gone, the popular business management and healthcare offerings — professional in focus but imbued with a liberal arts ethos — remained, and became integral to the college's curriculum. Holt School students were generally too busy with jobs, families and studies to be concerned with internecine campus conflicts, and paid little attention to the brouhaha.

Perhaps no president appreciated the Holt School on such a visceral level as Rita Bornstein, now president emerita, who is remembered for her fundraising prowess. Bornstein's Campaign for Rollins in the late 1990s secured $160.2 million and quintupled the college's endowment. But the native New Yorker, who once dreamed of being a dancer, dropped out of the University of Chicago, married and had children early. When she was ready to resume her education, she earned both her bachelor's and master's degrees in English literature from Florida Atlantic University and her Ph.D. in education leadership instruction from the University of Miami, primarily through evening programs not unlike the Holt School. "Every commencement, I resonated with the Holt School graduates," said Bornstein, who decreed during her presidency that the school should no longer offer an Associate of Arts degree. "I had been in their shoes: having difficulty finding time to study; feeling I was neglecting my children. Their hard work at the Holt School was often done while parenting or working, or both." In the school's graduates, Bornstein often saw herself.

PRESIDENT HAMILTON HOLT talked about "the four stages of man" and "teaching an old dog new tricks" when he announced the Adult Education Program in 1936. But Holt's

221

idea of adult education — within the context of Rollins, at least — was providing cultural diversions for winter visitors. It is intriguing to speculate what Holt might have done had he focused some of his attention on the adult education movement, which had begun to come into its own in the late 1920s. Even though his storied name adorns the Hamilton Holt School, it is difficult to locate even a tenuous connection between Holt and the kind of continuing education programs that exist today — beyond the fact that many of his tenets (a flexible curriculum, small classes, open discussion) are equally applicable to programs that cater to nontraditional students. Holt, who believed that adult education was best facilitated by preparing young people to be lifelong learners, apparently spent little time pondering what formal role a college might play in the intellectual lives of people in their 20s, 30s, 40s and beyond.

President Hugh F. McKean, perhaps, should have lent his name to the college's continuing education program when he was asked to do so in 1986. He did, after all, implement a degree-granting program for adult learners. But McKean could neither fully embrace nor entirely abandon the program during his presidency. He was often sidetracked by more exciting projects — the Rollins College Space Science Institute, for example — and seemed more eager to lambast George Sauté for the program's shortcomings than to offer him the tools required to make it worthy of respect. Taking nothing away from these two titans of college history, by all rights the Hamilton Holt School should be the Thaddeus Seymour School. Seymour — aided by Provost Daniel R. DeNicola and Dean Robert A. Miller — was the first president who not only fully embraced the continuing education program, but also implemented bold reforms that swapped cash generation for academic integrity. The program has, however, likely endured too many name changes, and Holt's moniker has served it well for more than 30 years.

"You have achieved your goals despite various challenges and hardships," said Barry Levis during his memorable 2013 commencement address to Holt School graduates and their families. "One young man did not own a car and had to depend on Lynx buses to get to campus from the other side of Orlando — a trip that took almost two hours each way. Another student was just recovering from an addiction problem and, despite warnings that now was not the time to return to college, she achieved an 'A' in my class and did not start drinking again. That student completed the B.A. degree with a praiseworthy GPA and went on to receive a master's degree from an Ivy League [institution]. I have worked with students who have gone through messy divorces, the birth of a child, a death in the family and a spouse or partner losing a job. Yet these students overcame their trials, forged ahead with their academic work and earned their degrees. And I know that most of you have had to juggle classes, a job — sometimes two jobs — community obligations and a family. Some of you are not only caring for children but also aging parents. Some of you drive long distances, from Tampa or Melbourne, because you want your degree from Rollins. You have foregone family vacations, movie nights, reading a favorite book. You have all shown real dedication, or you would not have reached this point."

As Prexy's colleague, adult education advocate A. Caswell Ellis, contended in 1932, education is not exactly wasted on the young — but it is by necessity incomplete: "Our vital moral, religious, social, civic and economic problems are studied now during adolescence, when we have little interest and very limited experience or capacity for giving them intelligent consideration. Then, after we get out into life and obtain the experience, the interests and the mental maturity that would enable us to think about these things more intelligently, we cease studying them and devote systematic study only to our personal, professional and business interests, and therefore continue through life living in a child's or adolescent's mental world in regard to those aspects of life that make civilization possible." In the 87 years since Ellis published that essay in *The Journal of Educational Sociology*, no more compelling argument for continuing education had been made.

Chapter 9

ADULT EDUCATION: AN OVERIVEW

BY PATRICIA A. BROWN

THE HISTORY OF American higher education encompasses politics, economics, traditional values, social standing and the dynamics of change. Its response to these factors has shaped its evolution. It is defined by the audiences it serves and is driven by mission and purpose. In these ways, the history of the Hamilton Holt School parallels the history of higher education in the United States.

Early Years

ROLLINS COLLEGE WAS founded by the Florida Congregational Association in 1885, toward the end of a period during which many liberal arts institutions were established by religious denominations. More than 500 colleges, in fact, were chartered by various groups, religious and secular, from the 1790s to the late 1800s. The actual number is hard to pinpoint, as some were chartered and never opened, while others provided courses but not degrees. Also, the terminology "college" embraced a wide range of entities including academies, technical institutes, seminaries and professional schools.

The first Colonial Era colleges — namely Harvard, Princeton, Yale and Dartmouth — mirrored early European-style institutions. From 1810 to 1860, most colleges in the U.S. were founded by religious denominations, including those established by Congregational, Presbyterian and Episcopalian churches, followed by those affiliated with Baptist, Methodist and Catholic churches.

An impetus for the rapid expansion of higher education came from the 1819 Supreme Court decision, *Dartmouth College v. Woodward*. When Dartmouth's trustees dismissed the president, the New Hampshire legislature tried to force the college — which was founded in 1769 through a corporate charter granted by the British crown — to become a public institution. Daniel Webster, a Dartmouth alumnus, eloquently argued the case against William H. Woodward, the state-designated secretary of the board of trustees. The court's ruling recognized the college's original charter as a contract and forbade states from passing laws that interfered with contracts between private parties. The landmark decision limited state power over private colleges, thereby giving "license for unrestrained individual and group initiative and the creation of colleges of all sizes, shapes and creeds" (Trow, 1989, p.12).

Early settlements supported the establishment of colleges as a means of legitimizing their communities and expanding their economies. Florida's development, however, lagged. It joined the Union in 1822 as an organized territory but did not become a state until 1845. And it did not begin to grow significantly until after the Civil War, when railroad lines made the south and central parts of the state more accessible. Rail service supported Florida's burgeoning agricultural industry and facilitated the annual migration of wealthy Northerners seeking refuge from harsh winters. Many of those snowbirds, enticed by booster-bought advertising, found their way to Winter Park.

The establishment of Rollins in 1885 was championed by local investors as well as a church leader with aspirations of becoming a college president. Certainly the bucolic (if still isolated) setting was ripe for development. Although the Florida Congregational Association made the selection process competitive, Winter Park enjoyed the advantage of having civic leaders who also served on the selection committee. In part because of insider knowledge, the town was able to offer an attractive package of incentives that far outstripped those of Daytona, Jacksonville, Mount Dora and Orange City.

While many colleges were established throughout the country prior to 1900, few were successful. Educational institutions were subject to free market pressures, and the federal government's influence was diminished by the conspicuous absence of education as a focus in the U.S. Constitution and the failure of attempts to establish a national ministry of education.

Rollins, in fact, barely survived its early years. Founders were able to marshal the key ingredients for a startup, yet the college remained financially strapped — in part because its mission centered on creating educated citizens, not an elite citizenry. As was the case with many small institutions, tuition was low in order to entice enrollment but inadequate to fully support operational costs. Donations, therefore, were crucial to financial viability.

Industrial Revolution

AGRICULTURE, MINING AND manufacturing created a national economic boom that was enhanced by advancements in technology. The ability to transport goods and materials via rail created a network for commerce and communication. Migratory patterns followed economic needs and the country experienced a swell of immigrants.

The growth in industry, capital and population was greatest in the North and West. The South retained an agrarian society that was so devastated by the Civil War that it lost half its wealth and was slow to recover. However, while the South struggled, the rest of the country saw tremendous economic expansion. The post-war years were marked by rampant speculation and fortune building, as many early industrialists grew rich and gained political as well as economic power. Their unfettered excesses contributed to several financial panics — in 1837, 1873 and 1907 — prompting the federal government to step in with legislation.

- 1887: The Interstate Commerce Act, which protected farmers and manufacturers from ruinous multiple-pricing tactics of the railroads.
- 1890: The Sherman Anti-Trust Act, which curbed interference with trade.
- 1906: The Pure Food and Drug Act, which regulated food and drugs moving in interstate commerce.
- 1913: The Federal Reserve Act, which established economic stability by overseeing monetary policy; and ratification of the Sixteenth Amendment, which established an income tax.
- 1914: The Federal Trade Commission Act, which focused on providing consumer protection.

Tighter constraints resulted in the growth of philanthropy, which directly benefited education while providing donors with standing as social leaders and power brokers. Testament to their influence can still be seen across the nation through family names emblazoned on academic buildings. Rollins, like many early colleges dependent on external funds, sought out wealthy benefactors and offered an outlet for their philanthropic endeavors.

University Movement

THE IMPACT OF technological advancements in agriculture and manufacturing in the early 1800s gave rise to demands for education and training, thereby spurring a movement to establish universities. Passage in 1862 of the Morrill Act meant that states received land grants for the building of institutions that would teach engineering, agriculture and military tactics (a concessionary amendment).

During the same year, President Abraham Lincoln signed legislation that financed a transcontinental railroad and established the Homestead Act, both of which encouraged western settlement. These actions gave rise to the development of the comprehensive university — a departure from the classical liberal arts institution — and set in motion the building of universities from coast to coast.

A second Morrill Act, passed in 1890, was directed at former Confederate states where segregation remained entrenched. The act required each state to show that its land-grant universities did not use race as an admissions criterion. If race was a factor, then the federal government withheld appropriations unless "separate but equal" facilities were provided for people of color. In all, 70 land-grant institutions were founded, including many of today's historically black colleges and universities.

The land-grant college system, with its focus on teaching, research and service, is seen as a major contributor to economic growth. It further solidified curricular focus on scholarship and applied science and technology. Enrollment growth was supported by an increasing number of secondary school graduates, many of whom were children of immigrant parents.

The land-grant system opened a pathway for professional programs of study that were aligned with the demands of the burgeoning industrialized economy. The growth of universities that followed created competition for students that challenged the viability of many liberal arts colleges. Rollins, established as a traditional liberal arts institution, nonetheless retained its traditional roots and focused on its students and the community.

Curriculum

INSTRUCTIONAL PROGRAMS THAT emphasized scholarship in technology and the sciences were rapidly replacing classical education, with its focus on character development. The curriculum imported during the early Colonial Era — and strongly supported by religious founders of colleges during that time — was giving way to more practical education models.

The Yale Report of 1828 became the foundation for courses of study in numerous institutions, and provided many small, religiously affiliated colleges a way to justify a curriculum that straddled the liberal arts and experimental sciences while still declaring that Latin and Greek were essential for the development of educated citizens (Cohen and Kisker, 2010). Many small colleges, including Rollins, touted fealty to the Yale Report as being indicative of their quality.

In the 1860s, Harvard University led another wave of change by taking major steps in defining the authority and governance of the institution while redefining its curriculum. From its inception, Harvard was governed by a board of overseers that included political leaders — among them the governor of the Commonwealth of Massachusetts — who were elected by a joint ballot of the two houses of the state legislature.

Influential Harvard graduates pressed for changes in

both the leadership and the offerings of the university. Eventually, oversight shifted to the alumni. In 1869, Charles Eliot was appointed to the presidency, and governed as a pragmatist who understood that education based on recitations and lectures was inadequate to achieve competency. Therefore, he shifted the focus to achievements and broadened the curriculum to enhance choice.

Rollins adhered to the Yale Report until 1925, when newly appointed President Hamilton Holt, recalling the rigidity of his own education at Yale, restructured the curriculum to incorporate experience and engagement. He sought faculty members who shared his belief that students and professors should be partners in learning, and set up his conference plan to actively encourage dialogue between students and faculty.

The conference plan provided intensive one-on-one interaction between students and professors, placing the student in the center of the learning process. He organized a high-profile campus colloquium, "The Curriculum for the Liberal Arts College," in 1931, inviting educational philosopher John Dewey to serve as its leader.

The colloquium brought together leaders in nontraditional education, whose ideas were incorporated into the conference plan. This furthered the college's reputation as a pacesetter in innovative teaching, and placed Holt's revolutionary approach squarely at the forefront of the progressive education movement — a movement that continues to shape education today.

Adult Education

FACTORS SHAPING THE establishment of a college in Winter Park, aside from a presumed enhancement of status, included the desire to attract more well-to-do Northerners who would purchase property and make their homes in the community.

Early students were predominantly from the Northeast until secondary education matured sufficiently to draw students from Southern communities.

As the town grew, the influx of winter residents became an important audience for the college's offerings. Lectures, performances and social events brought locals to campus and helped define the role of the college within the community. This sort of activity — at Rollins and elsewhere — would form the basis of the adult education movement. But to fully understand that movement, it is important to understand how social, economic and political factors played a role.

Adult education can be traced to the nation's beginnings. Many early settlers were illiterate, and those seeking to advance themselves sought tutors who primarily focused on reading, writing and numeracy. The influx of immigrants led to the emergence of English language classes, while the rapid growth of technologies — particularly in agriculture and manufacturing at the dawn of the Industrial Age — increased demand for vocational training and education in the sciences. Although liberal arts colleges set the foundation for higher education in the 17th and 18th centuries, they began to diverge from their classical roots as demand for vocational and professional instruction increased.

The history of the International Correspondence School (ICS) in Scranton, Pennsylvania, offers an example of education meeting a social, political and economic need. The school, which remains in operation today, was founded in 1891 after the state of Pennsylvania passed a law requiring miners and inspectors to satisfactorily complete examinations on safety or lose their jobs. ICS was started by Thomas J. Foster, a journalist at the *Colliery Engineer and Metal Miner,* who wrote columns for the publication on mining methods and machinery. The articles increased demand for information, leading Foster to develop correspondence courses related to coal mining. He eventually left the paper to establish ICS — and within eight years the company had 190,000 enrollees.

ICS enjoyed tremendous success as result of demand and the quality of the learning materials (Watkinson, 1996). The school's success accelerated in 1891, when the U.S. Postal Service introduced rural free delivery (RFD), thereby broadening the company's reach (Cushing, 1893). ICS's effectiveness was noted by the War Department, which contracted with the company during World War II to develop the department's training manuals.

Except for campus-based community education, early forms of adult education operated outside the domain of colleges and universities. Most adult education was driven by a need for skills development, which translated into social and economic advancement. The forces that shaped early adult education have continued unabated, although the key difference is that the academic community is now actively engaged in developing relevant curriculum.

The academic role in offering college credit for adult education first took place as an outgrowth of the Chautauqua Institute. The institute was established in 1874 as a summer educational retreat for Sunday school teachers. In 1876, the institute was expanded to provide a liberal arts experience for adults through a residential program that rose in prominence and attracted many national leaders. A variety of cultural opportunities were offered, including explorations of religious and secular thought and lectures and discussions covering civic, cultural and scholarly life.

In 1878, the institute developed the Chautauqua Literary and Scientific Circle, which offered study circles and a systematic homeschool plan that operated like a local book club. The circles provided the institute a means to extend liberal education to the middle class and became a vehicle through which college credit was offered when William Rainey Harper became president of the University of Chicago.

Harper was selected to organize the university by its founder, John D. Rockefeller. A strong proponent of life-long learning, Harper was also an advocate for the Chautauqua Institute and the Literary and Scientific Circle movement. He set high standards for academic quality and faculty productivity and implemented many firsts in higher education, including the nation's first extension school for working adults with evening and weekend classes. Harper is also credited with pioneering the junior college movement, which resulted in today's community colleges. Like Holt, he was committed to innovation espoused by the progressive education movement.

Harper applied the same educational standards applied to classroom instruction for the extension school and its correspondence offerings, thus validating correspondence study. As a result of his efforts, participants in the circles were able to complete courses and programs of study leading to degrees. Correspondence courses for credit grew as a means of educating adults while setting the stage for distance education.

Correspondence study expanded with technology, beginning with radio, moving to television and ultimately to the internet. Many colleges and universities now embrace technology as a valuable delivery system for courses and degrees, creating an attractive alternative not only for adult learners but for students of all ages and all levels of study, from preschool to graduate programs. Today, distance education and online learning are virtually synonymous.

Rollins, however, has held to its traditional classroom-focused instruction and commitment to faculty/student engagement. It has also demonstrated innovative leadership in serving adult learners. For example, in the 1950s the college developed a television course, "Mathematics and Western Culture," for Sunrise Semester, an early morning television series produced by the College of Arts and Sciences at New York University. Today the college, particularly the Holt School, continues to engage technologies to enhance instruction and support flexible options for students without undermining the college's foundational mission.

Aside from correspondence study and early forms of distance education, the greatest impetus for adult education was the passage of The Servicemen's Readjustment Act of 1944 — commonly known as the G.I. Bill. The bill provided a wide range of benefits, including low-cost mortgages, low-interest business loans and payments of tuition and living expenses to attend high school, college or vocational school. The impact of educational funding transformed higher education and expanded the field of adult education.

A post–World War II study commissioned by the American Council on Education described the bill's "profound" and likely lasting impact on adult education (Houle, et al., 1947). In the first decade of the program, the G.I. Bill served more than 2 million veterans and led to the establishment of a variety of nontraditional approaches to serve adult students.

Rollins joined in serving veterans and active-duty students in 1951 with an agreement to offer courses for credit at Patrick Air Force Base in Brevard County. Operation Bootstrap, a national program established by the U.S. Air Force, paid two-thirds of the tuition for participating students. At the same time, the college began a Courses for the Community program that established credit-based continuing education on campus and set the stage for degree programs that have been offered these past six decades.

Nationally, enrollment demands of veterans remained

strong for nearly two decades following World War II. The boost redefined higher education and brought many new players into the field, including proprietary colleges and universities whose primary markets were veterans and active-duty military personnel.

As enrollment numbers began to wane in the 1970s, the gap was quickly filled with baby boomers who dominated enrollments for the next decade. In 1960, the Rollins board of trustees approved establishment of the Institute of General Studies and supported launch of the Bachelor of General Studies degree. The program continued to serve a significant population of veterans and was opened to an expanding population of adults. Early students were predominantly males, but by the mid-1970s women had become — and would remain — the predominant population served by the college's evening program.

The 1960s was a time of great tumult and social change. Civil rights, the Vietnam War and the race to space played key roles in shaping individual identity. The landscape of higher education changed significantly to accommodate a bulging middle-class population of students from baby boomers to adults. Higher education — celebrated as the pathway to economic well-being, career development and personal enrichment — attracted an increasingly diverse population of students.

Enrollments, though sustained for more than two decades, began to decline in the 1970s as the baby-boomer population graduated from college and the high school population declined. To fill the gap, colleges and universities began offering a wide range of creative options to attract adult students. Women — emancipated by the birth control pill and encouraged by new opportunities in fields outside the secretarial, teaching and nursing arenas — were actively recruited to higher education as a pathway to careers and self-fulfillment.

Colleges and universities began to broaden their offerings to attract these students. Liberal arts institutions, likewise, deviated from their traditional curriculum to include business and professional degree programs in an effort to remain relevant and financially viable.

Adult education in the 1970s blossomed as colleges and universities sought to tap the adult population. However, the focus on enrollment first, quality second, created a great deal of angst in the higher education community — in part because most adult education degree programs operated independently of their parent institutions and were supported solely by adjunct faculty who had little professional development as educators. Concurrently, many full-time faculty did not want to teach in adult education programs that they believed to be substandard.

College administrators saw such programs as cash cows and had a difficult time reining in entrepreneurial adult education leaders. Support from external sources, such as business and government entities, gave colleges and universities high-level visibility and enabled the nimbleness and flexibility required for the creation of new adult education programs as opportunities presented themselves.

Rollins, under the leadership of President Thaddeus Seymour (1978-90), redirected adult education to the college's core mission. In doing so, he stabilized the focus of the evening program and gave clarity to the role of the college in serving adult students. It can be said that Seymour's action served as a pivot point for Rollins while other institutions continued to follow revenue-generating strategies.

For the next two decades, colleges and universities across the country struggled with the role of adult education within their institutions. Rollins was no exception — a fact demonstrated by the evening program's many name changes. The result was significant separation of adult education from traditional undergraduate education. In response, accrediting bodies challenged adult education programs to align themselves with the institutional mission and quality parameters of the institution's primary curriculum.

The push to define and validate learning outcomes has broken many of the barriers dividing programs for traditional and nontraditional students. Adult education will continue to influence and shape higher education as it ebbs and flows with changes in demographics, economic demand, technological advancements and workforce needs.

The Holt School is well positioned to respond to current and emerging learning needs of adult students — and its focus on degree completion and graduate education is positioned to strengthen even as new and innovative ways are found to serve its constituencies.

The school, for example, has assumed a major role in outreach with its senior enrichment programs, STARS (Senior Tars). Integration of community engagement within instructional programs is helping to build bridges between academic and community initiatives. Meanwhile, the school has maintained and reinforced its core mission in alignment with its liberal arts foundation. Through changing times, the Holt School has remained steadfast in its commitment to serving the community and the many adult populations seeking an enriched learning environment.

Works Cited

Cohen, A. M., & Kisker, C. B. (2010). *The Shaping of American Higher Education: Emergence and Growth of the Contemporary System* (2nd ed.). San Francisco, CA: Jossey-Bass.

Cushing, M.H. (1893). *The Story of Our Post Office.* Boston: A.M. Thayer & Co. 47-67.

Houle, C. Orvin., American Council on Education. Commission on Implications of Armed Services Educational Programs. (1947). *The Armed Services and Adult Education.* Washington: American Council on Education.

Lane, J. C. (2017). *Rollins College Centennial History: A Story of Perseverance, 1885-1895.* Winter Park, FL: Story Farm.

Trow, M. (1989). "American Higher Education — Past, Present and Future." *Studies in Higher Education*, 14(1), 5-22.

Watkinson, J. D. (1996). "Education for Success." The International Correspondence Schools of Scranton, Pennsylvania. *The Pennsylvania Magazine of History and Biography*, 120(4), 343-369.

Chapter 10

FINDING THEMSELVES

BY MICHAEL McLEOD

HISTORY HAPPENS IN classrooms, too. We were determined not to overlook that when we envisioned this book to celebrate the 60th anniversary of the Holt School. Toward that end, I began collecting individual stories from the school's graduates, teachers and current students as a companion to Randy Noles' history of Holt leadership through the years and Patricia A. Brown's broader analysis of how adult education changed in the U.S. over those same six decades.

Their work is methodical. Mine is a mosaic, a core sample representing the views and experiences of 22 graduates, two iconic professors and two current Holt School students. Beginning with an 85-year-old Class of 1964 graduate who came to Orlando as a Cold War–era engineer and ending with the stories of two current international students who came here to escape repression, their remembrances represent significant changes and steadily increasing diversity over the decades.

Yet what emerged most vividly, in interview after inter-

view, were not differences but similarities. This genera-
tion-spanning contingent is, overall, a stubborn lot, like the
grandmother who pursued a degree even harder after being
told she didn't need one. Adventuresome, too: A surprising
number traveled the world, either before or after their years at
the Holt School, on endeavors either charitable or exploratory.

Most striking of all was the through-line of camaraderie
among them. They were inspired nearly as much by their classmates as their professors, imbued with a rapport – an *esprit
de corps,* as one Holt School student proudly put it, in among
nontraditional learners with a variety of trajectories and goals
– and one thing in common: They had turned up at Rollins,
after dark. And that was where they found themselves.

Steve Sekulich
Rocket Man

All Steve Sekulich was looking for was a bump in pay. He
wound up getting quite a bit more than that out of the bargain.

He had just landed a job as part of an influx of aerospace
engineers who migrated to Orlando in the early 1960s to work
at the Martin Marietta Corporation's new missile-manufac-
turing base. Hired on the strength of a high school education, a mind for math and a handful of engineering extension
courses, he was told by a supervisor that earning a college
degree of any sort would elevate him to a higher pay scale.
He arranged to couple his day job of testing intercontinental
ballistic missile systems with night classes devoted to somewhat more peaceful subjects.

Steve had always aced math and science courses. What
made him uneasy about being confronted with a liberal arts
education was the prospect, as he saw it, of studying "all the
subjects I'd been avoiding." Those misgivings would evapo-
rate — in no small part because of an encounter with a teacher

who represented the college's late–19th century foundations. His name was Arthur Teikmanis. He was pastor of the First Congregational Church of Winter Park, whose members had been instrumental in founding Rollins in 1885, and taught a History of Religion class at the college's night school, which was then called the Institute for General Studies.

Steve was in the midst of contending with a traumatic event in his life when the course turned up on his schedule. "My wife and I had a baby in 1963," he said. "She came down with the measles, then spinal meningitis. By the time they got it under control, she was deaf and blind in one eye. Here was this terrible thing happening to an innocent child that would change her life forever. I was angry. I was irate. It was so unfair. I had been raised by devout Catholics. All that 'God's will' stuff they came up with, it just left me cold."

But in class discussion, and then in a series of private conversations with Teikmanis, Steve found consolation in the theological views of Charles Hartshorne, an influential and widely published Episcopalian minister and professor of philosophy who posited a God who was not a creator but rather a co-creator — an all-loving but not necessarily all-powerful force in a multifaceted universe dominated by free will and its consequences.

Steve, who graduated in 1964, will turn 85 this year. He lives alone in the home he bought for his family when he first moved to Central Florida. His wife died years ago; his daughter lives comfortably out west with a roommate who cares for her. He has arranged for her to be financially independent for life. He is also leaving a substantial gift to the Holt School in his will.

He is an affable man, clearly at peace with himself. He always has a new joke to tell — one that will usually have a punch line so sly that it takes a beat or two to register. Ever the hands-on engineer, he is usually involved in a home-improvement project that would intimidate less savvy do-it-yourselfers. His conversation is often filled with offhand references to the likes of parabolic trajectories, ionization and magnetic closed loops, with an occasional sentimental foray into the dawn of the UNIVAC computer and the complexities of the Pershing missile system.

He can even make theology sound like an engineering issue.

It is just the way his mind works: Matters metaphysical are still to be addressed in a practical, cause-and-effect sort of way. "What I came to realize from that class I took and the talks we had is that when a bad thing happens, it's just like two spatial vectors that intersect," he mused. "Sometimes, you're just in the wrong place at the wrong time. I remember, when I told that to Professor Teikmanis, he looked at me for a second and then said: 'That sounds about right.'"

Rick Bommelje
The Golden Pause

Rick Bommelje possesses all the usual academic credentials — published works, post-graduate degrees, recognition in his field. He also enjoys the rarer distinction of surely being the only tenured professor in Holt School history who interviewed for his first job at Rollins while wearing a meter-reader's uniform.

A returning Vietnam veteran, Rick was working full-time reading electric meters for the City of Orlando when he enrolled in the college's day school in the early 1970s. A month after graduating with a degree in business in 1974, he heard of an opening as an assistant to Daniel F. Riva, dean of the School of Continuing Education, as the program was then called, and turned up in Riva's office in full municipal regalia. He not only got the job but rose through ordinarily impermeable ranks, from staffer and administrator to instructor and tenured professor.

Rick has seen so many changes at what came to be known as the Holt School that to explain them all he rose from his desk, walked to the white board in his office at Cornell Hall for the Social Sciences, and with marker in hand filled the surface with a flurry of names, dates, names and directional arrows, looking a bit like a retired general recounting a pivotal military campaign. In truth, he's played a humbler role: He listens.

Rick's devotion to the art, science, scholarship and subtleties involved in that seemingly simple activity has made the 71-year-old professor of organizational communications both a nationally recognized expert and one of the school's most beloved and influential instructors. "When you really listen to somebody, you're telling them something," he said. "You're telling them: *You matter.*"

Rick's preoccupation with effective listening tracks to his earliest years at Rollins, when he came to the realization that he was not communicating as well as he wished with either Riva or his wife, Quin (who has a fascinating a story in her own right as a ballroom dancer who, in 2018, at age 71, earned a coveted "golden buzzer" while competing in *America's Got Talent*).

Determined to elevate his listening skills on behalf of both his marriage and his career, he began studying with Lyman Steil, founder of the International Listening Leadership Institute. Eventually, the two collaborated on a book, *Listening Leaders: The Ten Golden Rules to Listen, Lead and Succeed,* and Rick began incorporating its concepts into his classes.

He has enjoyed a four-decade career at the college. Yet he glows with the enthusiasm of a newly minted prof and talks about the connection between listening and leadership in the revved-up tone you would expect from a fiery football coach half his age. Teaching three classes every semester is considered a full load for a tenured professor. Rick teaches four. Each class begins with silence; he strikes a small gong, and he and his students spend a few moments collecting their thoughts — or, better still, keeping them at bay.

The interlude, which he calls "the golden pause," bespeaks yet another distinction: He is surely the only tenured professor in Rollins College history who prefers to start a class with something other than the sound of his own voice.

Rita K. Roney
Hearts of Texas

Apropos of a native Texan, Rita Kathryn Roney has had a big life — one that has encompassed owning a 550-acre ranch in the hill country west of San Antonio with her financial-wizard husband; traveling the world to rub shoulders with international financiers and even ringing the bell one heady morning to signal the opening of trading at the Nasdaq Stock Exchange; and quite likely being the only School of General Studies graduate who can say that she and her young son once shared a home with a Rollins College fraternity.

"Rita K.," as she prefers to be called, grew up in McAllen, Texas, a Hidalgo County border town at the southern tip of the state that was still rural enough in her childhood days for her father to keep a horse for her in the pasture next to their house — an arrangement that elevated her social status among neighborhood playmates.

Years later, as a single mother in the 1970s, she moved to Orlando for a job as a designer for a new-home developer. Eventually, she decided to change careers, and enrolled in night classes with the goal of becoming an elementary school teacher. She and her son, Mark, lived in a small rental unit at

Pflug Hall, once a private home owned by Winter Park Mayor J. Lynn Pflug but purchased by the college and occupied mainly by the Phi Beta Delta fraternity. "The fraternity boys more or less adopted Mark. They would take him out to the soccer field with them to kick the ball around," she said. "And Dinky Dock was right behind our apartment. To this day, Mark always says we had a tiny little place, but a million-dollar backyard."

There were real millions yet to come.

After graduating in 1977, Rita K. and her son returned to McAllen, where she met and married Glen Roney, a banker and philanthropist who rose from a small-town upbringing much like her own to establish a chain of banks that reshaped both the skyline and the economy of the Rio Grande Valley. They became a southwest Texas power couple. He built banks; she helped to decorate them, gradually weaning the boardrooms and lobbies of the state's financial institutions from a devoted overreliance on paintings of cowboys and horses. It was in 1994 that Rita K. and her husband rang the bell to open trading on the New York Stock Exchange when the enterprise he stewarded, Texas Regional Bankshares, went public.

They travelled widely as he developed national and international business ties, losing several close friends when the World Trade Center towers collapsed in the 9/11 attacks. For years afterward, they would bring shell-shocked Manhattan acquaintances who needed to escape the city and memories of the attack to McAllen for annual visits that were as much about healing as connecting.

Over the years, the couple also included Rollins in their many philanthropic endeavors, coming to Winter Park annually as members of a Rollins Leadership Council. "Glen was a giver," said Rita K. "I would ask him to help with some organization that needed help, and when I would suggest an amount, he would always say, 'Oh, let's give them a little more.'"

Glen Roney died in November 2018 at age 88. Rita K. and Mark still live in McAllen. Pflug Hall, the haven they loved, was demolished in 2006. But a tribute to the time they shared there as mother and son endures, thanks to an endowed Holt School scholarship for single mothers that was established that same year by two small-town Texans — one with a generous heart, the other with a grateful one.

Susan Porcaro Goings
"You're too big for this town."

When senior year rolled around, graduation loomed, and all her University of Florida classmates started worrying about paying off their student loans, a fifth-generation Floridian named Susan Norris took a different approach: She decided to do something about it.

Typical.

Susan had a streak of resourcefulness and independent thinking that began manifesting itself when she was a student at Lyman High School in Longwood, just north of Orlando. She landed a job at Disney World and turned down a chance to be Snow White, choosing instead to work as a tour guide, a position that provided her first experience at rubbing shoulders with celebrities who merited one-on-one tours.

As a sophomore at UF, she would be selected as queen of the Tangerine Bowl, the annual college football matchup held in Orlando and now known as the Citrus Bowl. In an encounter that was prophetic in a way neither could have imagined at the time, she was encouraged by one of the judges, Brownie Wise, vice president for marketing of Tupperware Brands and legendary creator of the Tupperware Party, who told her: "You're too big for this town."

It wouldn't take long for Susan to prove her right.

Two years later, when the student debt issue came up,

her solution was to withdraw from UF, move back to Central Florida and enroll at the School of Continuing Education — a name that struck her as being stilted and patronizing, "especially since my courses and teachers were just as good as those I'd had in Gainesville," she said.

Taking classes at night and working full-time during the day, she would earn her diploma and pay off the student debt by dividing her time between studying on campus and working as the first female advertising executive at WFTV, the Orlando ABC affiliate. She would rock the city's male-dominated advertising-sales market by introducing an inventive, lone-wolf strategy: She convinced strip-mall merchants to band together so they could share the cost and afford the rates.

By the time she graduated in 1978, her success had attracted the attention of executives at the network-owned station in Los Angeles, who hired her as *their* first female ad rep. Then she broke another barrier, becoming the first ever to move from sales to the news as a reporter, anchor and entertainment show host.

Susan was assigned one day to interview the members of a rock band she had never heard of. Her producer had to tell her how to pronounce the group's name — and explain that it had just been awarded seven Grammys. The band: Toto. The group, which caught fire in the late 1970s and early 1980s with "Africa," "Rosanna," "Hold the Line" and other hits, revolved around three brothers, one of whom she would fall in love with and marry: drummer Jeff Porcaro. Over the next nine years, the couple would have three sons — Christopher, Miles and Nico — and Susan would become an activist city council member and mayor pro tem of Hidden Hills, an exclusive gated community in Los Angeles County.

It was a fabulous life until tragedy struck: Jeff died of a heart attack in 1992. Susan returned to Orlando with her children to grieve, be with family and in time embark on yet another phase of her life — this time as a businesswoman, philanthropist, and advocate for women and children. In 1998, in a charmed stroke of chance, she married Rick Goings, chairman and CEO of the empire that had employed the late Brownie Wise: Tupperware Brands. Susan soon became a global ambassador for the company, collecting the stories of women around the world who leveraged themselves out of poverty by selling Tupperware.

Susan and her husband also become impassioned advocates for Boys & Girls Clubs. During their extensive global travels, they recognized a need for clubs outside the U.S. and started one in Tijuana, Mexico, then another in Soweto, South Africa, eventually fostering more than 100 clubs in 18 countries and founding the nonprofit World Federation of Youth Clubs.

The couple also began serving on college boards and funding scholarships for both Holt School and Rollins day school students. In the process, they became close friends with former Rollins President Rita Bornstein, who once surprised Susan with a small but meaningful gift: a new diploma. On the line that had read "The School of Continuing Education," another name now appeared: "Rollins College."

Warren "Chip" Weston
"I didn't have a game plan."

Here are a just a few of the big adventures Chip Weston embarked upon after graduating as a Rollins day student in 1970 with a degree in behavioral science: joined the Peace Corps; authored an anthology of Canadian folk music; created a line of hand-painted greeting cards; played in a band that performed at the Grand Ole Opry; drove around the country in a balky 1956 Plymouth; made stained-glass windows in the garage of a house on four acres that had just been vacated by a motorcycle gang; and partnered with a friend to invent a spray-on makeup device.

Here are a few of the interests he went on to develop: marketing, digital arts, archetypal imagery, symbolism, sublimation, yoga, color theory, sound theory, new urbanism, economics, physics, emerging technology and artificial intelligence.

And here is where he learned to knit all those threads together: the inaugural class of the Master of Liberal Studies program, which was launched in 1987 — the same year the School of Continuing Education was renamed for former President Hamilton Holt. Chip, who was awarded a scholarship to the 48 credit-hour program devoted to the great ideas of Western Civilization, emerged with a focus, both artistic and civic, that had previously eluded him. "I didn't have a game plan in life," he says. "The MLS program changed everything."

Among all his other interests, Chip had studied the writings of George Washington and Thomas Jefferson devoted to civic engagement. He emerged from the Holt School determined to apply what he had learned.

"The most valuable part of my educational experience was the connection to the Winter Park community — the behind-the-scenes access that we got," he said. Chip would go on to become a key figure in the city's civic and cultural life. He served as Winter Park's director of economic development and was later a course director of new media, social media and sports marketing at Full Sail University as well as a lobbyist for United Arts of Central Florida.

He has flourished artistically as well, joining a consortium of painters and sculptors that comprise the McRae Art Studios and serving on the boards of the Florida Alliance for Arts Education and the State of Florida Council on Arts and Culture. He has also been chairman of the Walt Disney World

Festival of the Masters. Rollins left its mark on Chip, and he returned the favor: His artwork — mostly digitally manipulated photography — may be seen on the walls of the Crummer Graduate School of Business.

Barbara van Horn
"Keep in mind, this was the '60s."

Barbara van Horn's first effort at higher education took her to the University of Colorado, but not for long. She dropped out with a 1.53 GPA — the result, as she put it, of "having too much fun." She moved on to a stint at art school in Boston, but dropped out again, this time to work as a nurse's aide, become involved with the Vietnam-era draft resistance movement and eventually travel overseas with her new husband to backpack through 43 countries in Europe and Asia.

"Keep in mind, this was the '60s," she drolly noted.

Barbara and her husband would sustain that flower-power theme into the 1970s and beyond, returning to the U.S. and relocating to Central Florida, where they became early organizers of the StoneSoup School — an alternative school for children based on the anti-authoritarian educational philosophy of Scottish educator Alexander Sutherland Neill. (The school's name was inspired by a fable about a traveler who visits a village during a famine and coaxes everyone to share their meager resources to create a bowl of soup big enough to serve them all.)

It was not until she had raised a daughter in that school's Putnam County retreat, which featured 10 staff members, 24 students and an array of geodesic domes made from found materials, that Barbara's educational forays took a traditional turn. "I wanted to get a B.A. in psychology, and I had two choices: I could go to UCF or Holt," she said. "To be quite honest with you, I picked Holt because I didn't want to deal with the parking at UCF. But it's a choice I've never regretted."

At the Holt School, she blossomed intellectually under the guidance of psychology professor Sandra McIntire, who enrolled her in a study involving interviews with men who had been convicted of domestic-violence crimes. "She was just such a brilliant mentor," said Barbara. "She was dedicated to the project and to having her students make the most out of the opportunity. But the greatest gift she gave me was when I graduated and was named the Outstanding Senior. I had to give a speech that I very much wanted her to be present for. But she couldn't make it. I was very upset. I was ready to give the award back. And she told me: 'You don't need me anymore. You have all you need now. You can go forward on your own.'"

Her mentor's confidence was well founded. Barbara, who graduated summa cum laude in 1995, had clearly left her counterculture years behind. She would go on to earn her M.S. and Ph.D. from the University of North Texas; complete her clinical internship at the University of Miami/Jackson Memorial Medical Center; and become a tenure-track professor at Indian River State College in 2001, where she would eventually serve as chair of the social sciences department. She retired in 2014.

Chris Ramsey
Rising Up

It all goes back to that one classroom for Chris Ramsey. The one in the basement of his old high school that was reserved for students like him: underachievers and problem kids who were tucked away to keep them at a distance from the students who occupied the classrooms upstairs.

Attleboro, Massachusetts, was a failing factory town when Chris was growing up there in the 1970s and 1980s. His working-class neighborhood was not just sketchy but outright dangerous. "Most of those kids who were in that room with me are dead now," he said. "I had friends who didn't make it past 40. Crime. Drugs. The opioid epidemic."

It would be nice to say that a caring teacher saw his potential and rescued Chris. Actually, it was a television set that saved him, one that was kept on in that basement class-room as a way of keeping the warehoused outcasts occupied. Whenever local news came on, Chris was captivated: Here was a world filled with people who were going somewhere — and others who were tasked with telling their stories. When he wrote to the station manager, asking for a job, the station manager invited him to come in for a tour.

"Walking into that newsroom was like landing on the moon for me," said Chris, who was offered a part-time job covering local sports. Energized, he not only finished high school but parlayed the experience at the station into a full-time career that would bring him to Orlando and a news-pro-duction position at WOFL, the Orlando Fox affiliate. Even-tually, hoping to expand his horizons, he began splitting his time between his day and night classes at the Holt School.

"I was 31 years old and I hadn't been in a classroom since high school. I didn't know if I belonged. But something trans-formative took hold almost immediately. I entered a world of working adults hungry to reengage with the learning process. This was a community dedicated to the goal of finding their voices, speaking their truths, and embracing their fears, their sacrifices and their dreams."

Chris earned an English degree in 2004 and went on to complete the Holt School's Master of Liberal Studies program. He is now chair of the creative writing for entertainment program at Full Sail University. He also volunteers as a story-teller with the Boys & Girls Clubs of Central Florida and hopes to establish a scholarship program for disadvantaged youths at Full Sail. Having climbed up the down staircase himself, he would like very much to help other young people make the same journey.

Barbara Leach
"You are too smart for this."

"None of them knew the color of the sky."

That is the first sentence of *The Open Boat*, a short story written by Stephen Crane, the great 19th-century American novelist who authored *The Red Badge of Courage*. Based on his own experience of being stranded at sea off the Florida coast near Key West, *The Open Boat* is about four exhausted, shipwrecked men in rough waters, clutching the oars of their tiny craft, their eyes too riveted on the monstrous waves that threaten to swamp them to register anything else.

Barbara Leach could relate.

When she read that sentence as part of an assignment for a late-1990s Holt School literature course, it seemed a perfect metaphor for her life up to that point. "If you grow up poor and uneducated, you see everything in small, discreet blocks, paycheck to paycheck," she said. "You don't see the big picture. My father was a convenience-store clerk. My mother taught ceramics classes. I was a waitress, making a couple thousand dollars a month. I couldn't see any further ahead than that."

Leach was 22 when a waiter at the Daytona Beach steakhouse where she worked took her aside. "Do you know what the biggest disappointment at this restaurant is?" he asked her. "You. You are too smart for this. You should go to college.'"

Inspired by her co-worker's challenge, she earned her A.A. degree, moved on to the Holt School two years later after taking a break to care for her terminally ill mother, and graduated in 1999 with a degree in English and recognition as the program's Outstanding Senior. It took three more years and a series of soul-sucking jobs for her to settle on one more step: She applied to law school and was accepted into the Florida State University College of Law.

"I had zero concerns about integrating the information I needed in law school," Barbara recalled. "Some of the other students were afraid to track down the teachers and ask them for advice. I made a habit of it. The rapport I had with my Rollins professors gave me confidence."

Barbara passed the bar exam on her first try. She is now a well-established Orlando family law attorney. Much of her work day is spent handling divorces, helping clients thread their way through taxing chapters in their lives. What she learned in law school gave her what she needs to hash out the legal issues. She also helps her clients, as well as she can, to see beyond the emotional ones. That story about the shipwrecked men, struggling to survive in rough waters, is never too far from her mind.

Jamie Snead Cricks
A Letter from Dumbledore

"I was bad in school," said Jamie Snead Cricks. That is "bad" as in the only high school subject that held her interest was theater, and the thrill of performing in campus productions. She would hide scripts in her math book and memorize lines during class, and after graduating talked her parents into sending her to a performing arts school in New York City.

Jamie supported herself by serving late-night cocktails at the TGI Fridays in Grand Central Station. She lived in a cramped Manhattan apartment that was essentially a women's dorm, with long lines outside the single, shared bathroom every morning. The early morning classes and her first northern winter took the stars out of her eyes. "I didn't love theater quite so much when I was learning how to do it eight or nine hours a day," she said.

So back to Orlando it was, for a job driving a beer cart around at a local golf course. She became a voracious reader, from Kurt Vonnegut novels to political commentary, and soon found herself employing a variation of her old math-class book trick. After one golfer teased her about the serious reading she was doing, she bought a Harlequin romance, left it in plain sight and hid the books she was actually reading. Soon afterward, she left the golf course behind and enrolled at the Holt School, majoring in English.

The class she remembers most vividly was the result of a scheduling mistake. It was a 400-level poetry course devoted to Walt Whitman, a course meant not for beginners such as herself but for upper-level students. In her first week, she said "the teacher used at least two dozen words I didn't understand." But when she got home, she looked up the words, determined to will her way through the class.

The professor, Steve Phelan, had no qualms about setting people straight when they were off course in their thinking. In looks and disposition, he reminded her of Dumbledore, the wizard of Harry Potter renown. For their final project, Phelan had his students create an anthology of poems — 20 by Whitman and 10 by poets Whitman had influenced — complete with explanatory notes about each. She worked hard on the project and her efforts were rewarded in the form of a hard-won compliment from her professor.

"He wrote me the kindest letter about it," she recalled. "He said he liked it so well, he wished he could publish it."

Jamie graduated from the Holt School in 2004. She is now the regional manager of a college-level tutorial service and is working toward a master's degree in instructional technology at the University of Central Florida. She still has the Whitman anthology. Also, the letter from Dumbledore.

Christine Dalton
"I'm going to paint all these buildings."

Of all the fond memories Christine Dalton has from her Brooklyn childhood, none are more enduring than the crosstown subway rides she remembers taking with her father to Coney Island. The wonders of the iconic amusement park surely preoccupied the other children. Meanwhile, Christine had urban renewal on her mind.

Face glued to the dirty subway window, she watched the timeworn Brooklyn neighborhoods slip by in a blur of scruffy shops and weathered brownstones. "I would wonder why nobody was taking care of those places," she recalled. "One day I told my father: 'I know what I'm going to do when I grow up. I'm going to paint all these buildings.'"

Eight years old, and she had a plan.

Whether they know the backstory or not, anyone who encounters Christine these days is likely to gets a sense of the impression those clattering train rides made on one young passenger, and the single-minded enthusiasm for historical preservation that began blossoming in her on the way to the Stillwell Avenue station.

As the product of a broken home, Christine would grow up fast. She was caretaker for four younger siblings by the time she was 11 — by which time her favorite television show was *This Old House*. She married at 16 and was divorced three years later. Soon afterward, she headed for Central Florida at a friend's invitation — having never wavered, through it all, from the journey that started on that crosstown train.

"I always knew I was going to do some sort of work in preserving historic homes and neighborhoods in some way," she said. "I think maybe one of the things that drove me was never having a solid home life of my own. I always wanted a stable and solid home — and what could be more stable and solid than a historic building?"

After moving to Orlando on her own, she got a job managing kiosks at two area malls, saving enough money to enroll at Seminole State College to earn an A.S. in architectural design and construction. She followed that up by earning a B.A. in environmental and growth management studies at the Holt School. Her career has included work as an architectural researcher at Glatting Jackson, an influential Orlando urban planning firm, and 12 years as the Historic Preservation Officer for the City of Sanford, where she helped steer an award-winning streetscape initiative and launched efforts to revitalize the city's African-American communities.

Anything but a staid bureaucrat, Christine takes protecting and enlivening neighborhoods and historical buildings personally. As part of her crusade, she has recently developed a YouTube channel devoted to demystifying the subject and engaging everyday people in the cause. She works as a historic preservation consultant and teaches at both Seminole State College and the Holt School with an unabashed enthusiasm that was typified when one of her classes fell on Valentine's Day. Instead of lecturing in the classroom she took her students on a tour of historic buildings on campus, inviting them to bring their significant others along. Their homework: Write a love letter — not to their sweethearts, but to each one of those venerable old buildings.

Wendy Goodard, Mary Ann de Stefano, Julie Dunsworth, Kären Blumenthal
The Book Club

Major in English and you know you are going to be reading

a lot of books. You would not expect to be called upon to *write* one. But that was the challenge taken on in 2004 by four ambitious Holt School English majors: Wendy Goddard, Mary Ann de Stefano, Julie Dunsworth and Kären Blumenthal, under the tutelage of Lezlie Laws, who arrived at the school in 1989 and directed its writing program for the next 23 years.

Laws learned quickly that the more traditional teaching style she had used at her previous post as director of the first-year writing program at the University of Missouri would not work with the adult learners in her night school classes. Instead she adopted a broader, holistic teaching approach that often extended beyond Orlando Hall's classroom walls. That included creating a monthly, open-to-all, town-and-gown discussion group called First Friday that gave students a chance to mingle with local writers to socialize and solicit feedback about works in progress.

By the early 2000s, Laws had noticed a trend. Her writing classes were often filled with women, many of them empty-nesters, who were facing turning points in their lives, either personal or professional or both. She found herself wondering: Why not seize that as a theme and build a tailor-made writing class around it? So she created an experimental class in which students would write personal essays about transitions or challenges they were going through, solicit and edit similar essays from other Holt School students, and turn the best of the results into a book.

"These students were incredibly eager to learn, but they had also been outside the traditional classroom situation for so long that they tended to be unsure of their intellectual capabilities, wondering whether they even belonged in college at all," Laws recalled. "Yet they had life experience, capabilities, accomplishments and incredible potentials. I realized I had to find a way to cut through those insecurities and tap into what was already there, draw out their innate capacities to be inquisitive and discover patterns and designs — to allow these students to wake up to a new version of themselves."

"We took it very seriously," said one of the four students, Kären Blumenthal, whose essay about dealing with her grief about the loss of a friend was included in the book. "It was very rigorous. This was going to be a book, not something just stapled together. We reviewed over 100 submissions from other students and then acted as editors for those we selected. We met in Orlando Hall on Saturday mornings. It was inspiring to work with Lezlie. She was like a border collie. She would just round us all up."

The book, which was entitled *Shifting Gears*, included 21 stories and essays. Lezlie Laws, irrepressible as ever, is retired from Rollins but maintains a spiritual and creative coaching practice — and a friendship, and ongoing tutelage, with all four of the editors and many of the writers of *Shifting Gears*.

Laura van den Berg
The Accidental Learner

Some students have a goal in mind when they enroll at the Holt School. Others discover themselves along the way, often with dramatic results. Such was the case with Laura van den Berg — once a high school dropout, now teaching at Harvard University.

As a child, Laura had moved from Nashville to Orlando with her parents, Caroline Merritt and the late Egerton van den Berg, an influential attorney who helped found the Legal Aid Society of the Orange County Bar Association and the Greater Orlando Aviation Authority. While a student at Lake Howell High School, she battled depression and an eating disorder, and had difficulty socializing or focusing on her classes.

"I had no motivation whatsoever," she said. "I also had a

serious health issue. I was 5-foot-9 and weighed 108 pounds. I needed inpatient treatment." She rebounded after months of therapy, earning a GED rather than returning to Lake Howell and transferring to the Holt School after two semesters at a community college.

"It was liberating to me, being among nontraditional students, all of us there to try and do something with our lives," she said. Yet, her struggles to focus continued. She was on the verge of leaving school yet again when she took a writing class with the late Phil Deaver, an award-winning author who was fiercely dedicated to his students, and fell in love with contemporary short stories.

Writing had never been an interest of hers — "I never even read anything, let alone write" — but with workshopping assistance from another English professor, Bruce Aufhammer and guidance from creative writing professor Connie Mae Fowler, she began writing short stories of her own.

"Writing was the first thing I ever wanted with real and lasting force," she said. "You might say that the lighthouse of the soul switched on for me."

After graduating with a degree in English in 2005, Laura continued to write, prolifically. Her first volume of short stories, *What the World Will Look Like When All the Water Leaves Us,* was published in 2009. That was followed by another collection of short stories, then by two widely acclaimed novels: *Find Me,* which is about life in a mysterious, post-apocalyptic world besieged by a plague that robs people of their memories, and *The Third Hotel,* about a woman who travels to Havana for a horror-film festival, and while there finds herself encountering — or believing she is encountering — her dead husband.

Laura's stories are rich with surreal oddities, expansive in their geographical and psychological reach, and a little unsettling to read while you are alone. She has been unanimously praised by book critics as one of the most promising fiction writers in the country. At Harvard, she has taught creative writing while writing a book of short stories set to be published in late 2019, and has begun working on a new novel, this one set, for the first time, in Central Florida.

She and her husband, Paul Yoon, who is also a writer, divide their time between an apartment in Cambridge and a home in Sanford, both of which they share with a boisterous Labrador named Oscar.

When Laura looks back at her time at the Holt School and tries to explain why she succeeded there when she had failed to do so elsewhere, she boils it down to this: "Holt gave me the space to fail." Her first few stories, in her own estimation, "were probably terrible." (One of them was published in *Shifting Gears*.) But what she discovered in writing them was how much she wanted them to be good, and how hard she was willing to work to make that happen.

At Rollins, she said, "I found out the world was a much larger place than I thought it was."

"When I think of Laura van den Berg and what a liberal arts education can do, I think of accidental learning," noted English professor Carol Frost, director of the college's Winter with the Writers program — which is now supported, in part, by Laura and her family. "Accidentally, she found what she was meant to do for the rest of her life."

Mike Edwards
Imagining a Future

What is interesting about the extended gap-year expedition that Mike Edwards crafted for himself after graduating from Lake Howell High School is just how sensible he makes it all sound. He tried the traditional route first, enrolling in general studies at Palm Beach Atlantic University in 2003. But when he took stock after his freshman year, he noticed two things. One, he was already $20,000 deep in student-loan debt, and two, he was no further along at knowing what he wanted to do with his life — or as he put it: "I just extrapolated it out and said to myself: 'This is dumb.'"

So, off to Kyrgyzstan he went with a church group to teach English to university students. He took a similar trip to do the same for the children of squatters living in an impoverished inner-city *favela* in Rio de Janeiro. By the time he returned to Orlando, he was fluent in Russian and Portuguese, grateful for things he had taken for granted, surer than ever that he was not the cookie-cutter type and determined to incorporate what he had learned about himself into a career. He just did not know how. As it turned out, there was an answer in his own backyard.

After earning his A.A. degree, Mike enrolled at the Holt School, majoring in international studies and energized most of all by professors and classes that explored the creative process, with sources that ranged from the father/son bonding exploration recounted in *Zen and the Art of Motorcycle Maintenance* to the blend of discipline and spiritualty outlined in *The Artist's Way.*

"The teachers were amazing and extremely accessible," he remembered. "There was a support mechanism baked in the culture."

By the time he graduated in 2010, Mike knew he wanted to devote himself to a creative endeavor, eventually discovering it in Maven Creative, a creative and branding agency operated by three former Lake Howell classmates. Clients range from an artificial intelligence company in Texas to the Orlando Magic and the Orlando Economic Partnership, for whom the agency developed an ad campaign revolving around the slogan: "You don't know the half of it."

It's just too bad that slogan is already taken. As far as Mike is concerned, it could just as easily apply to the Holt School.

Kay Mullaly
"I don't like it when people tell me what I can and can't do."

Kay Mullaly took a long time getting herself to college. Once she arrived, she was in no great hurry to leave. "People would ask me when I was going to graduate. I'd say 'I'm trying not to. I'm having way too much fun.'"

For Kay, the desire to pursue a college education had simmered for decades as she raised five children, juggled part-time jobs to make ends meet and dealt with the challenges of being a military wife, holding down the fort as her husband's career as a Marine and his tours of duty in Vietnam took him far from home. She loved her children, she loved her husband, she loved her life. But she could not help but wonder: What would it be like to be defined "as something other than somebody's mother, somebody's wife?"

The Holt School gave her a chance to find out. In 1994, when the children were raised and the chance came her way, she enrolled at age 58. Some people tried to discourage her, telling her that she did not need a degree. "I don't like it when people tell me what I can or can't do," she said. And she just laughed at the joke among her children, who pretended to be scandalized that their retirement-aged father was dating a college freshman.

Kay really had only one worry, which had to do with younger classmates. "I told everyone when I started that the only thing that would keep me from doing it would be if the other students start treating me like their mother," she said. Working as an administrator and security officer to pay her own tuition, Kay took one class per semester, and finished in 16 years.

Her entire family — husband, sons, daughter, their assorted spouses and grandchildren, including one who drove all night from Raleigh, North Carolina — were present at commencement when she graduated with a degree in English in 2011.

Lisa Caldes
Making the Grade

Lisa Caldes remembers a professor whose teaching method was to work his way through the textbook chapter by chapter, class after class, all semester long. "Someone asked him why he was teaching that way, why there was never any class discussion," she recalled. "He told us: 'You paid a lot for this textbook. I want to make sure you get your money's worth.'"

Even under the best of circumstances, that was not going to be easy for Lisa, who has a learning disability that makes it difficult for her to take tests in close quarters, absorb information by rote and screen out distractions during lectures. She passed the class at a large university "by the skin of my teeth" and kept at her studies with such dogged determination that one of the many college counselors she visited along the way told her: "You're very good at finding a way around your disabilities. You don't let them stop you. You should write a book someday.'"

It took Lisa six years to earn a two-year degree, but she did it, and then went on to earn another one from UCF's Rosen College of Hospitality Management. But after a 15-year career in that profession, she grew restless. She kept thinking back to how engaged she was as a Girl Scout, fascinated by plants and animals on field trips.

She also thought back to a moment of triumph as she

was just barely passing classes on the way to that two-year degree. She had enrolled in a tough-as-nails biology class, and announced in the first session, when the instructor asked why she was taking the course: "I need to raise my GPA." Eyebrows were raised, but Lisa got a B in the class. "That was like getting an A-plus for me," she said.

Then someone told her that she would do well at the Holt School, with its small classes and approachable professors, and she enrolled to earn a degree in environmental studies. When some of her old attention-disorder issues came back to haunt her, some teachers allowed her to do extra credit makeup work.

She graduated in 2016, and now works as an environmental specialist with the Florida Department of Health, a job that calls for her to inspect food-preparation facilities and swimming pools for public safety issues — and occasionally involves a bit of role-reversal. Rollins is in her territory. When she comes to campus to perform inspections, she said, it does not feel like a job. "It feels more like coming home."

Aloma Bratek
"A judgement-free zone"

For most parents, singing to a small child is a simple pleasure. For Aloma Bratek, it was a labor of love. Struggling to connect with a 2-year-old son who has autism, she developed a strategy. She would sing a simple melody to him, over and over. Once the song had become familiar to the child, she would leave out a word at the end of a phrase. Eventually, he would perk up, notice its absence and make eye contact — if only for an instant. It took years, but eventually he began filling in the missing word, thereby taking a precious, painstaking step through the window into that outside world.

This small victory, and others that followed, would ultimately inspire Aloma, who already had some musical training at the University of North Carolina, to enroll at the Holt School to finish her degree in hopes of becoming a music therapist.

In 2016, when it came to creating a capstone senior-year project — which is required of all music majors — she decided, with the help of fellow students, to stage a concert for children with autism and their parents, who could relax in a public setting, free from feeling judged by onlookers who did not understand the spontaneous outbursts and other behaviors common of children with autism. What is commonplace for most parents felt miraculous. "The most profound things happened that day," recalled Aloma.

The concert inspired her to begin staging regular such concerts through a nonprofit initiative called SHARP, which stands for "sharing harmony and raising possibilities." A SHARP concert at Rollins — with the assistance of students and professors — is now an annual event. Shows are also staged at Wekiva Presbyterian Church.

The stated mission of SHARP is "to enrich lives and strengthen communities by providing a variety of musical events for individuals with Autism Spectrum Disorders and other forms of developmental disabilities than can cause significant social, communication and behavioral challenges, and for the families of these individuals." John V. Sinclair, chair of the college's music department, calls the annual SHARP concert at Rollins "a judgement-free zone" — one where music is free to work its magic. For everyone.

Doragnes Bradshaw
A Life of Service

Like many students asked to deliver a commencement address, when Holt School graduate Doragnes Bradshaw rose to address teachers, families and friends as the class of 2018's Outstanding Senior, she began by expressing her gratitude.

To her family for their support. To favorite teachers. To Rick Bommelje, a professor of organizational communication, for his listening lessons. To Christine Jubelt, a Crummer Graduate School of Business lecturer, for her guidance on handling challenges. To Mattea Garcia, an assistant professor of communication, for introducing her to the power of serving others. And to Knowles Memorial Chapel, for just being there.

Doragnes — the unique name is a combination of "Dora" and "Agnes" — had good reason to seek out time to compose herself in the stained-glass solitude of the venerable campus chapel during her studies at the Holt School.

She had enrolled after she and her husband were laid off from the company where they both worked. Then her adoptive father developed Alzheimer's disease. Her younger brother, still in Puerto Rico, died at the age of 35. And her husband contracted a rare form of viral throat cancer. As he was undergoing the radiation treatments and chemotherapy that would eventually cure him, she found strength and refuge in her studies, in the relationships she was developing at school and in volunteer efforts with campus, professional and community organizations — ranging from Student Government posts to the Women's Executive Council of Orlando to Heart of United Way.

"It was Rollins that kept me grounded," she recalled. "My studies, my teachers and the relationships I was developing gave me the strength to keep going." Doragnes not only kept going but became the recipient of the Fiat Lux Award for leadership and was named the Outstanding Senior of the Class of 2018. Soon afterward, she was offered a newly created position of communications manager for the Holt School Office of Admissions, a job to which she will devote herself while pursuing an MBA in the Crummer School.

Doragnes sees the Holt School position as an opportunity to share both the struggles and the rewards of her own journey. "Life is for service," she said. "That's what I discovered about myself at Holt. Now I want to deliver a message to people who feel the way that I did when I started out. I was fearful that I wouldn't fit in, and so worried that what I wanted wasn't attainable. It was for me. It can be for them, too."

Shannon Burrows
The Longest Walk

Nothing helps to put everything in a fresh perspective like a nice long walk. The one that Shannon Burrows took in March 2015 is an interesting example. She and her husband, Patrick, owner of an Orlando-based software firm, had lunch on Park Avenue that day, shared a bottle of wine and decided to take a walk to clear their heads before driving home.

The walk took them to the Rollins campus, where by chance they wandered into the English Department lobby on the first floor of Carnegie Hall. That was where Shannon, who had always been an aspiring writer, found herself eyeing posters, sifting through brochures — and remembering how much she had regretted it, several years before, when family obligations forced her to postpone her work toward a college degree. "I'd always wanted to finish my education, and Patrick knew it," she recalled. "He said: 'Well, here we are. Let's go talk to somebody.'"

An hour later, Shannon had signed up as a Holt School student, majoring in psychology and minoring in writing. She had a general notion of someday becoming a writer, and an equally general notion that she would need a grasp of human behavior to be any good at it.

The writing part was a great adventure, particularly the creative calisthenics involved in a collaborative fiction class she took with Professor Matt Forsythe. But it was the psychology classes that stretched her the most. Workshop classes required a degree of sometimes painful self-revelation that stretched her even further. A class about the sources of prejudice, she said, "took me out of my shell as a middle-class white woman, made me question what I thought I knew. I walked away not just with what I needed for a profession, but with a sure-footed idea of who I wanted to be in the world."

For centuries, the Greeks and Romans believed that there was a connection between wisdom and wine. Ever since that walk she once took to clear her head — the one that started on Park Avenue and ended when she walked across a stage, having graduated summa cum laude, to deliver her class's commencement address as its Outstanding Senior — so does Shannon Burrow.

May Phan

Finding Her Tribe

May Phan has found her tribe. She had to come halfway around the world to do it.

"We can talk about literally anything," she said of her Holt School classmates. "They get my sense of humor. Most of them are older than me, and I appreciate their advice."

Some students might take casual classroom rapport for granted. Not May.

She grew up in Saigon, a city she remembers as being so loud, dirty and crowded that "there was no room to think." Nor was there much room for contemplation at her high school. "In class, they had us study Chinese poems, which I never understood, because there are many very good Vietnamese poets," she said. "And there was always only one approved interpretation of a poem. It was an unwritten rule: If you expressed your own feelings, you were guaranteed to have a bad grade."

May's father, a translator and tour guide, saw the independent spirit in his daughter and encouraged it. He taught her English, gave her Hillary Clinton's autobiography and brought home CDs of American movies that they would watch together. They weren't exactly Hallmark Channel material; much to her mother's distress, many of the movies, which were directed by Quentin Tarantino, featured his trademark of stylized, over-the-top violence. But what May saw beyond that were people who differed from one another — wore what they wanted to, said what they wanted to, moved through a world that made her own look monochromatic by comparison.

With money she saved while working at her mother's shop in Saigon, financial assistance from her grandparents and a scholarship she earned at Rollins via its International Program, May was able to come to Central Florida on a student visa to study computer science at the Holt School. She hopes to graduate in the summer of 2022 and find work as a software engineer.

She misses her parents. She catches herself remembering visits with her grandparents, who lived in the countryside north of Saigon in a house surrounded by a garden so lush with jackfruit, guava, durian and mango trees that she could hide among them.

But sentiment is one thing. Reality is another. That was home once. This is home now.

"I feel like I miss the memories more than the actual place," May said. "If I were to go back now, it would be different. Because things have changed without me — and I have changed myself. This is where I belong."

Wendy Parra

Safe at Last

Like many Holt School students, Wendy Parra juggles

eight-hour workdays with a full load of classes. She has had plenty of practice at it. Wendy has been her family's breadwinner since age 14.

Wendy was a student at Bishop Moore High School when her mother fell seriously ill with thyroid cancer. The teenager supported the two of them with after-school jobs, from clerking at a jewelry store and a dry-cleaning shop to lifeguarding. It was a hard life, but not so hard as the one they had left behind. She and her mother had moved to the U.S. when Wendy was a 5-year-old to escape one of the most dangerous cities in the world, infamous as an epicenter of terror: Medellin, Colombia, where killings and kidnappings were routine thanks to the powerful drug lord Pablo Escobar and the so-called Medellin Cartel.

Wendy adapted quickly to her new life, excelling in her studies at Bishop Moore and becoming a star on the school's tennis team — a talent she hoped to parlay into a college scholarship. A broken wrist during her senior year made that impossible. But she won a scholarship to Rollins from a church where she had worked as a volunteer and is currently enrolled in the 3/2 Accelerated Management Program, which combines a four-year B.A. with a two-year MBA.

Recently, for the first time, she and her mother, who recovered from her illness, were able to return to their homeland for a visit with the extended family they left behind. Wendy's aunts and uncles have been working for years to find and re-acclimate the people of the caves: a generation of adults and children who fled Medellin during the years of terror to live in caves in the mountains that ring the city. Over the years, many died of hunger. Many of those who survived do not know any other way of life and are afraid to return to civilization.

"My family has a halfway house," she said. "We're bringing the people back from the mountains. We teach them how to farm, how to have gardens, and that it's safe to come back. We teach the children little things, like how to ride bikes. We show them they don't have to be afraid anymore."

The 22-year-old business major returned to Orlando with a fresh perspective on the future she is building for herself at the Holt School. She is hoping for a career in international exporting. She is grateful, in the meantime, to be safe in her own skin, to live without fear.

Like most Holt School students, she combines classes in the evenings with employment by day. She has her first full-time job, rising at 5:30 weekday mornings to head for the Winter Park Tennis Center, where she is an assistant manager, before heading to campus for late-afternoon and evening classes.

"I'm more relaxed right now than I've ever been in my life," she said. "Sometimes, there are moments in my day when I look around and I think: 'Oh, I don't have anything to do right this second.'"

Given the life she has led so far, it's a very strange feeling indeed.

Ephemera

A FOND FAREWELL

When Hamilton Holt spoke at his final commencement ceremony in June 1949, he shared with faculty, students, trustees and community leaders many nuggets of wisdom that are as applicable today as when he uttered them more than 70 years ago. Here are some excerpts:

"This morning there are two things that keep vibrating in my mind and heart — first gratitude for your kindness and goodness to me during the past 24 years, and second, the memories of the good fight we have fought and the faith we have kept in our common adventure. Our adventure, thank God, has been fundamentally an adventure of service, and service always begats love."

"This is my commencement as well as that of the seniors. The seniors go out into the morning sunshine. I go out into the evening shade. So be it. I cannot speak for the seniors, but I may speak for myself. Therefore, I would say a word of affection and farewell to each of the four groups assembled here with whom I have been so long and so closely associated — the trustees, the faculty, the staff and the students."

First, My Fellow Trustees

"I have spent most of my life on the firing line, trying to turn minorities into majorities. That usually makes trouble. I must have tried your patience many a time, but if so, you never complained. At all events you have never brought me on the carpet before you."

"Make the chief aim of your stewardship the maintenance of greater and ever greater security and freedom of the faculty, staff and student body. After all, those are the chief reasons for your existence."

"Keep the college small but make it a great small college. Material growth for its own sake is only a confusion of greatness with bigness."

"Do not curtail the powers you have wisely delegated in bylaws to the faculty. Continue to grant them complete supervision over the curriculum and the students."

"Pay the faculty and staff the highest salaries you can possibly afford, not the lowest salaries they will accept. Nothing will keep up their morale more than that."

"Never dismiss a faculty member because his views differ from yours, unless you would be willing in turn for a majority of faculty to dismiss one of you for your opinions."

"Do not treat the students nor permit them to be treated as children."

"Fill vacancies on the board with young, vital and liberal men and women of both achievement and promise. Otherwise your board will grow conservative with the passing years and reactionary."

"Businessmen are essential to any well-balanced board of trustees but keep them in the minority. Rollins is an educational institution, not a bank or a department store. Imagine a successful business concern filling its board with educators."

"When the president and the faculty break new paths, do not become frightened just because some powerful institutions like Harvard or the Rockefeller Foundation or the American Council on Education raise their eyebrows. Welcome advice but think and act for yourselves."

"Balance the budget and keep it balanced. Be satisfied with nothing else. Small colleges will not survive the competition of state-supported institutions unless they adopt policies that fit the post-war age. Dare to formulate those policies."

"Have a heart. Do not make the president do all the money raising."

To the Faculty and Staff

"I have never known you as a group to meet any obstacle you could not surmount by free discussion, tolerance of each other's opinion and the will to cooperate. Though we have gone through many trials and tribulations together, yet somehow the light has always emerged at the end."

"The trustees have never been able to pay what you deserve, yet I am proud to say that they have let me fulfill the promise I made to them when I first assumed office, namely that every year I would expect to increase the total amount of money spent for faculty and staff salaries."

"Seek truth wherever truth is found; follow truth wherever truth may lead; teach truth and nothing but the truth."

"Achieve and hold your mastery of your chosen art or science. Break paths bravely where you may. Follow humbly where you must. You promised all these things when you were installed in the faculty, but you may have forgotten them."

"If the trustees or the president should become lax in academic leadership, take the leadership into your own hands. After all, you are the educators."

"Teach students rather than subjects. Give students the same courtesy, respect and affection that you crave of them."

"Minimize marks, grades, recitations, lectures, examinations, certificates, diplomas and degrees. Maximize personal contacts within and without the classroom. Imitate Socrates. You may get a Plato."

"Cut out cliques, gripes, gossip, pedantry and highbrowism – the chief of faculty sins."

"Jesus preached to the multitude, taught his disciples and cast out devils. Follow His example: lecture to the many; teach the few; wrestle with the individual."

"The three paramount functions of a faculty are teaching, research and public service. But the greatest of these is teaching."

To the Students

"We of the older generation hold the entrenched positions. You cannot share them with us unless you fight us and drive us out of our strongholds (which is usually impossible). Or unless we invite you to join us. We do not invite you, however, if we do not like you, and we do not like you unless we approve of you. So, it is wise for you to cultivate us a little. ... You will have to do the same when you become old and set in your ways."

"I have learned more from you than you have learned from me. Youth is idealistic; age is cynical. You think success is beckoning you; that you will be happily married; that you will be healthy, wealthy and wise. Keep on thinking these things, for faith moves mountains and faith will make them come true."

"You have not yet gained the wisdom we have, for wisdom comes from experience. So, I do not blame you for not having much wisdom. But I do blame myself and people my age for losing their idealism. You have helped me keep my idealism."

"If I had my life to live over again there are not a few things that I would do differently, but I will mention only two. First, I would cultivate my parents more than I did or more than most young people do. After they are gone it is too late. Second, I would try to fulfill in myself at the earliest moment Huxley's definition of an educated man – namely one who knows everything about something and something about everything."

"Those who are returning next year will find another man in my place. Please give him all the support, friendship and affection you have given me."

"For those of you who are graduating into the world, where realities pervade, I wish you all happiness and success. But do not expect to be treated as grownups by older people until you are about 30 years of age. And do not expect results without sustained effort. Nothing in life worthwhile has come easily."

Self-Evident Truths

"No college can educate you. All college is self-education. The college can stimulate, advise and point the way. But the path must be trod by you."

"The human race has never and will never put physical prowess above mental or moral achievement. Do not, therefore, put athletics first."

"Budget your time and your money. You will be surprised what will happen."

"Get happiness from your contemporaries. Get wisdom from your elders. Cultivate, therefore, your college mates and the faculty."

"If you mistake liberty for license, both liberty and license will be taken away from you."

"Cultivate and enjoy the opposite sex. But let not love-making be a public exhibition. Love-making should be a personal, not a vicarious, experience."

"If fraternities are good for the few, they are good for the many. But cut the memberships down to about 20, which is the limit of intimacy."

"Major in courses that you like and therefore come most easily. Minor in the courses you dislike and therefore come the hardest."

"Choose the professor rather than the course. The professor may be alive!"

"I shall miss you, my sons and daughters, in the coming days. I shall miss your happy laughter coming through the open windows of my office. I shall miss the waving of your hands as we pass on the campus. I shall miss the quiet talks I have had in my home with you, whether singly or in groups. Write me sometimes and tell me of your trials and triumphs. May the latter far exceed the former."

A Last Word

"If any of you ... find yourself in the northeast corner of Connecticut, near the ancient and temple-hilled town of Woodstock, stop in at my old colonial homestead on the village common for an old home week together for overnight or at least a meal. I will show you my ancestral walk of stepping stones which originated the Rollins Walk of Fame. I will take you on a personally conducted tour of my antiques, including a document printed and published by my 'Uncle Ben' Franklin (I am descended from his sister, Mary); a woodcut by Paul Revere and a ladder-backed caned chair that Lincoln made with his own hands for Ann Rutledge.

I will take you back of the barn to the brow of the hill and there let you behold one of the most beautiful pastoral scenes of peace and plenty in all of New England. If you stay for the afternoon, I will give you a ... buggy ride behind my big, gentle white farm horse, George, who is a family institution and whom I raised from a colt. We will jog over some of the elm-shaded back country ribboned roads while Poin, my setter (poin-setter) accompanies us, jumping over the roadside walls to sniff for rabbit and quail, cooling himself in each running brooklet and having a near fight with every farm dog.

We will light a log fire in the big open stone fireplace with the Dutch oven at the side, bring a dish of walnuts and a pitcher of cider and spend the evening talking over the little college we all so love — the struggles of its past, the achievements of its present and the promise of its ever-broadening future."

A WAY TO DISARM:
A PRACTICAL PROPOSAL
BY HAMILTON HOLT

At the outbreak of the Great War in 1914, Holt revisited the topic of an international federation in "The Way to Disarm: A Practical Proposal." The editorial, which appeared in The Independent *and other publications in September of that year, was widely praised. The response to it encouraged Holt and Theodore Marburg, a long-time activist in international peace movements and a previous U.S. minister to Belgium, to form The League to Enforce Peace, subsidized by industrialist Andrew Carnegie's World Peace Foundation, in 1915. Now-former President William Howard Taft, at Holt's behest, agreed to chair the new organization, which is said to have provided the philosophical underpinnings for the League of Nations.*

IN HIS FAMOUS ESSAY, Perpetual Peace, published in 1795, Immanueal Kant, perhaps the greatest intellect the world has ever produced, declared that we never can have universal peace until the world is politically organized and it will never be possible to organize the world politically until the people, not the kings, rule. And he added that the peoples of the earth must cultivate and attain the spirit of hospitality and good will towards all races and nations.

If this be the true philosophy of peace, then when the Great War is over, and the stricken sobered peoples set about to rear a new civilization on the ashes of the old, they cannot hope to abolish war unless they are prepared to extend democracy everywhere, to banish hatred from their hearts, and to organize the international realm on a basis of law rather than force. The questions of the extension of democracy and the cultivation of benevolence are domestic ones. They can hardly be brought about by joint action of the nations. World organization and disarmament, however, can be provided for in the terms of peace or by international agreement thereafter. As the United States seems destined to play an important part in the great reconstruction at the end of the war, this is perhaps the most important question now before American statesmanship.

Law or War

THE ONLY TWO powers that ever have governed or ever can govern human beings are reason and force—law and war. If we do not have the one, we must have the other. The peace movement is the process of substituting law for war. Peace follows justice, justice follows law, law follows political organization. The world has already achieved peace, through justice, law and political organization in hamlets, towns, cities, states and even in the forty-six sovereign civilized nations of the world.

But in that international realm over and above each nation, in which each nation is equally sovereign, the only final way for a nation to secure its rights is by the use of force. Force, therefore — or war as it is called when exerted by a nation against another nation — is at present the only final method of settling international differences. In other words, the nations are in that state of civilization today where, without a qualm, they claim the right to settle their disputes in a manner which they would actually put their own subjects to death for imitating. The peace problem, then, is nothing but the problem of finding ways and means of doing between the nations what has already been done within the nations. International law follows private law. The "United Nations" follow the United States.

At present international law has reached the same state of development that private law reached in the tenth century. Professor T. J. Lawrence (in his essay The Evolution of Peace) distinguishes four stages in the evolution of private law:

1. Kinship is the sole bond; revenge and retaliation are unchecked, there being no authority whatever.

2. Organization is found an advantage and tribes under a chief subdue undisciplined hordes. The right of private vengeance within the tribe is regulated but not forbidden.

3. Courts of justice exist side by side with a limited right of vengeance.

4. Private war is abolished; all disputes being settled by the courts.

It is evident that in international relations we are entering into the third stage, because the nations have already created an international tribunal which exists side by side with the right of self-redress or war.

Like the American Confederation

FURTHERMORE, A CAREFUL study of the formation of the thirteen American colonies from separate states into our present compact Union discloses the fact that the nations today are in the same stage of development that the American colonies were about the time of their first confederation. As the United States came into existence by the establishment of the Articles of Confederation and the Continental Congress, so the "United Nations" came into existence by the establishment of The Hague Court and the recurring Hague Conferences; The Hague Court being the promise of the Supreme Court of the world and The Hague Conferences being the prophecy of the parliament of man.

We may look with confidence, therefore, to a future in which the world will have an established court with jurisdiction over all questions, self-governing conferences with power to legislate on all affairs of common concern, and an executive power of some form to carry on the decrees of both. To deny this is to ignore all the analogies of private law and the whole trend of the world's political history since the Declaration of Independence. As Secretary of State Knox[1] said not long ago: "We have reached a point when it is evident that the future holds in store a time when war shall cease, when the nations of the world shall realize a federation as real and vital as that now subsisting between the component parts of a single state."

It would be difficult to recall a more far-visioned statement than this emanating from the chancellery of a great state. It means nothing less than that the age-long dreams of the poets, the prophets and the philosophers have at last entered the realms of practical statesmanship. But now the Great War has come upon us. "When the storm is spent and the desolation is complete; when the flower of the manhood of Europe has passed into eternal night; when famine and pestilence have taken their tithe of childhood and age" will then the exhausted and beggared that live on be able to undertake the task of establishing that World Government which the historian Freeman has called "the most finished and the most artificial production of political ingenuity?"[2]

---

1 Philander Chase Knox (1853-1921) was the U.S. Secretary of State under President William Howard Taft.

2 Edward Augustus Freeman (1823-1892) is best known for *The History of*

The Hague or the League of Peace

IF IT CAN BE done at all it can only be done in one of two ways. First. By building on the foundations already laid at The Hague, the Federation of the World. Second. By establishing a great Confederation or League of Peace, composed of those few nations who through political evolution or the suffering of war have at last seen the light and are ready here and now to disarm. It is obvious that the time is scarcely ripe for voluntary and universal disarmament by joint agreement. There are too many medieval-minded nations still in existence. The Federation of the World must still be a dream for many years to come.

The immediate establishment of a League of Peace, however, would in fact constitute a first step toward world federation and does not offer insuperable difficulties. The idea of a League of Peace is not novel. All federal governments and confederations of governments, both ancient and modern, are essentially leagues of peace, even though they may have functions to perform which often lead directly to war.

The ancient Achaean League of Greece, the Confederation of Swiss Cantons, the United Provinces of The Netherlands, the United States of America, and the Commonwealth of Australia are the most nearly perfect systems of federated governments known to history. Less significant, but none the less interesting to students of government, are the Latin League of 30 cities, the Hanseatic League, the Holy Alliance, and in modern times, the German Confederation. Even the recent Concert of Europe was a more or less inchoate League of Peace. The ancient leagues, as well as the modern confed-

---

the *Norman Conquest of England,* published in six volumes. As a professor of modern history at Oxford University, he studied and wrote about federalism. The rest of the quote Holt references is: "It is hardly possible that federal government can attain its perfect form except in a highly refined age, and among a people whose political education has already stretched over many generations."

erations, have generally been unions of offense and defense. They stood ready, if they did not actually propose, to use their common forces to compel outside states to obey their will. Thus, they were as frequently leagues of oppression as leagues of peace.

The Problem of Force

THE PROBLEM OF the League of Peace is therefore the problem of the use of force. Force internationally expressed is measured in armaments. The chief discussion which has been waged for the past decade between the pacifists and militarists has been over the question of armaments. The militarists claim that armaments insure national safety. The pacifists declare they inevitably lead to war. Both disputants insist that the present war furnishes irrefutable proof of their contentions.

As is usual in cases of this kind the shield has two sides. The confusion has arisen from a failure to recognize the threefold function of force:

1. Force used for the maintenance of order — police force.
2. Force used for attack — aggression.
3. Force used to neutralize aggression — defense.

Police force is almost wholly good. Offense is almost wholly bad. Defense is a necessary evil and exists simply to neutralize force employed for aggression. The problem of the peace movement is how to abolish the use of force for aggression, and yet to maintain it for police purposes. Force for defense will of course automatically cease when force for aggression is abolished. The chief problem then of a League of Peace is this: Shall the members of the League "not only keep the peace themselves, but prevent by force if necessary its being broken by others," as ex-President Roosevelt suggested in his Nobel Peace Address delivered at Christiania, May 5, 1910?

Or shall its force be exercised only within its membership and thus be on the side of law and order and never on the side of arbitrary will or tyranny? Or shall it never be used at all?

Whichever one of these conceptions finally prevails the Great War has conclusively demonstrated that as long as War Lords exist defensive force must be maintained. Hence the League must be prepared to use force against any nations which will not forswear force. Nevertheless, a formula must be devised for disarmament. For unless it is a law of nature that war is to consume all the fruits of progress disarmament somehow and some way must take place. How then can the maintenance of a force for defense and police power be reconciled with the theory of disarmament?

The Constitution of the League

IN THIS WAY: Let the League of Peace be formed on the following five principles:

First. The nations of the League shall mutually agree to respect and guarantee the territory and sovereignty of each other.

Second. All questions that cannot be settled by diplomacy shall be arbitrated.

Third. The nations of the League shall provide a periodical assembly to make all rules to become law unless vetoed by a nation within a stated period.

Fourth. The nations shall disarm to the point where the combined forces of the League shall be a certain percent higher than those of the most heavily armed nation or alliance outside of the League. Detailed rules for this pro-rata disarmament shall be formulated by the Assembly.

Fifth. Any member of the League shall have the right to withdraw on due notice or may be expelled by the unanimous vote of the others.

The advantages that a nation would gain in becoming a member of such a league are manifest. The risk of war would be eliminated within the League. Obviously, the only things that are vital to a nation are its land and its independence. Since each nation in the League will have pledged itself to respect and guarantee the territory and the sovereignty of every other, a refusal to do so will logically lead to compulsion by the other members of the League or expulsion from the League. Thus, every vital question will be automatically reserved from both war and arbitration while good faith lasts. All other questions are of secondary importance and can readily be arbitrated.

By the establishment of a periodical assembly a method would be devised whereby the members of the League could develop their common intercourse and interests as far and as fast as they could unanimously agree upon ways and means. As any law could be vetoed by a single nation, no nation could have any fear that it would be coerced against its will by a majority vote of the other nations. By such an assembly the League might in time agree to reduce tariffs and postal rates and in a thousand other ways promote commerce and comity among its members.

As a final safeguard against coercion by the other members of the League, each member will have the right of secession on due notice. This would prevent civil war within the League. The right of expulsion by the majority will prevent one nation by its veto power indefinitely blocking all progress of the League.

The Scrap of Paper

BUT IT WILL BE said that all these agreements will have no binding effect in a crisis. A covenant is a mere "scrap of paper" whose provisions will be violated by the first nation which fancies it is its interest to do so. In order to show that their faith is backed up by deeds, however, the nations on entering the League agree to disarm to a little above the danger point. This is the real proof of their conversion to the peace idea.

It will be noticed that no attempt is made to define how the force of the League shall be exerted. This is left for the decision of the Assembly of the League. The suggestion that "the nation shall disarm to the point where the combined forces of the League shall be a certain percent higher than those of the most heavily armed nation or alliance outside the League," implies that the forces of the League shall be used for the neutralization of the aggressive force of nations outside the League — that is, for defense. But shall not the force of the League be also used as police power, that is, aggressively to maintain international law and order? A League with power to exert its will without any constitutional limitations might easily become a League of Oppression. It would have the right to be judge and sheriff in its own cause, a violation of the first principles of justice.

It would not be over-sanguine to expect that the Assembly of the League would vote that the armaments of the League should be brought into regular and concerted action for compelling obedience to the judicial decisions of the Court of the League both among members of the League and those outside who have agreed to this method of settling their disputes. It may even be anticipated that the force of the League will be used to assist one of the members of the League in a controversy with a nation outside the League that has not previously agreed to resort to arbitration and that refuses so to agree upon request.

Such an agreement would tend to enthrone law and suppress arbitrary action. Entering a League with such a policy would not subject the United States to the necessity of waging war thru the erroneous action of its allies in an "entangling alliance," but only to extend the reign of law. This is the fundamental purpose of our Government and perhaps the United States is now ready to go thus far.

Thus, the nations which join the League will enjoy all the economic and political advantages which come from mutual cooperation and the extension of international friendship and at the same time will be protected by an adequate force against the aggressive force of the greatest nation or alliance outside the League. The League therefore reconciles the demand of the pacifists for the limitation of armaments and eventual disarmament and the demand of the militarists for the protection that armament affords. Above all the establishment of such a league will give the liberal parties in the nations outside the League an issue on which they can attack their governments so as sooner or later to force them to apply to the League for membership. As each one enters there will be another pro rata reduction of the military forces of the League down to the armament of the next most powerful nation or alliance outside it; until finally the whole world is federated in a brotherhood of universal peace and armies and navies are reduced to an international police force.

This is the plan for a League of Peace. Is the hour about to strike when it can be realized? If only the United States, France and England would lead in its formation, Belgium, Holland, Switzerland, Denmark, Norway, Sweden, Argentina, Brazil, Chile and others might perhaps join. Even if Russia and Germany and Japan and Italy stayed out, the League would still be powerful and large enough to begin with every auspicious hope of success.

The Destiny of the United States

IT WOULD SEEM to be the manifest destiny of the United States to lead in the establishment of such a league. The United States is the world in miniature. The United States is the greatest league of peace known to history. The United States is a demonstration to the world that all the races and peoples of the earth can live in peace under one form of government, and its chief value to civilization is a demonstration of what this form of government is.

Prior to the formation "of a more perfect union" our original 13 states were united in a confederacy strikingly similar to that now proposed on an international scale. They were obliged by the articles of this confederacy to respect each other's territory and sovereignty, to arbitrate all questions among themselves, to assist each other against any foreign foe, not to engage in war unless called upon by the confederation to do so or actually invaded by a foreign foe, and not to maintain armed forces in excess of the strength fixed for each state by all the states in congress assembled.

It is notable that security against aggression from states inside or outside the American Union accompanied the agreement to limit armaments. Thus, danger of war and size of armaments were decreased contemporaneously. It is also notable that from the birth of the Republic to this hour every President of the United States has advocated peace through justice. From the first great Virginian to the last great Virginian, all have abhorred what Thomas Jefferson called "the greatest scourge of mankind." When the Great War is over and the United States is called upon to lead the nations in reconstructing a new order of civilization, why might not Woodrow Wilson do on a world scale something similar to what George Washington did on a continental scale?

Stranger things than this have happened in history. Let us add to the Declaration of Independence a Declaration of *Interdependence*.

WHISPERIN' BILL

BY IRVING BACHELLER

Irving Bacheller's first published work of fiction, which appeared in The Independent, *was a poem called "Whisperin' Bill." In it, an elderly farmer describes the impact of the Civil War on his son, a soldier who was injured and returned home after "a bullet killed his mind but left his body livin'." The timeless message about the toll of war, even on those who physically survive the experience, sparked the poem's revival in the years preceding World War I and World War II. In 1933, Metro Goldwyn Mayer adapted "Whisperin' Bill" as a short film starring character actor and one-time vaudevillian Charles "Chic" Sale. In the film, unlike Bacheller's poem, the person to whom the farmer relates his story is not a census taker but a candidate for Congress. It was broadcast for the first time in decades in 2014 on Turner Classic Movies. The poem, which remains as timely today as ever, is reproduced here as it was first published in 1890.*

So you're takin' the census, mister? There's three of us livin'
    still,
My wife an' I, an' our only son, that folks call Whisperin' Bill;
But Bill couldn't tell ye his name, an' so it's hardly worth
    givin',

For ye see a bullet killed his mind an' left his body livin'.

Set down for a minute, mister. Ye see, Bill was only fifteen
At the time o' the war, an' as likely a boy as ever this world
      has seen;
An' what with the news o' the battles lost, the speeches an' all
      the noise,
I guess every farm in the neighborhood lost a part of its crop
      o' boys.

'Twas harvest time when Bill left home; every stalk in the
      fields o' rye
Seemed to stand tip-toe to see him off an' wave him a fond
      good-bye;
His sweetheart was here with some other girls — the sassy
      little miss!
An' pretendin' she wanted to whisper 'n his ear, she gave him
      a rousing' kiss.

Oh, he was a han'some feller, an' tender an' brave an' smart,
An' though he was bigger than I was, the boy had a woman's
      heart.
I couldn't control my feelin's, but I tried with all my might,
An' his mother an' me stood a-cryin' till Bill was out o' sight.

His mother she often told him, when she knew he was goin'
      away,
That God would take care o' him, maybe, if he didn't fergit to
      pray;
An' on the bloodiest battle-fields, when bullets whizzed in
      the air,
An' Bill was a-fightin' desperit, he used to whisper a prayer.

Oh, his comrades has often told me that Bill never flinched a
bit
When every second a gap in the ranks told where a ball had
hit.
An' one night, when the field was covered with the awful
harvest o' war,
They found my boy 'mongst the martyrs o' the cause he was
fightin' for.

His fingers were clutched in the dewy grass — oh, no, sir, he
wasn't dead.
But hey lay sort o' helpless an' crazy with a rifle-ball in his
head;
An' if Bill had really died that night I'd give all I've got worth
givin';
For ye see the bullet had killed his mind and left his body
livin'.

An officer wrote an' told us how the boy had been hurt in the
fight.
But he said that the doctors reckoned that they could bring
him around all right.
An' then we heard from a neighbor, disabled at Malvern Hill,
That he thought in the course of a week or so he'd be comin'
home with Bill.

We was that anxious t' see him we'd set up an talk o' nights
Till the break o' day had dimmed the stars an' put out the
northern lights;
We waited an' watched for a month or more, an' the summer
was nearly past,
When a letter came one day that said they'd started fer home
at last.

I'll never fergit the day Bill came — 'twas harvest time again —

An' the air blown over the yellow fields was sweet with the
    scent o' the grain;

The dooryard was full o' the neighbors, who had come to
    share our joy,

An' all of us sent up a mighty cheer at the sight o' that soldier
    boy.

An' all of a sudden somebody said: "My God! Don't the boy
    know his mother?"

An' Bill stood a-whisperin', fearful like, an' starin' from one
    to another:

"Don't be afraid, Bill," he said to himself, as he stood in his
    coat o' blue;

"Why, God'll take care o' you, Bill, God'll take care o' you."

He seemed to be loadin' an' firin' a gun, an' to act like a man
    who hears

The awful roar o' the battle-field a-soundin' in his ears;

I saw that bullet had touched his brain an' somehow made it
    blind,

With the picture o' war before his eyes an' the fear o' death in
    his mind.

I grasped his hand, an' says I to Bill, "Don't ye remember me?

I'm yer father — don't ye know me? How frightened ye seem
    to be!"

But the boy kep' a-whisperin' to himself, as if 'twas all he knew,

"God'll take care o' you, Bill, God'll take care o' you."

He's never known us since that day, nor his sweetheart, an'
    never will;

Father an' mother an' sweetheart are all the same to Bill.

An' many's the time his mother sets up the whole night
   through,
An' smoothes his head an' says: "Yes, Bill, God'll take care
   o' you."

Unfortunit? Yes, but we can't complain. It's a livin' death
   more sad,
When the body clings to a life o' shame an' the soul has gone
   to the bad.
An' Bill is out o' the reach o' harm an' danger of every kind —
We only take care o' his body, but God takes care o' his mind.

TIMELINE

1890: Irving Bacheller, founder of the first syndicated news service in the U.S., submits a poem called "Whisperin' Bill to *The Independent*. The poem is published, although Holt does not yet work at the magazine. Bacheller and Holt become acquainted in the late 1890s.

1894-95: Back-to-back freezes decimate Central Florida's citrus crop and the Winter Park Company defaults on payments to the estate of Francis Bangs Knowles, a former Rollins trustee whose daughter would fund Knowles Memorial Chapel. The company surrenders 1,200 building lots to the Knowles heirs.

1904: Chicago industrialist Charles Hosmer Morse, a seasonal resident and a Rollins trustee, buys the Knowles family holdings for $10,000 (the equivalent of about $280,000 today).

1910: Holt delivers a lecture, "The Federation of the World," on the Rollins campus. It is his first known visit to Winter Park.

1914: Holt again lectures in Winter Park and, at the invitation of Rollins President William F. Blackman, joins the college's board of trustees. He serves a two-year term but resigns due to other commitments.

1914: As the U.S. entry into World War I looms, Holt writes "The Way to Disarm: A Practical Proposal" that advocates world government. The article rallies internationalists and provides the philosophical underpinning for the League of Nations.

1917: Morse instructs his manager, Harold A. "Harley" Ward, to ensure that Bacheller, a Connecticut resident who winters at the Seminole Hotel, buys property in Winter Park and relocates permanently.

1918: Bacheller moves to Winter Park and builds a home he dubs Lake O' the Isles on the Isle of Sicily. He quickly establishes himself as Winter Park's foremost celebrity.

1920: Holt writes "The Ideal College President" for *The Independent*, which essentially offers an outline for how he would ultimately approach the presidency of Rollins.

1924: Holt again lectures at Rollins and informally discusses the vacant presidency with trustees. However, William Clarence Weir is hired.

1924: Holt, disillusioned by the U.S. Senate's failure to ratify the Treaty of Versailles and join the League of Nations, runs as a Democrat for the U.S. Senate from Connecticut.

1925: Weir abruptly resigns the Rollins presidency, ostensibly for health reasons, although he opens a real estate office in Orlando the following year.

1925: Bacheller, in his capacity as a trustee, writes Holt and offers him the Rollins presidency. After some negotiation, Holt accepts and is appointed.

1925: Holt hires the first of his "golden personalities," Edwin Osgood Grover, and gives him the whimsical title "professor of books."

1926: Holt launches a fundraising drive in which he seeks to raise $300,000 from locals. Although commitments exceeding that amount are made, the collapse of the Florida land boom makes much of it impossible to collect.

1926: Holt implements the two-hour conference plan, which establishes a four-period day, with two-hour classes meeting three times weekly.

1927: The first Animated Magazine is held, with Grover as "publisher" and Holt as "editor" of the outdoor event, which features speakers from the world of literature, including Irving Bacheller.

1929: Holt hires the first adult education star attraction, British-born lecturer John Martin. Martin is a socialist, while his wife, Prestonia Mann Martin, owns a rustic socialist resort in the Adirondacks.

1929: Essayist Corra Mae Harris, who came to Holt's attention when she wrote him a letter at *The Independent* defending lynching, writes "The Town that Became a University," which describes the impact Holt has had on Winter Park's intellectual ambience.

1929: Rollins earns accreditation from the Southern Association of Colleges and Schools.

1930: President Calvin Coolidge visits Rollins, but characteristically does not speak.

1931: Holt convenes "The Curriculum for the Liberal Arts College," a colloquium headlined by educational philosopher John Dewey. The results encourage Holt to adopt a new curriculum dubbed "individualization in education."

1932: John Martin is the victim of a brutal attack by a young acquaintance. The story of the erudite professor and "Hammer Boy" makes national headlines. Martin, however, fully recovers.

1934: President Franklin D. Roosevelt speaks at Rollins. He receives an L.H.D., while Eleanor Roosevelt receives the Algernon Sydney Sullivan Award.

1935: Grover founds a summer adult education program

called the Banner Elk School of English (later the Blowing Rock School of English) in the Blue Ridge Mountains of North Carolina.

1936: Alexena "Zenie" Holt and Mertie Grover, wives of Holt and Grover, die within 24 hours of one another and the Animated Magazine is cancelled for the first time.

1936: Holt announces the college's first formal Adult Education Program, which consists primarily of cultural enrichment lectures from faculty members and "winter faculty" visitors.

1943: Holt hires George Sauté, who would direct the precursor to the Holt School, as an assistant professor of mathematics.

1944: John Martin retires, but the John Martin Lecture Series continues as an adult education staple. Martin himself is a frequent lecturer, as is Prestonia Mann Martin.

1946: President Harry S. Truman visits Rollins and receives an L.L.H. as well as an "open sermon" on world government from Holt.

1946: Holt convenes the Rollins College Conference on World Government and issues "An Appeal to the Peoples of the World."

1947: Holt forms the Institute for World Government, which is directed by associate professor of English Rudolph von Abele.

1947: Von Abele leaves Rollins and Sauté is appointed director of the Institute for World Government.

1948: Holt submits his resignation.

1949: Paul A. Wagner is appointed to the presidency of Rollins. In anticipation of an enrollment drop due to the Korean War, he fires one-third of the faculty (including Sauté) and precipitates a campus crisis that makes national headlines. He belatedly resigns in 1951.

1951: Holt dies in Woodstock, Connecticut.

1951: Hugh F. McKean is appointed to the presidency of Rollins. (His administration and Wagner's briefly overlap when Wagner refuses to recognize the legality of his dismissal and remains in the president's office.)

1951: Operation Bootstrap, in cooperation with the U.S. Air Force, is launched. Classes are held on campus and at local military bases.

1951: McKean launches Courses for the Community, which includes programs for children and adults, and appoints Sauté as director. Sauté later says the program was started to rehabilitate the college's image in the wake of the Wagner Affair. As in the Holt Era, the courses are primarily cultural enrichment lectures.

1953: Alphonse "Phonsie" Carlo, a violinist and assistant professor of music, begins what would become the Florida Symphony Youth Orchestra through the School of Creative Arts, a division of Courses for the Community.

1954: Operation Bootstrap is placed under Sauté's purview. Courses at the Orlando Air Force Base and the Pinecastle Air Force Base are moved on campus, and Operation Bootstrap is phased out by 1960. Patrick Air Force Base becomes an extension operation of the college.

1957: The Martin Company relocates to Orlando, pressuring Rollins to offer technology-oriented courses. The only local alternative is Orlando Junior College, a discriminatory private school championed by publisher Martin Andersen, who has exerted political pressure to keep a state-supported junior college out of Central Florida.

1957: At the behest of the Martin Company, Rollins offers an evening program leading to a Master of Business Administration.

1959: Again at the behest of the Martin Company, Rollins offers a Master of Science in Physics degree.

1960: The Rollins College Institute for General Studies is launched. It encompasses Courses for the Community and the School of Creative Arts as well as the Graduate Programs and the School of General Studies, which offers a Bachelor of General Studies degree. The Patrick Air Force Base program becomes a branch of the Institute for General Studies. A Master of Arts in Teaching degree is added.

1961: McKean announces a Rollins College Space Science Institute at Andersen Hall, a downtown Orlando mansion given to the college by the *Orlando Sentinel's* publisher. The project never gets off the ground.

1965: The Rollins College Institute for General Studies is dissolved and replaced by the Central Florida School for Continuing Studies.

1964: A $1 million gift from businessman Roy E. Crummer is used to build and endow the Roy E. Crummer School of Finance and Business Administration (later the Roy E. Crummer Graduate School of Business).

1967: McKean proposes "Everyone's College" through which low-cost degrees are accessible through television, radio and videotape.

1967: Summer Day Camp for children begins through the School of Creative Arts.

1969: Sauté, who has reached age 65, is compelled to retire.

1969: McKean announces his retirement.

1969: Jack Critchfield is appointed to the presidency of Rollins.

1969: Daniel F. Riva is named director of the Central Florida Institute for General Studies.

1970: Riva, thanks to federal Law Enforcement Assistance Administration funds, introduces an undergraduate criminal justice curriculum at the Central Florida Institute for General Studies. Fire safety administration soon follows.

1972: The Central Florida School for Continuing Studies is renamed the School of Continuing Education, through which Bachelor of Arts, Bachelor of Science, Bachelor of General Studies or Associate of Arts degrees could be earned. Riva's position is upgraded to dean of the school.

1973: The Master of Science in Physics degree is dropped, but a Master of Arts in Teaching and a Master of Education (a post-master's program) are introduced.

1974: A Master of Science in Criminal Justice degree is introduced.

1977: A Master of Arts in Guidance and Counseling degree is introduced.

1978: Critchfield resigns to pursue a career in business.

1978: Thaddeus Seymour is appointed to the presidency of Rollins.

1978: Seymour appoints a College Planning Committee, headed by Daniel R. DeNicola, associate professor of philosophy, that evaluates all aspects of the college's operation including the School of Continuing Education.

1980: Based upon the committee's findings, Seymour orders sweeping changes to the School of Continuing Education, most notably dropping the criminal justice degrees and business administration programs. (Business administration is eliminated in the day school as well.)

1981: Riva announces his retirement.

1982: The School of Continuing Education is replaced by the Division of Continuing Education and the Division of Non-Credit Courses. The Division of Non-Credit Courses encompasses the School of Creative Arts.

1984: Robert A. Miller is named associate director and dean of the Division of Continuing Education and begins to add core faculty through joint appointments with the day school and to strengthen academics by requiring completion of four core courses before a student can matriculate (be a candidate for a degree).

1985: Undergraduate degree programs in organizational behavior and organizational communication are introduced.

1985: The Division of Continuing Education is replaced by the School of Continuing Education and Miller is named dean.

1986: A Board of Advisors is created for the School of Continuing Education.

1987: Barry Levis, associate professor of history, wins for the college a $150,000 grant that is used to establish the Master of Liberal Studies program.

1987: Miller suggests that the school be renamed for former President Hugh F. McKean, who declines. Miller then suggests that the school be renamed for former President Hamilton Holt.

1987: The newly branded Hamilton Holt School is introduced during a special convocation at Knowles Memorial Chapel.

1990: Rita Bornstein is appointed to the presidency of Rollins.

1994: The Master of Human Resources degree is introduced.

1996: Establishment of the University Club Endowment for Holt School scholarships.

1997: The first Starry Starry Night scholarship benefit is held, which has to date raised $2 million in scholarships to assist 500 Holt School students.

1998: The Master of Arts in Corporate Communication and Technology degree is introduced.

2000: The Holt School celebrates its 40th anniversary.

2003: The Department of Music begins cross-listing its courses with the Holt School and offers the same music major for both day school and night school students.

2004: Rollins Brevard, which had begun at Patrick Air Force Base, is closed.

2004: Lewis Duncan is appointed to the presidency of Rollins.

2006: The Holt School adopts the Rollins College Academic Honor Code.

2006: The Master of Arts in Corporate Communication and Technology program closes.

2007: Rollins trustee Alan Ginsburg, also a member of the Holt School board of advisors, pledges $5 million to the Holt School for a scholarship endowment and for promoting curriculum and faculty development. It is the largest gift ever received by the Holt School.

2009: A Study on the Strategic Direction for the Hamilton Holt School is conducted.

2009: The Department of English begins cross-listing its courses with the Holt School and offers the same English degree for both day school and night school students.

2010: The Holt School celebrates its 25th anniversary.

2010: The Master of Planning in Civic Urbanism degree is introduced.

2012: The Hamilton Holt School Student Services team is awarded the Rollins Service Excellence Departmental Award.

2013: The Rollins Center for Lifelong Learning is established and offers noncredit courses for adults age 50 and older. The RCLL is initially funded by a grant from the Winter Park Health Foundation. The program is later known as STARS (Senior Tars).

2013: Minors in Jewish Studies, Dance and African-American Studies are introduced.

2013: The undergraduate major in business management returns when President Lewis Duncan forms the College of Professional Studies.

2014: The Master of Planning in Civic Urbanism program closes.

2015: Grant Cornwell is appointed to the presidency of Rollins.

2015: The college's popular summer day camp is dropped.

2015: The Health Services Management degree is introduced, as are the Master of Applied Behavior Analysis and Clinical Science and the Master of Health Services Administration degrees.

2016: The Master of Public Health degree is introduced.

2018: The Master of Health Services Administration program closes.

2019: Robert Sanders, previously associate dean of graduate studies at Appalachian State University, is appointed dean of the Holt School as it prepares for its 60th anniversary.

INDEX

———— **66** ————

No college can educate you. All college is
self-education. The college can stimulate,
advise and point the way. But the path
must be trod by you."

—Hamilton Holt